IMAGES
of America

EMPORIA

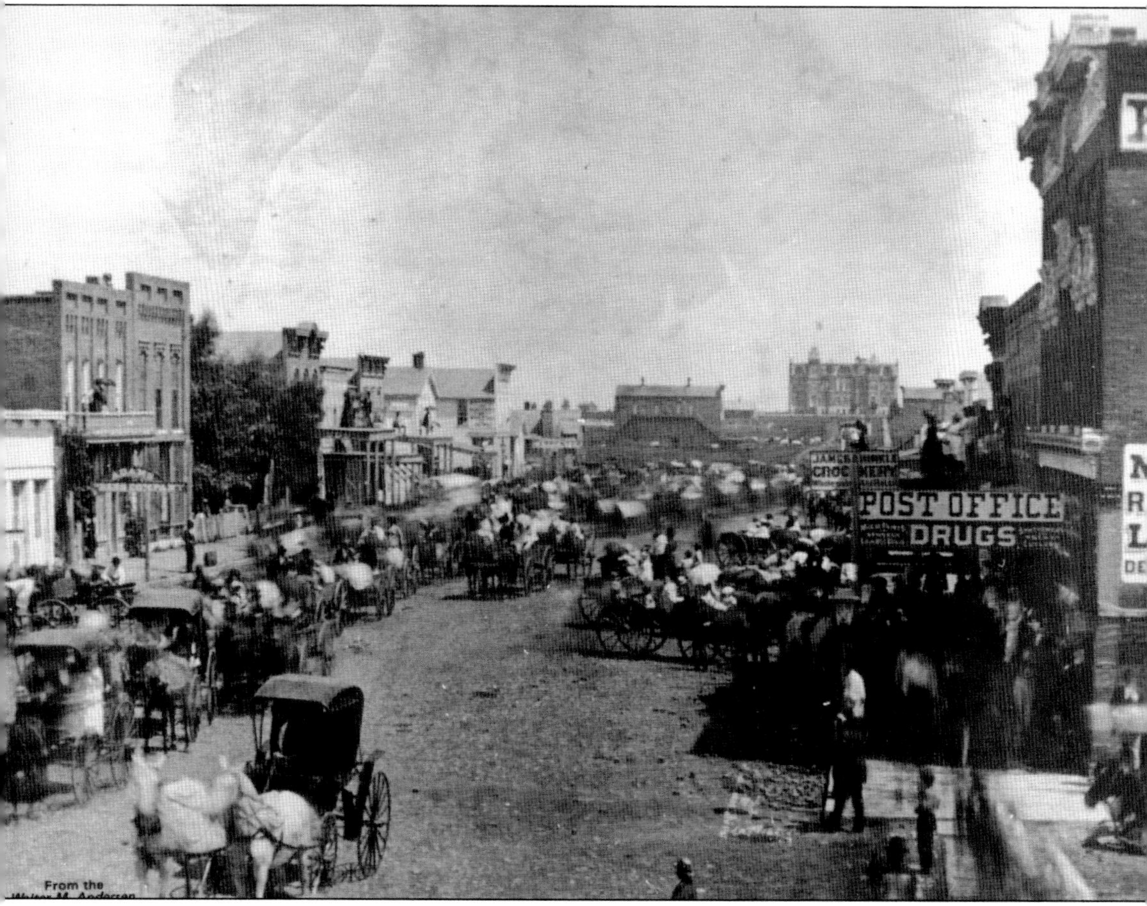

During the middle of February 1857, five men set out from Lawrence to scout the Kansas Territory for the ideal location to establish a new town. Traveling southwest about 75 miles, they staked their new town on the prairie between two rivers on February 20. The town company named the new town Emporia after the great Carthaginian financial center, hoping to rival the commercial trade that city had long ago. Before long, Emporia was one of the most bustling cities on the eastern edge of the famous Flint Hills. (Courtesy of Lyon County Historical Society Research Center.)

On the Cover: Since Emporia's founding in 1857, the citizens of the town and community have supported national and world wars through the giving of their men and women, supplies, finances, and other resources to help bring peace to the world. This 1898 image shows willing Emporians boarding the train at the Atchison, Topeka & Santa Fe Railroad ("the Santa Fe") depot to fight in the Spanish-American War. (Courtesy of Lyon County Historical Society Research Center.)

IMAGES
of America

EMPORIA

Steven Hanschu and Darla Hodges Mallein

ARCADIA
PUBLISHING

ISBN 978-1-4671-1318-2

Published by Arcadia Publishing
Charleston, South Carolina

Printed in the United States of America

Library of Congress Control Number: 2014942397

For all general information, please contact Arcadia Publishing:
Telephone 843-853-2070
Fax 843-853-0044
E-mail sales@arcadiapublishing.com
For customer service and orders:
Toll-Free 1-888-313-2665

Visit us on the Internet at www.arcadiapublishing.com

To all the citizens of Emporia who have given of their time, talents, and treasures to make this a great community today and for the future.

Contents

Acknowledgments

As we began to search for photographs and research the history of Emporia, we soon realized that it would take years and volumes to do justice in capturing all the images and stories that tell the history of the community. We also quickly recognized that the completion of this book was dependent on the assistance of many people.

First, we must thank the staff and volunteers of the Lyon County Historical Society Research Center for allowing us to plow through all their boxes of photographs and dig through the endless newspaper clippings, documents, and records to uncover such wonderful stories. Unless otherwise noted, all images are from their collection. Special thanks go to Ryann Brooks, archivist, and Jan Huston, research center volunteer, for cooperation, knowledge, and encouragement to make the completion of the book much easier.

Second, we would like to thank the staff at the Emporia State University Archives and Special Collections for their assistance in locating and scanning photographs from the Walter M. Andersen Collection.

Finally, we would like to thank our spouses, Beth Hanschu and Mike Mallein, for their support and patience in allowing us to spend the many hours in research and writing to meet our deadlines to publish this book.

Introduction

On February 20, 1857, the surveyor for the Emporia Town Company drove four stakes into the cold winter ground, marking the corners of the newest settlement in the Kansas Territory. The town company included George Brown, G.W. Deitzler, Lyman Allen, and Columbus Hornsby, all of Lawrence, as well as 19-year-old Preston B. Plumb, who became the town's founding father.

After scouting the territory southwest of Lawrence, the men finally settled on land located between two rivers, the Cottonwood and Neosho. To the west of the settlement was the lush grassland of the Flint Hills, providing abundant feed for cattle. To the east, north, and south, the fertile soil of the two river valleys offered rich farmland. The name *Emporia* came from a prosperous ancient trading colony in northern Africa. Likewise, the Emporia Town Company had hopes that Emporia would become a great financial center in the Kansas territory.

While the other members of the company went back to Lawrence, Preston Plumb made Emporia his home. By the first week of June 1857, Plumb had published the first issue of the *Kanzas News*. The newspaper touted the virtues of coming to Emporia. A Free State advocate, Plumb sent advertisements back East encouraging people to settle in Kansas and ensuring that it would enter the Union as an antislavery state. As settlers continued to move west seeking good land and an opportunity to gain wealth, Emporia became an attractive destination and quickly grew into a thriving community.

Following the Civil War, a steady stream of settlers headed to Kansas and other Western settlements. Many of them took advantage of the Homestead Act of 1862 and found the fertile soil of Lyon County to their liking. The grassland of the Flint Hills also offered ranching opportunities. In 1869, the Missouri, Kansas & Texas Railroad, known as "the Katy," reached Emporia, and in 1870, the Santa Fe followed. With transportation now available, the hope of Emporia to develop into a great financial center was becoming a reality. Banks, a variety of businesses, education, and cultural institutions were populating the city. Wooden buildings were being replaced by substantial brick and stone structures. Large Victorian residences were home to prominent and wealthy citizens.

Despite some years of poor crops and the Panic of 1893, it was the closure of the First National Bank that brought Emporia into a financial slump in 1898. Many citizens lost their life savings and their confidence in trusted leaders. To help overcome this tragedy, William Allen White promoted a street fair in 1899 to showcase all the bounties of the area. It was not long before Emporia was again a thriving financial center.

At the beginning of the 20th century, Emporia was becoming one of the state's cultivated cities offering educational, cultural, economic, religious, and social opportunities. In 1904, a new post office was constructed, and in 1906, the new Carnegie Library was completed. Streets were being paved. Electricity was replacing gas lighting. Citizens could ride the streetcar from Soden's Grove on the south edge of town to the College of Emporia on West Twelfth Avenue. Theaters, the Chautauqua, an aerodrome, a natatorium, parks, fraternal and civic organizations, and study clubs provided abundant entertainment and cultural opportunities.

City directories referenced Emporia as the "Educational Center of the West." In 1863, the Kansas legislature passed a bill establishing the Kansas State Normal School at Emporia. The normal school became the 13th higher-education institution in the country to train teachers. Classes began in February 1865 on the second floor of the Emporia School District's new building. In 1867, classes moved to the first building on the present campus located at Twelfth Avenue and Commercial Street. In 1923, the name was changed to Kansas State Teachers College as the normal school transitioned into a liberal arts college. Today, Emporia State University is still recognized as one of the best colleges in the nation to receive a teaching degree. In 1882, the Presbyterian-supported College of Emporia was established. For many years, the citizens of Emporia marked on their calendars the College of Emporia and Emporia State football games as their rivalry was one of the fiercest in the state. Because of financial difficulties, the College of Emporia had to close its doors in 1974. An active alumni association and the renovation of some of the key buildings keep the former college alive in mind and spirit. The Emporia Business College was established in the early 1880s. Classes were held in the upper stories of several business buildings until the college closed. For over 50 years, Emporia has been home to the Flint Hills Technical College, where students receive a two-year associate's degree in a variety of trade and professional occupations.

Over the years, industry, along with agriculture, has played an important part in the growth of Emporia. During the early years, Emporia boasted a cheese factory, brickyard, cigar factory, mercantile company, and a host of other small industries and companies. Following the post–World War II boom, Emporia became home to the Iowa Beef Processors, Dolly Madison Bakery, Modine Manufacturing, Menu Pet Foods, and home-developed companies such as Didde Web Press and Sauder Custom Fabrication.

With the completion of the railroad line through Emporia in 1870, the city became a major hub and division point for the Atchison, Topeka & Santa Fe Railroad. A large stone depot was built in 1882 at Third Avenue and Neosho Street. To the west of the station were a large roundhouse and other buildings used to maintain the trains. In 1926, Tudor-style additions were made to the stone depot. Hundreds of immigrants from Mexico came to work on the railroad and make Emporia their home. Next to the depot were the Harvey House restaurant and several hotels and boardinghouses. The railroad was a major economic component in Emporia through the 1950s. As trucks and airplanes became more common for transportation, the Emporia offices moved to Topeka in the late 1980s. The last remnant of the once-mighty Santa Fe headquarters in Emporia was lost forever when the old depot was destroyed by fire in 1999.

Emporians have always enjoyed and fostered the arts, sports, and other recreational activities. By the early 1880s, two opera houses provided cultural entertainment. Today, the restored Granada Theatre provides a venue for a variety of entertainment. Many bands have wowed the young and old with music. The Emporia Municipal Band still plays during the summer months from the restored bandstand in Fremont Park. The William Lindsey White Auditorium hosts local, state, and regional basketball games and other civic events. In recent years, Emporia has become nationally known for the annual Glass Blown Open professional disc golf tournament and the Dirty Kanza Gravel Grinder race through the Flint Hills.

What makes Emporia a great community is its people. From the early settlers hoping for a great commercial center to the citizens of today who continue that dream, Emporia remains what William Allen White claimed to be the epitome of small town America. It is a place where friends, families, and neighbors come together to support each other during floods, fires, and tornadoes, to honor military heroes as the founding city of Veterans Day, to recognize teachers and fallen educators, and to celebrate the victories of sports and debate teams as well as the joys of everyday living. It is always a great day in Emporia, Kansas.

One

The Founding Years

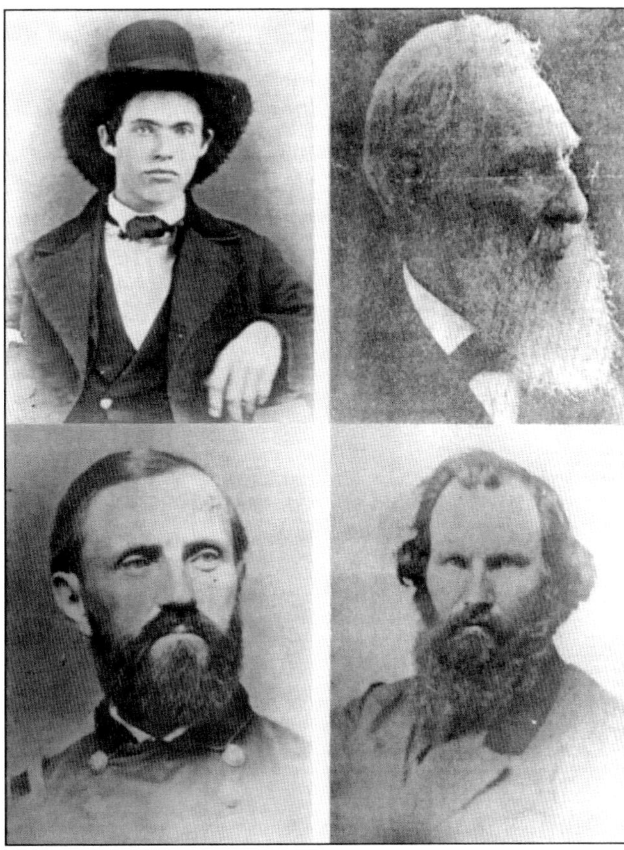

In the middle of winter in 1857, five men from Lawrence rode southeast on the prairie looking for the perfect spot to build a trade center. These men staked their claim on February 20 between two rivers called the Cottonwood and Neosho. They named the town Emporia after the great trade center in Carthage. At the top left is Preston B. Plumb, who was only a teenager and the only one who made Emporia home. At the top right is G.W. Brown, who took the lead in forming the town company. Pictured at bottom left is Gen. G.W. Deitzler, town company secretary. At bottom right is Lyman Allen, a Lawrence merchant. Not pictured is Columbus Hornsby, another Lawrence merchant.

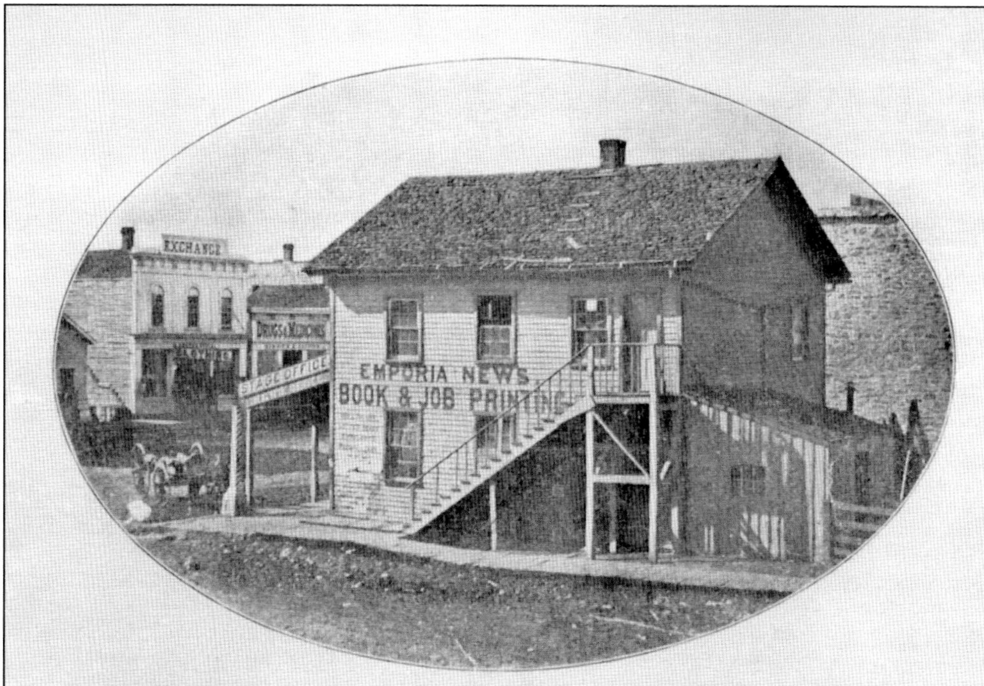

EMPORIA'S FIRST HISTORIC BUILDING—ERECTED 1857

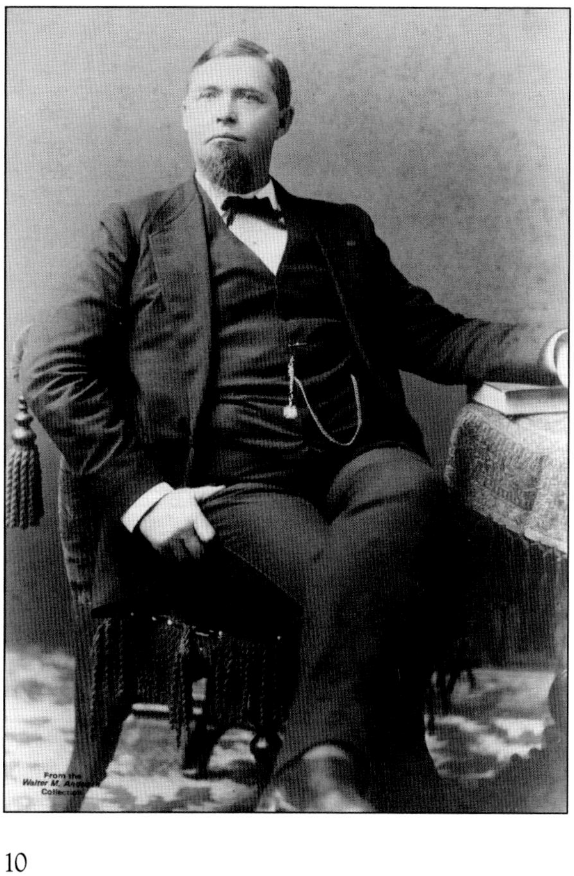

This building was the home of Emporia's first newspaper, the *Kanzas News*, founded in 1857 by Preston Plumb. Its first issue was printed on June 6, 1857. Early settlers credited the newspaper with saving the town because it gave citizens the confidence to stay and encouraged others to make their homes in Emporia. In 1859, Jacob Stotler took over the paper and changed its name to the *Emporia News*.

The Honorable Preston B. Plumb was one of the original town company members who founded Emporia in February 1857. He established Emporia's first newspaper, the *Kanzas News*. Plumb's career pursuits varied from newspaperman to lawyer to bank president to state representative and US senator. Plumb served in the US Senate from 1877 until his death on December 20, 1891. Plumb Hall on the Emporia State University (ESU) campus is named after him.

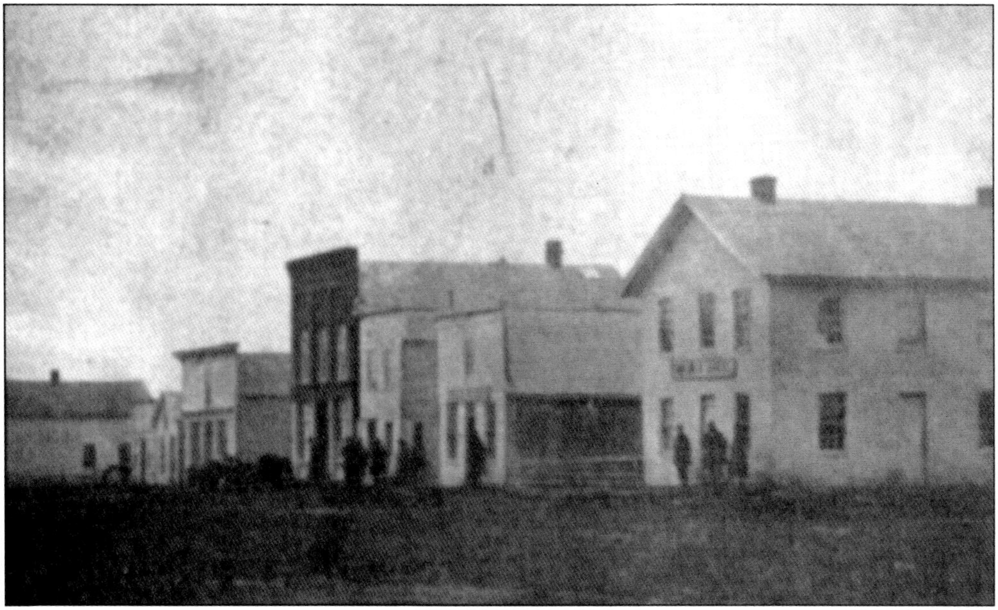

The second building constructed in Emporia was the town company's hotel, the Emporia House (far right). Located on the southwest corner of Sixth Avenue and Commercial Street, the Emporia House was managed mostly by Nathaniel and Elizabeth Storrs from 1857 to its closing in 1869. The Storrses were popular landlords, well known for their great hospitality.

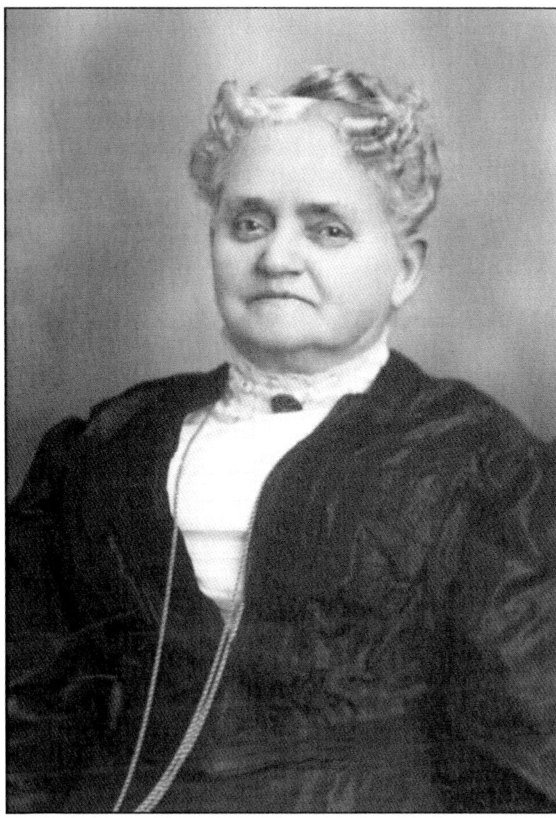

Elizabeth Storrs, Emporia's first landlady, ran the town's first hotel, the Emporia House. The hotel also served as a church, community center, and more. Storrs was very active in the town's development. Her only daughter, Nellie, married G.W. Newman, who established Newman's Dry Goods Company in the 500 block of Commercial Street.

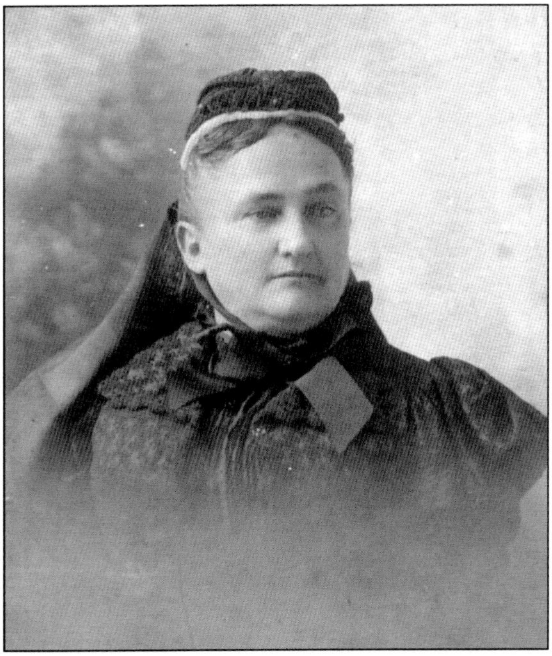

Caroline "Carrie" Plumb, wife of Preston B. Plumb, was one of the most influential women in Emporia. She was active in the Congregational Church for more than 50 years. She also participated in community affairs and donated the land on which Emporia's Carnegie Library was built. In 1917, she set aside one room of her home for the surgical-dressing department of the Emporia Red Cross.

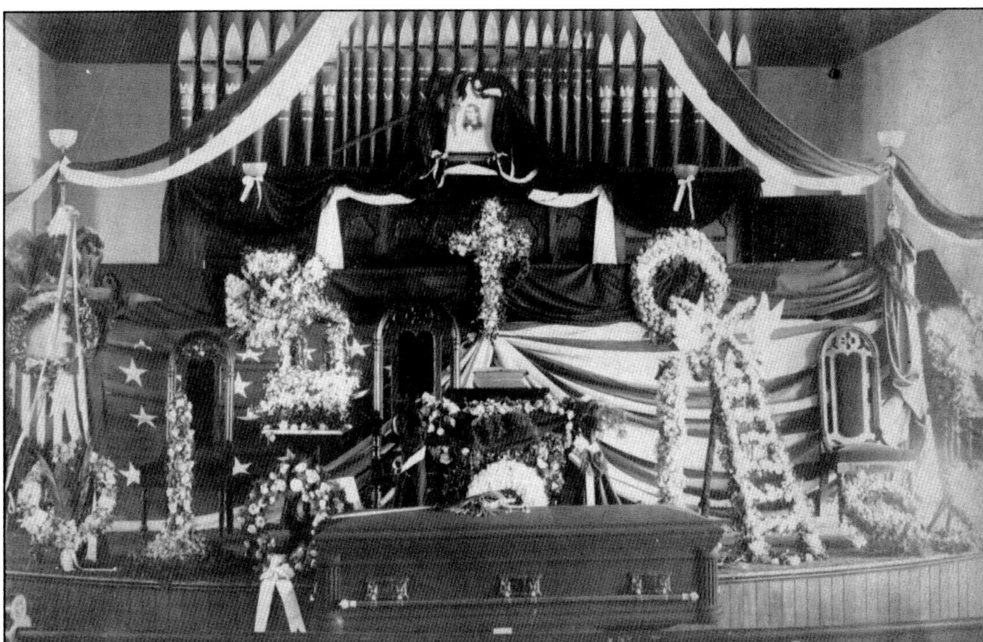

US senator Preston B. Plumb died unexpectedly from apoplexy on December 20, 1891. After memorial services in Washington, DC, and the state capital in Topeka, Plumb's body was brought to his home at Sixth Avenue and Union Street on December 23. The next day, Dr. Richard Cordley, former pastor of Emporia's Congregational Church, conducted a brief private service in the family home followed by a public service at the church. The cedar casket was surrounded by decorations that included an American flag, shield, and eagle, all festooned with black crepe. A photograph of Plumb was hung above the choir loft. Plumb was buried at Maplewood Ceremony with full military honors.

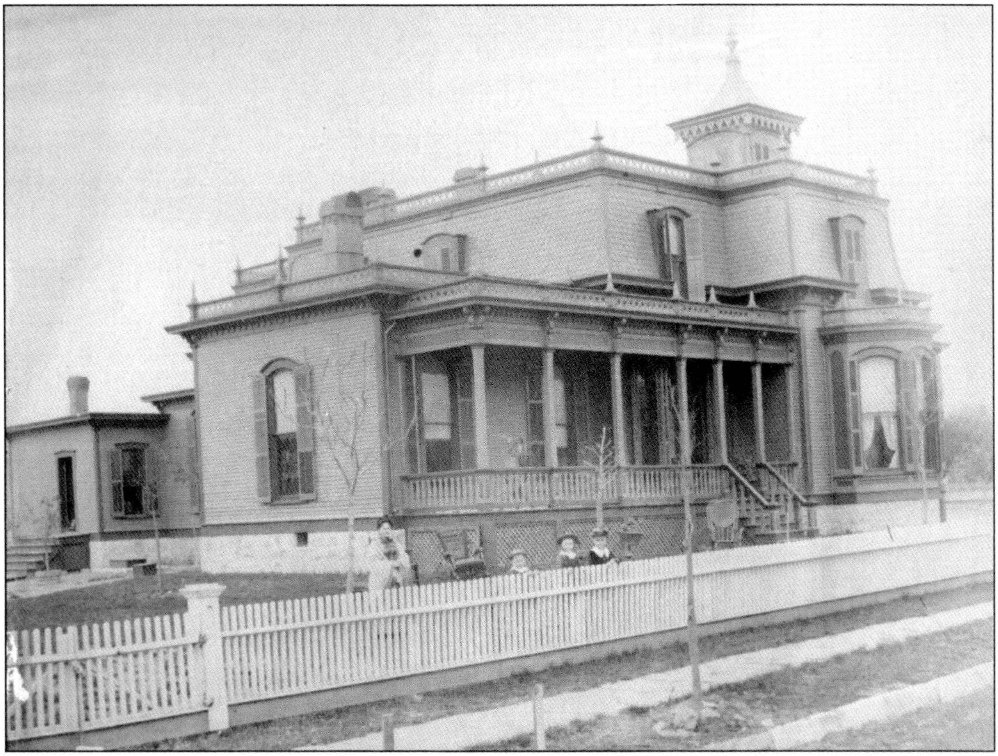

The original Preston B. Plumb house was built in the 1870s and served as the Plumbs' home from 1880 to 1895, when Carrie Plumb built the house below around it as a memorial to her husband.

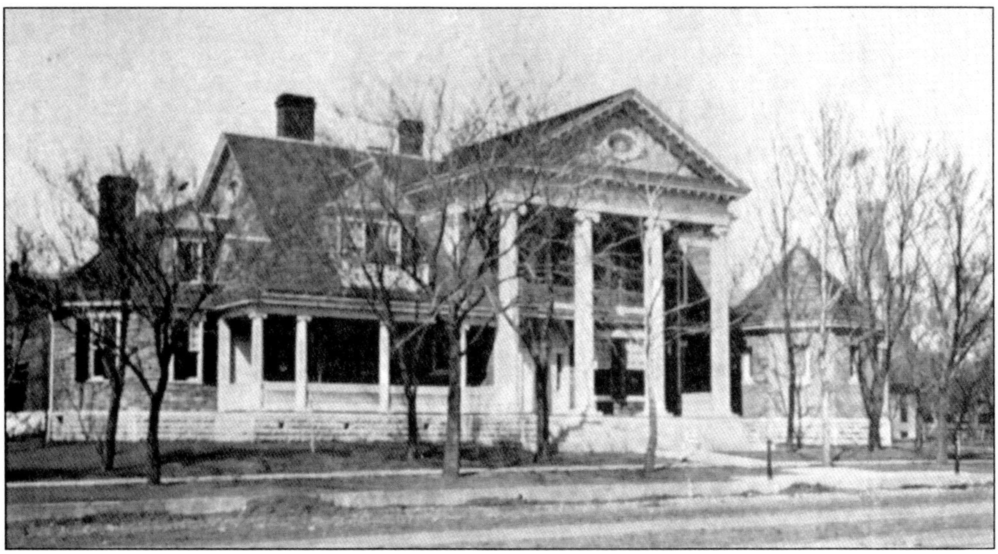

Located at 224 East Sixth Avenue, the Plumb home is an elaborate example of the Neocolonial style. It was quite the showplace in the social life of Emporia. On Carrie Plumb's death, the house was inherited by her three daughters, who immediately offered the property to the National Young Women's Christian Association as a home for working women. An additional gift of $20,000 was given by Plumb's two sons for the purpose of moving the carriage house to the north end of the home, where it was attached to make dormitories.

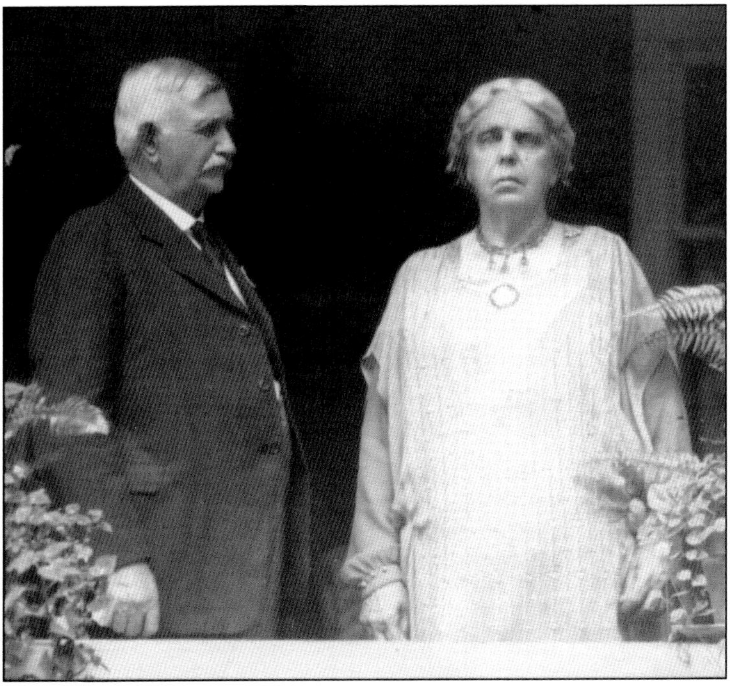

George Plumb, brother of Preston B. Plumb, and his wife, Ellen Cowles Plumb, were early Emporia pioneers. He was a soldier in the Civil War, rancher, railroad commissioner, state representative, and city finance commissioner. She was a member of the first class enrolled at the Kansas Normal School and was active in the Christian Science church and various clubs. The Plumbs celebrated 62 years of marriage in their home at 628 Exchange Street.

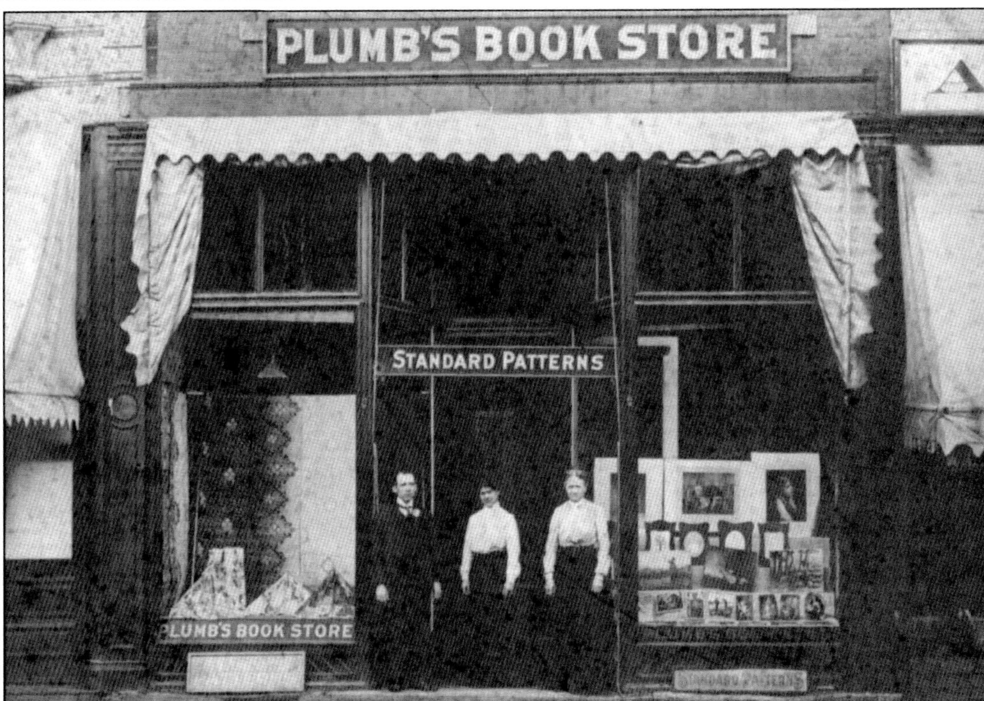

Ellen Plumb (far right) ran her book and stationery store from 1870 to 1907. Located at 523 Commercial Street, it was the third-oldest business on Commercial Street when she sold it in 1907. In addition to selling books and stationery, Plumb also sold photographs, picture frames, china, wallpaper, curtains, dolls, cheap toys, and even fireworks on the Fourth of July. Ellen was the sister of Preston and George Plumb.

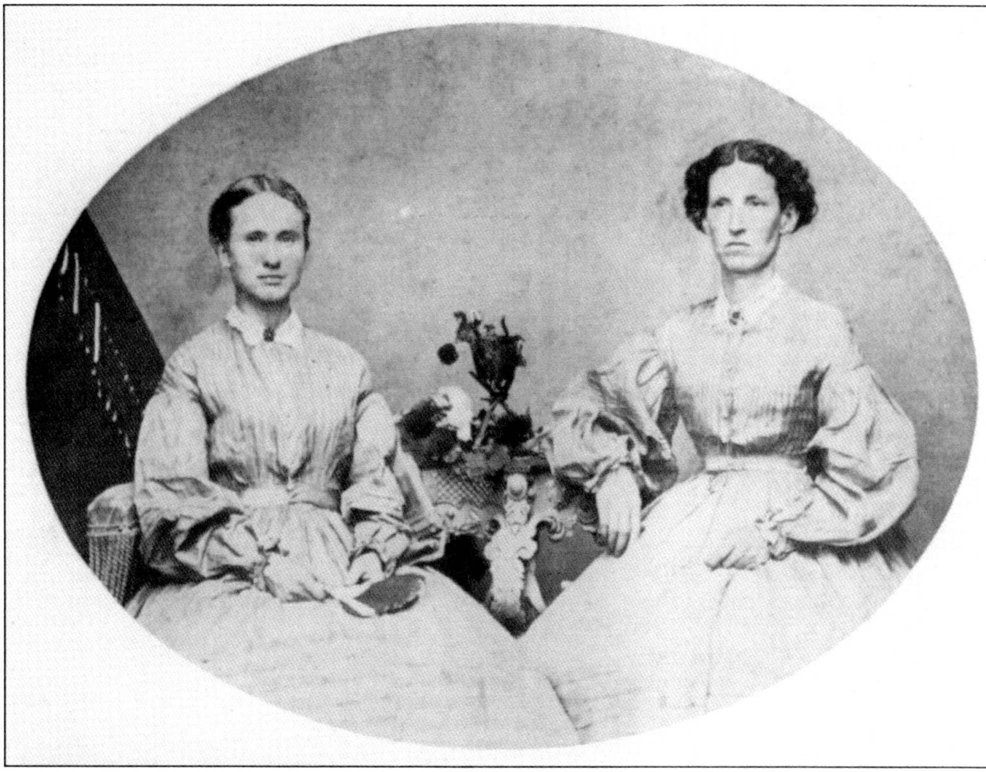

Ellen Plumb (left) and Mary Jane Watson (right) were the first two graduates of the Kansas State Normal School in June 1867. Plumb later served as principal of the Model School (1868–1870) and treasurer of the alumni association (1880–1913). Watson also taught at the normal school but is best known for opening Emporia's first subscription school in 1858 on the northwest corner of Sixth Avenue and Commercial Street.

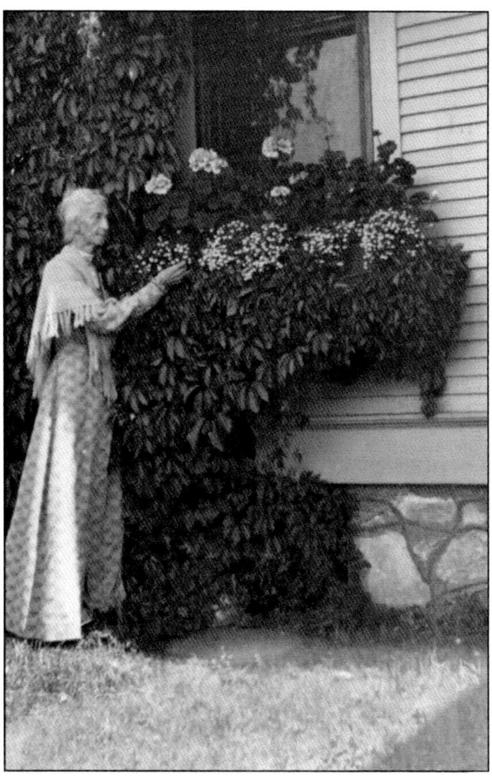

Anna Margaret (Watson) Randolph moved from Ohio to Emporia in 1858 with her parents. Her father, John Hampton Watson, served as 5th Judicial District judge from 1864 to 1872. She married Joseph Vance Randolph on December 22, 1859, and theirs was the first marriage on the town site of Emporia. Randolph was passionate about abolition, prohibition, and women's suffrage. Her diary expressing her convictions of social issues inspired a local television production entitled *Glad Spirit: Anna Watson Randolph*.

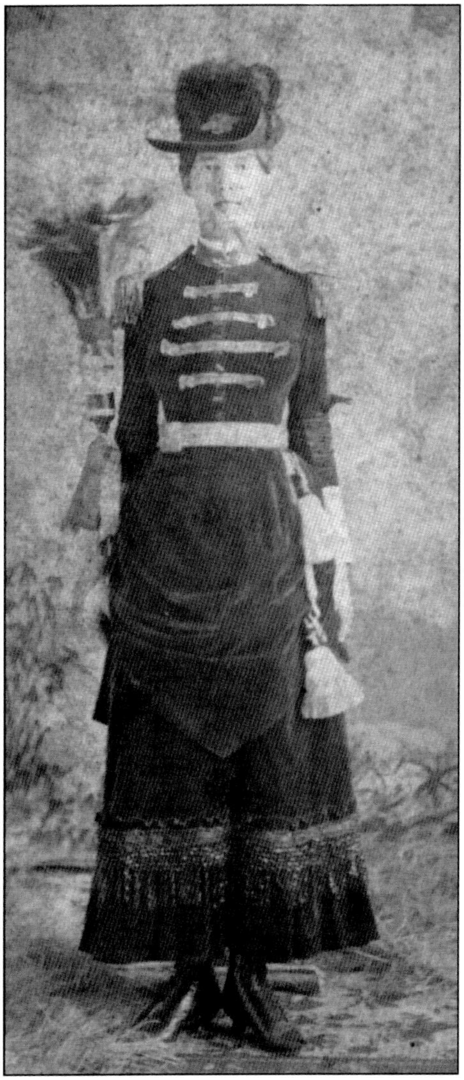

Fannie Randolph Vickery, daughter of Anna Watson Randolph and Joseph V. Randolph, is pictured here in her broom brigade costume in 1883. Broom brigades were composed of young ladies who dressed in a uniform costume and performed infantry drills with brooms instead of muskets. After Vickery graduated from Emporia High School in 1883, she taught in the Emporia schools and then served as county superintendent of schools from 1911 to 1915.

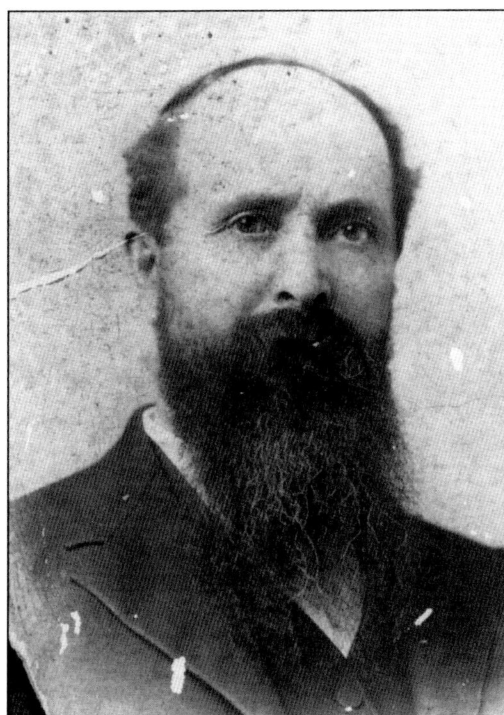

Of Irish descent, W.T. Soden came from New York to Lyon County in 1857 from New York, where he worked at Joel Hayworth's sawmill south of the Plymouth community. In 1860, he moved to Emporia, where he bought two tracts of land on both sides of the Cottonwood River south of the city limits and built a flour mill. Highly respected as a businessman, Soden was heavily involved in the development of the Emporia community and served on various boards and committees.

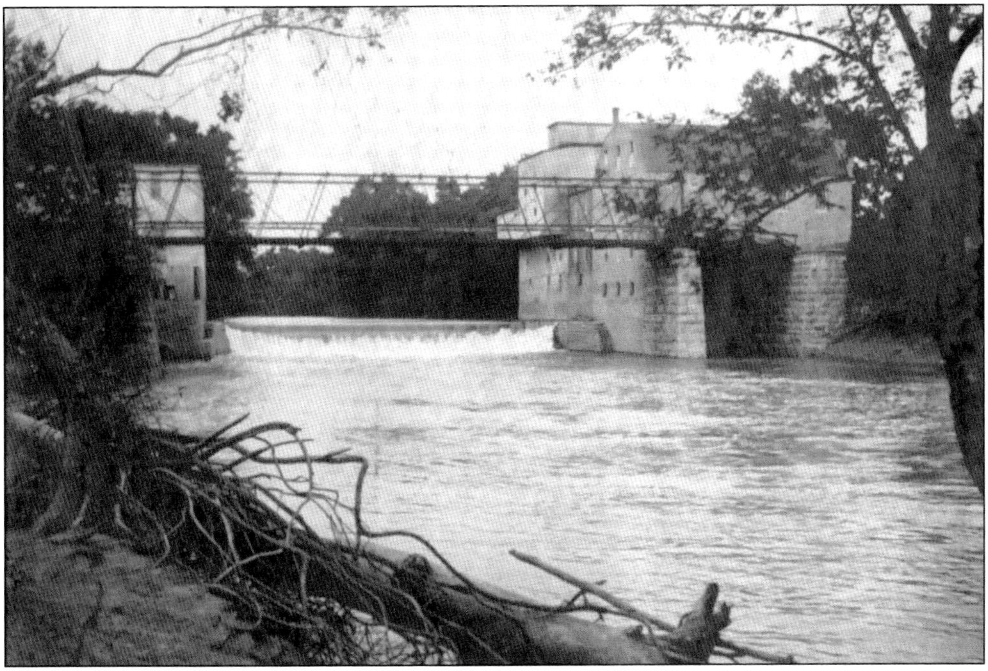

Upon the success of the flour mill, Soden added a woolen mill and furniture factory to his developments along the Cottonwood River. At the peak of production, the flour mill could produce over 650 bushels of flour per day. Many fine pieces of walnut furniture gracing Emporia homes today came from the furniture factory. The mill and factory burned to the ground in the 1930s, leaving the dam as the only reminder of these once successful early businesses.

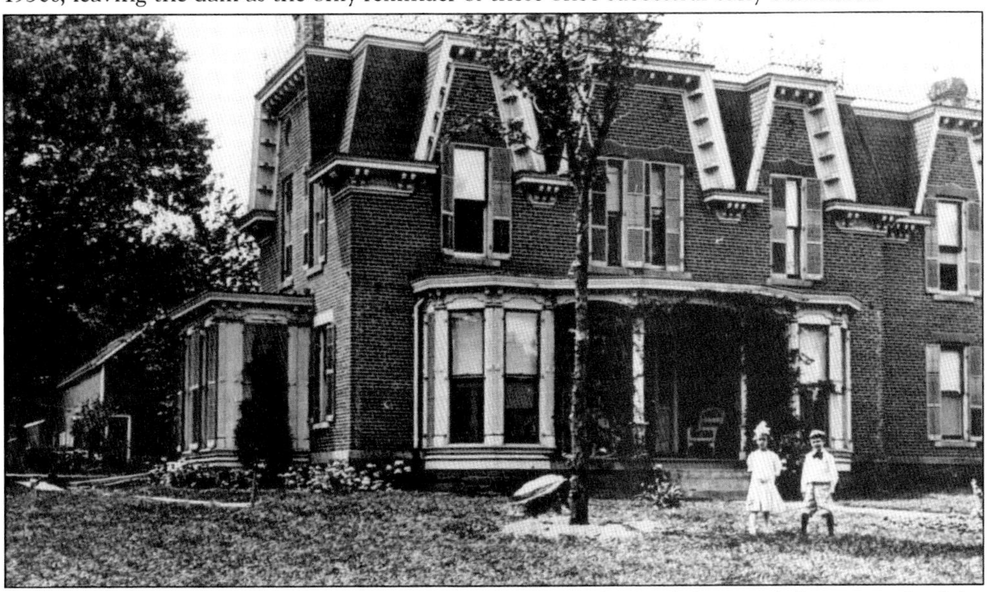

Reflecting the Second Empire architectural style, W.T. Soden built his stately home north of the mill and lived there until his death in 1906. Not only did Soden build this home, but he also built two homes across the streets for his daughter Hallie and son Justin as marriage gifts. Close by is Soden's Grove Park, where customers traveling from a distance would camp while waiting for products from Soden's flour mill and furniture factory.

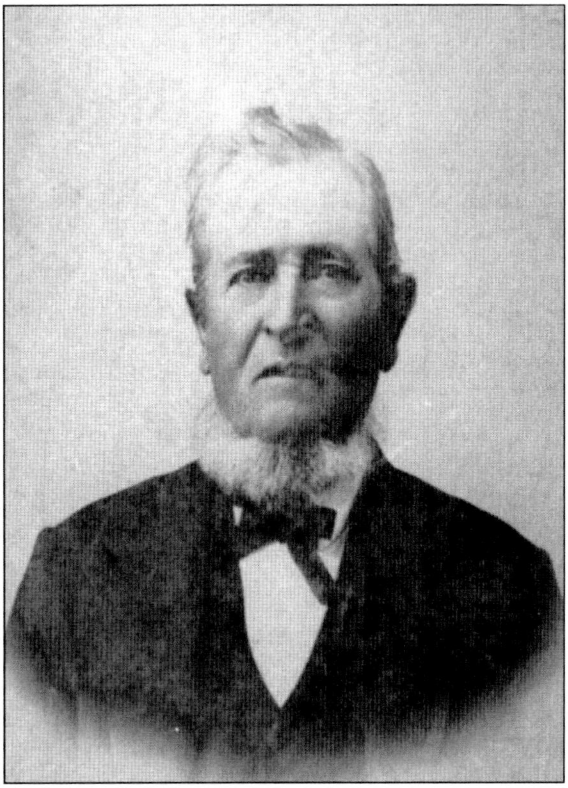

As a stonemason, Richard Howe constructed several of Emporia's first public buildings. These include Lyon County's first courthouse, the Kansas State Normal School main building, Lyon County School District No. 1 building, the Chase County Courthouse, and several residences. The family home on East Logan Avenue is the only surviving residence constructed by Howe.

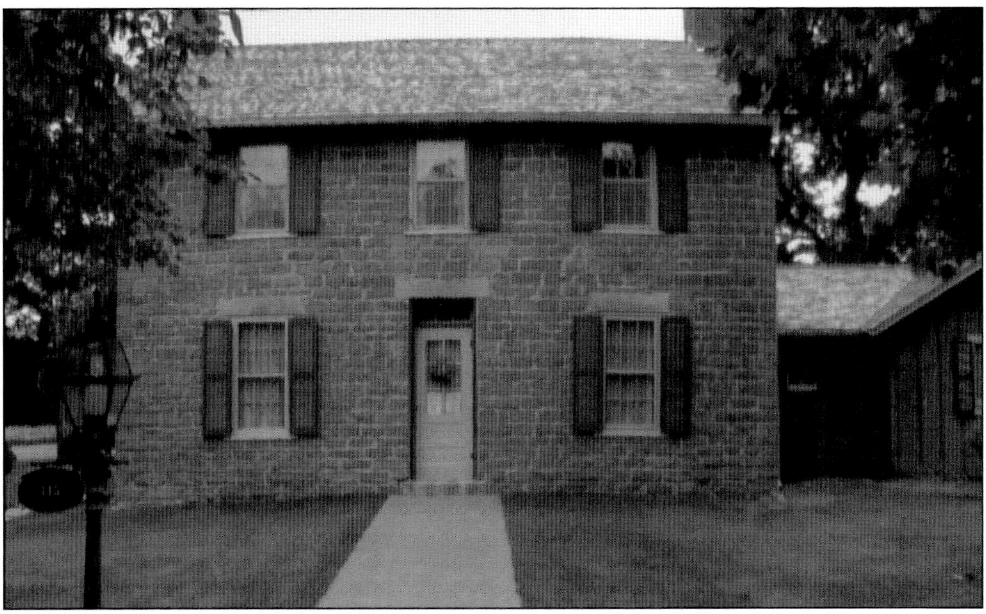

This small stone house is located at 315 East Logan Avenue. It was built by Welshman Richard Howe, a stonemason, who settled in Emporia in 1858. Howe began construction on the house before the Civil War but was unable to complete it until 1867. Built with native limestone and walnut woodwork in the interior, the house remains in its original condition. The property was gifted to the Lyon County Historical Society in 1995.

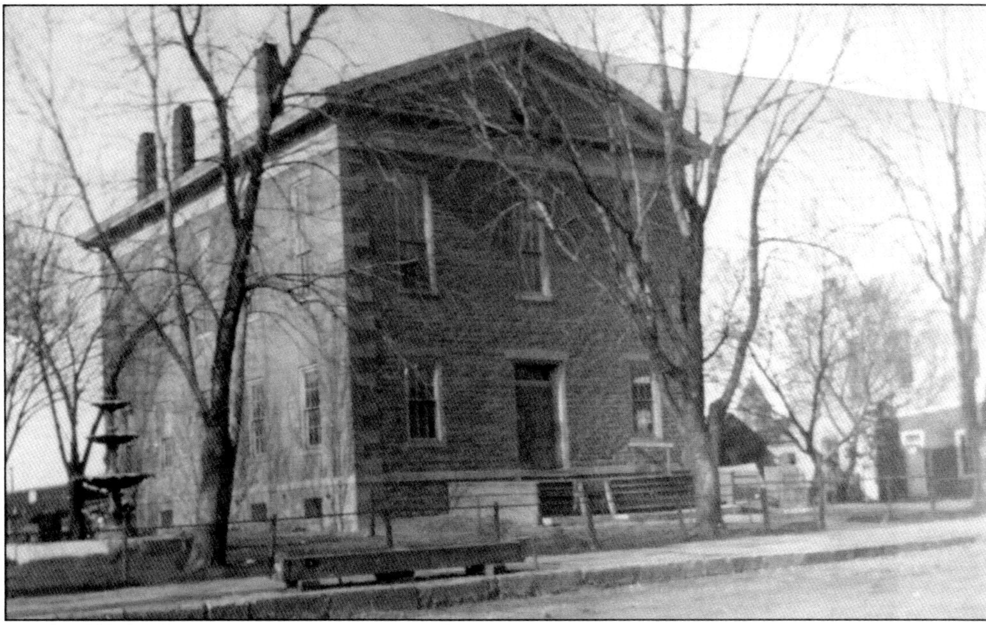

Lyon County's first courthouse was built in 1866 at the southwest corner of Third Avenue and Commercial Street. It was constructed of native limestone by Richard Howe. Near the entrance of the courthouse was a three-tiered water fountain. At the time it was built, the Santa Fe Railroad tracks had not yet been laid next to it. Following completion of the 1901 courthouse, the first one was demolished, and the land became the site of the Poehler Mercantile Company.

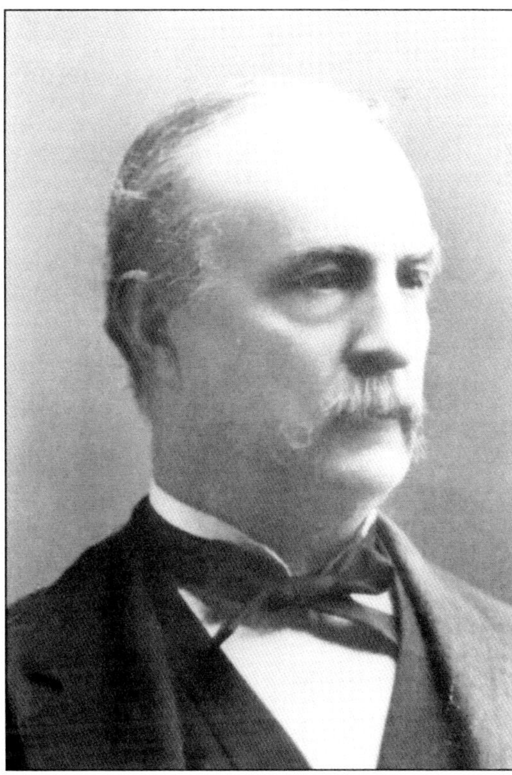

C.V. Eskridge was one of Emporia's most prominent citizens. Arriving in 1857, he became the town company agent. Eskridge established himself as a newspaperman by editing and publishing the *Emporia Republican*. Active in local and state affairs, he was instrumental in locating the Kansas State Normal School at Emporia. In 1863, Eskridge was appointed to the governor's staff with the rank of colonel. He was elected a state senator in 1864 and lieutenant governor in 1868.

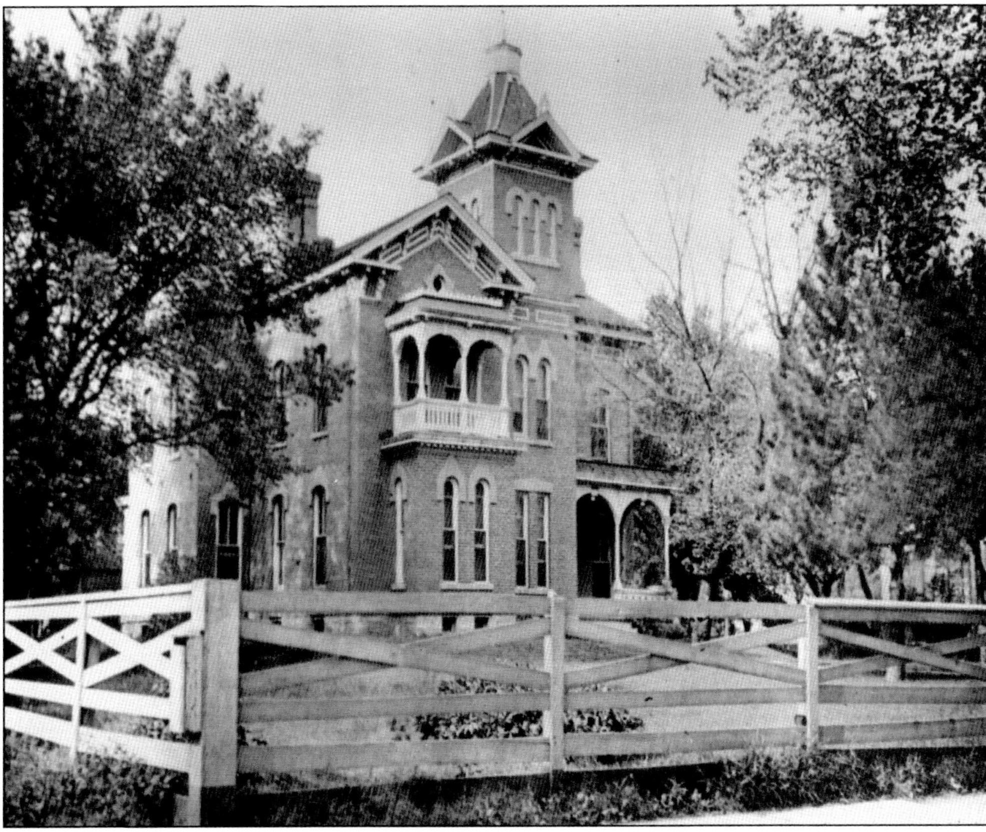

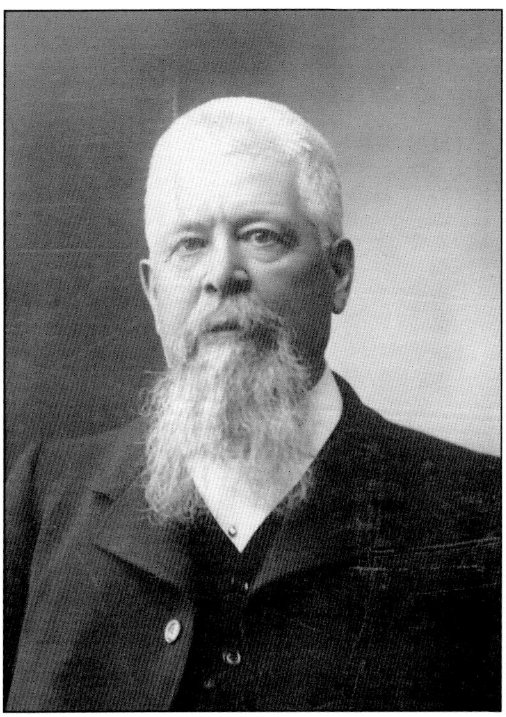

C.V. Eskridge's real estate developments and newspaper business allowed him to build a large Victorian home for his family at 28 East Twelfth Avenue. The house was located next to the normal school's campus. Following his death, the home was acquired by the normal school and renovated to meet the growing needs of the music department. Eskridge's home was torn down after the completion of Beach Music Hall in 1926.

When Dr. John Allen Moore arrived in Emporia in 1860, he immediately opened his doctor's office and became one of the most respected doctors in town. In 1866, Moore added a drugstore to his practice. He and his wife, Clara Weaver, lived at 710 Union Street. Moore also served on the school board and the city council and was president of the Emporia Canning Company.

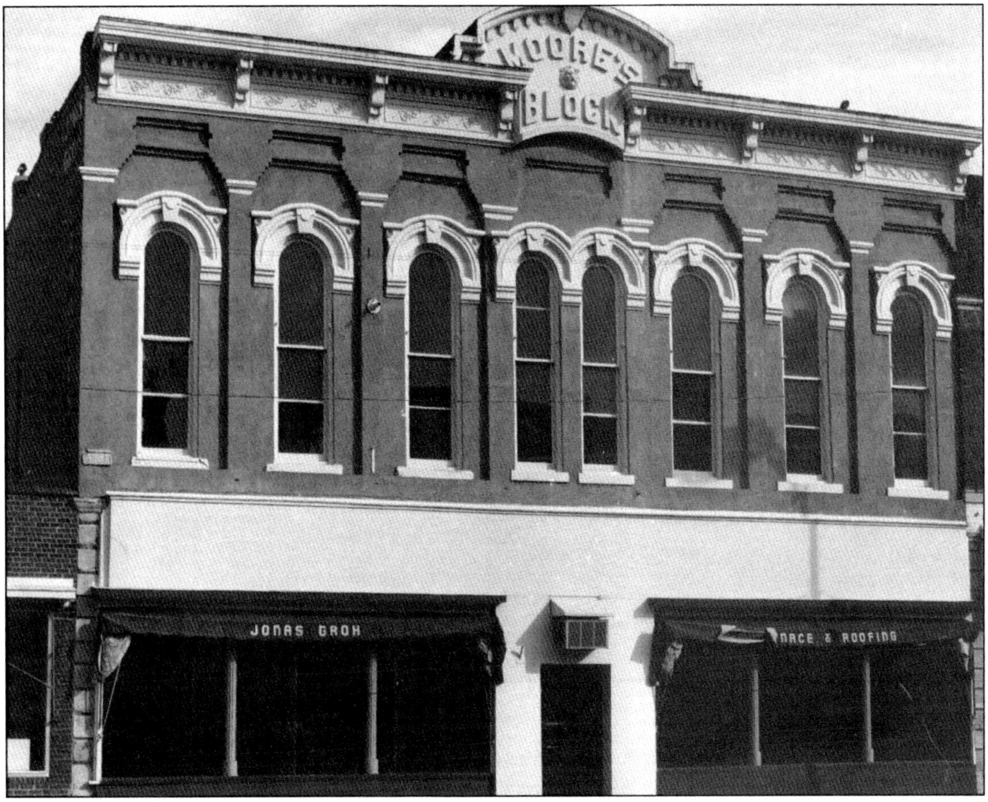

In addition to owning the building that housed his doctor's office and drugstore, Dr. Moore also owned Moore's Block, located at 324 North Commercial Street. In 1884, the building housed a cigar factory and saloon. Other uses for the building included boarding rooms, billiards hall, wholesale fruit and produce warehouse, and a new- and used-furniture store.

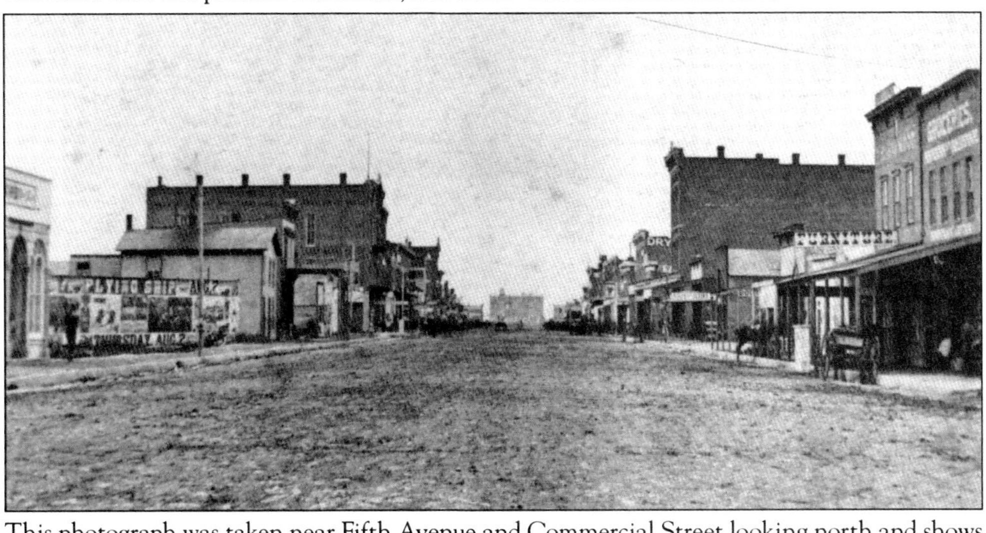

This photograph was taken near Fifth Avenue and Commercial Street looking north and shows the commercial development of Emporia in the 1880s. On the left are many wooden structures remaining from the 1860s and 1870s. At the end of the street is the Kansas State Normal School building that was constructed in 1873.

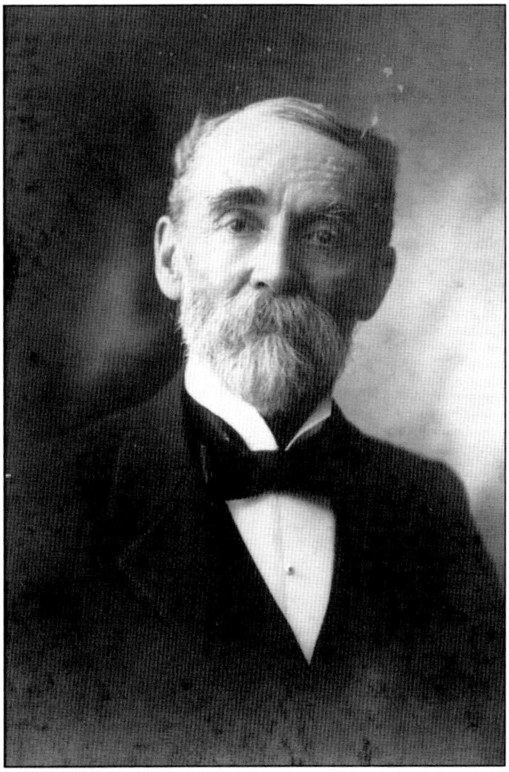

Maj. Calvin Hood called Emporia home from 1872 until his death in 1910. Hood formed a partnership with Preston B. Plumb, and together they made a fortune in the Texas cattle trade. In 1880, Hood was chosen to be the president of Emporia National Bank. He remained at the bank for 25 years; however, after retiring for only a week, he moved his desk into the Citizen's National Bank and worked there until his death. In 1898, he ran unsuccessfully for governor. Hood was a member of the First Presbyterian Church, a charter member of the board of trustees at the College of Emporia, and a member of the Masons. He was known for being a generous, charitable man of high character.

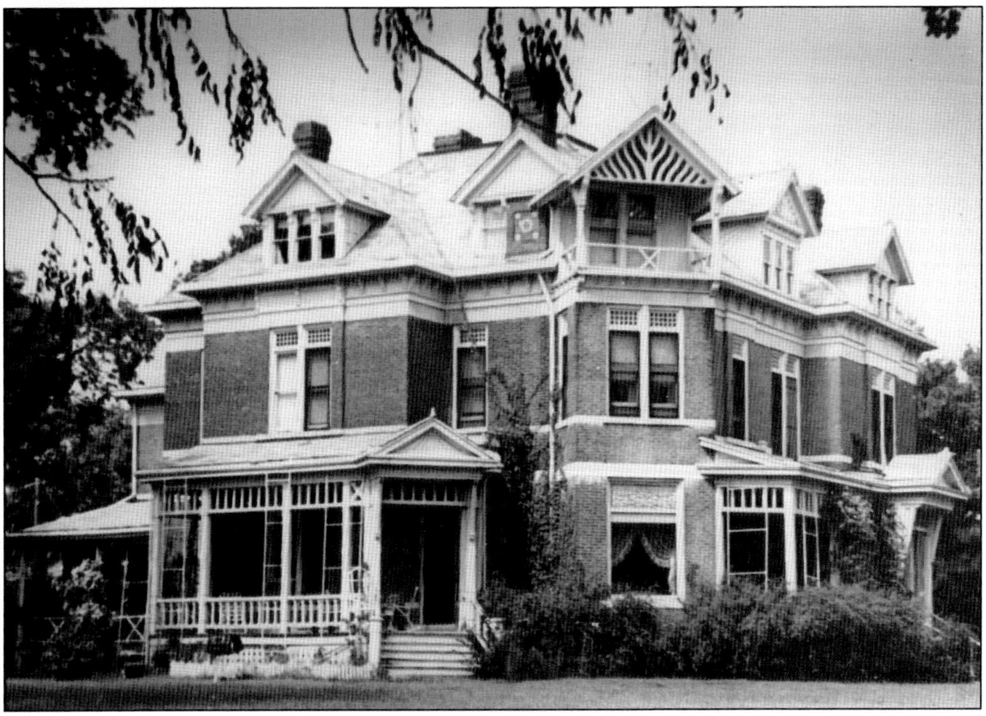

Hood and his wife, Fannie Platt Hood, lived in the Victorian house located at Eighth Avenue and State Street. The house was demolished in the 1960s and replaced with an apartment building.

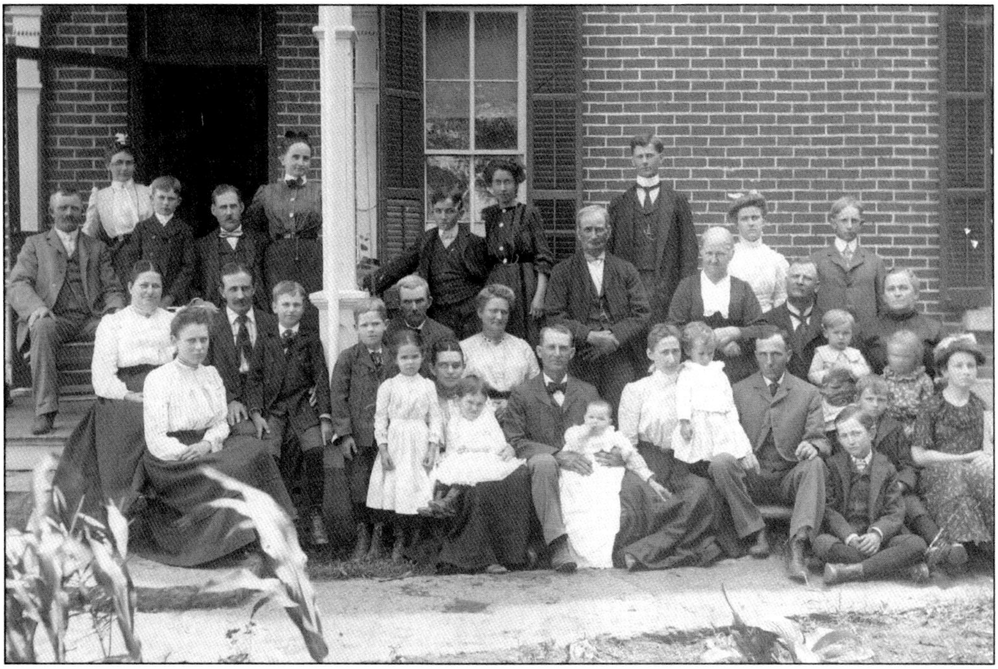

Pictured with their children and grandchildren in 1903, Andrew Hinshaw and Sarah Hiatt Hinshaw were pillars in the Society of Friends community. Andrew followed his "most beloved" to Kansas when Sarah moved with her parents to the Emporia area in 1856. Married in 1857 by Rev. Solomon G. Brown, the Hinshaws made their home outside of the city limits of east Emporia. They helped establish the Society of Friends in Emporia and were active in the Friends meeting house at First Avenue and Sylvan Street.

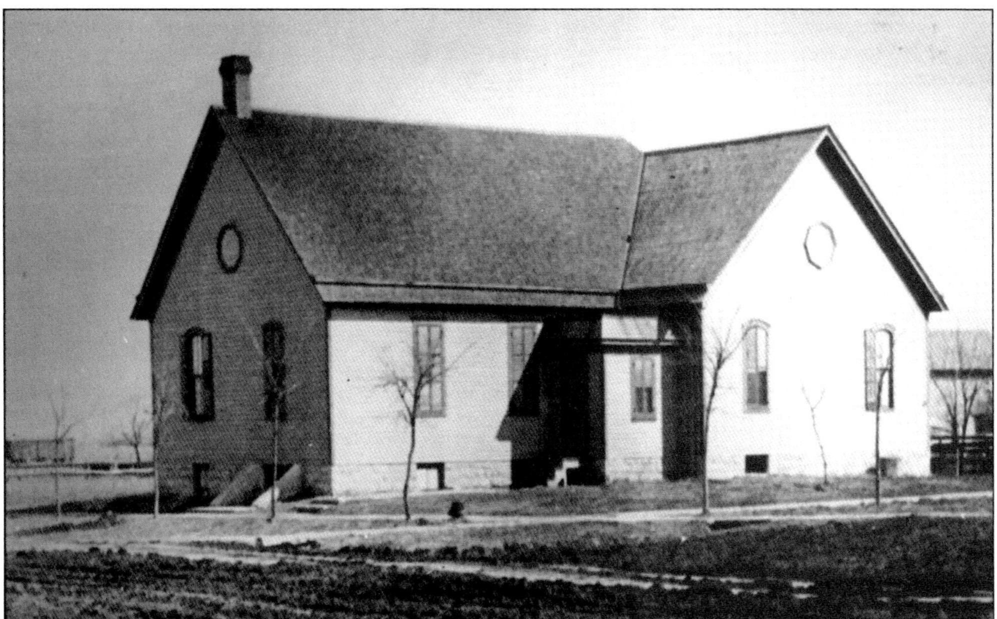

The first Friends Church was located at the corner of Sixth Avenue and Sylvan Street. This photograph was taken around 1890.

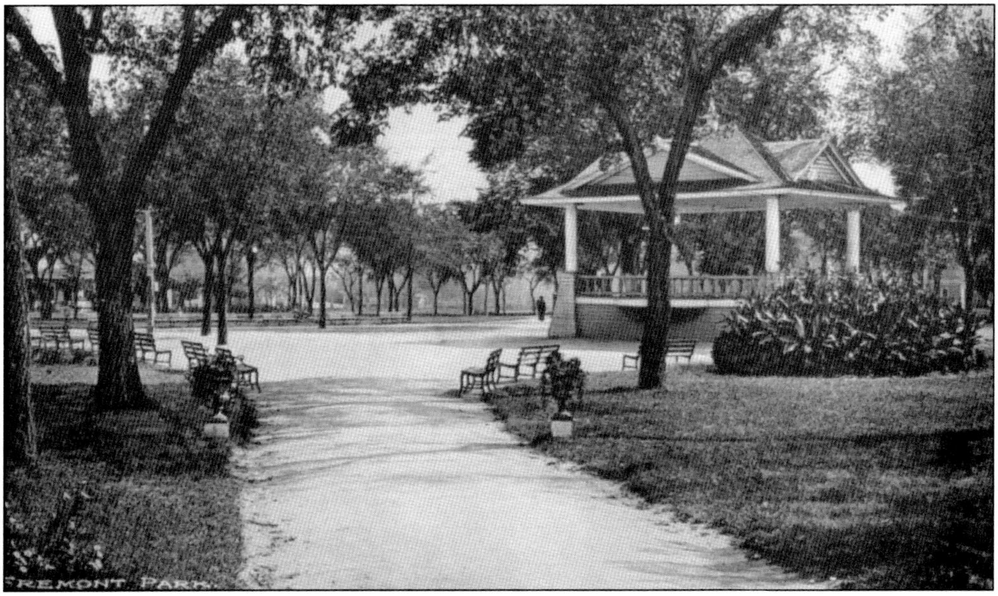

When Emporia was platted in 1857, several parks were included in the original town site, which was two sections of land running from South Avenue to Twelfth Avenue and from West Street to East Street. The parks were near the middle of the town, and each had a bandstand and water fountains where citizens could go for concerts and walks. In the early 1870s, the railroad came through Emporia, and tracks were laid on the south side of each park. Pictured here is Fremont Park, located in the 300 block between Exchange and Union Streets. In recent years its bandstand has been restored, and concerts are held there during the summer.

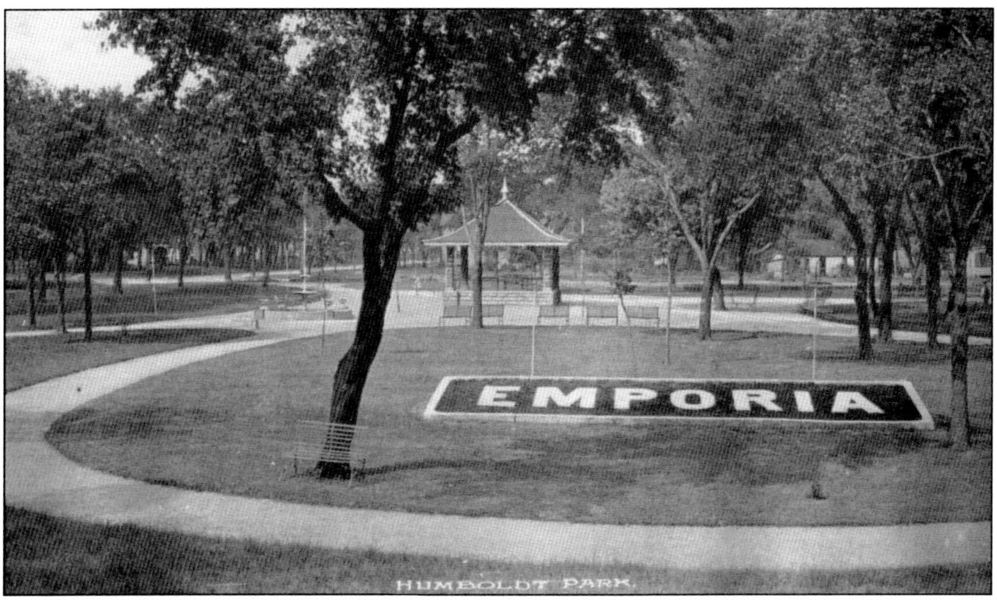

Shown here is Humboldt Park, located in the 300 block between Congress and State Streets. After the railroad came through Emporia, large cement letters painted in white and spelling Emporia were placed in the park so train passengers would know the town they were passing through. The bandstand in Humboldt Park was later removed, and today the site is the home of the Emporia Recreation Center.

Two

Prosperous Years

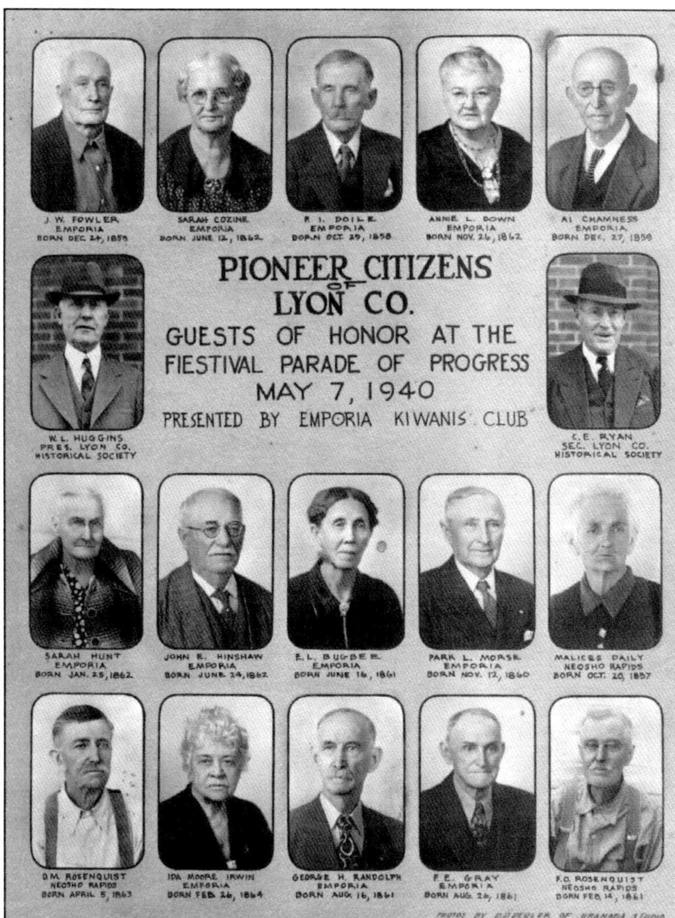

The pioneer citizens featured in this photograph were born in Lyon County prior to 1865. They were the guests of honor during the Fiestival Parade of Progress on May 7, 1940. Organized by the Kiwanis Club, the parade consisted of a moving pageant that showed human life from pioneer to modern times. More than 1,200 people participated in the parade, which was viewed by an estimated crowd of 45,000.

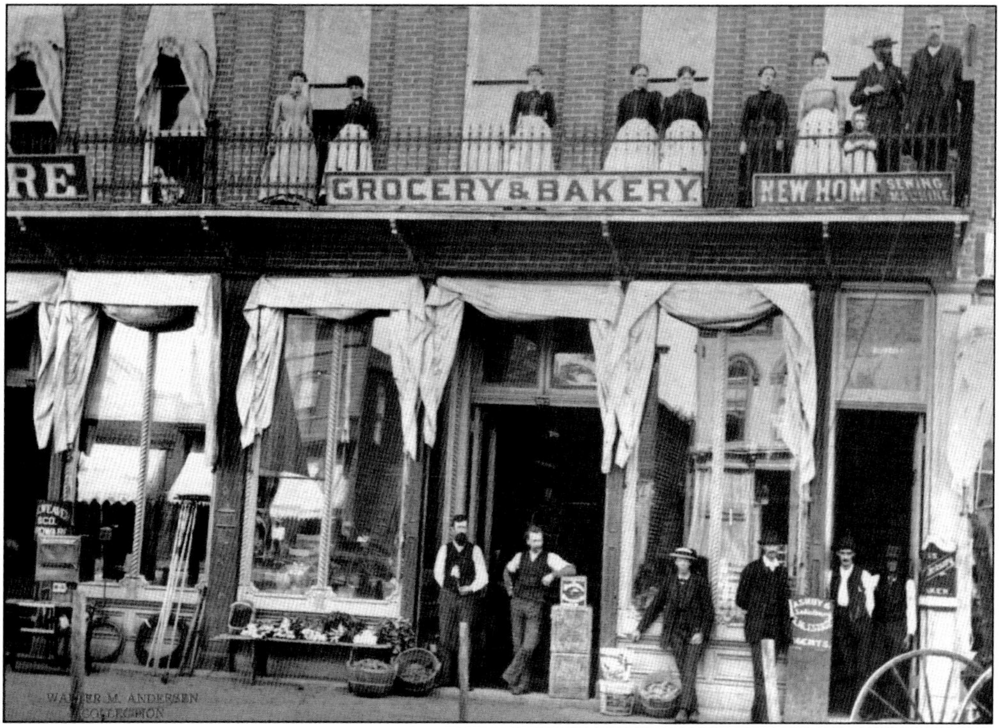

Taking a break from the rigors of making a business succeed are store employees and families who worked and lived in the building that housed one of Emporia's grocery and bakery stores. This image was taken in the 600 block of Commercial Street in the late 1870s. Note the men and women standing on the balcony of the second story.

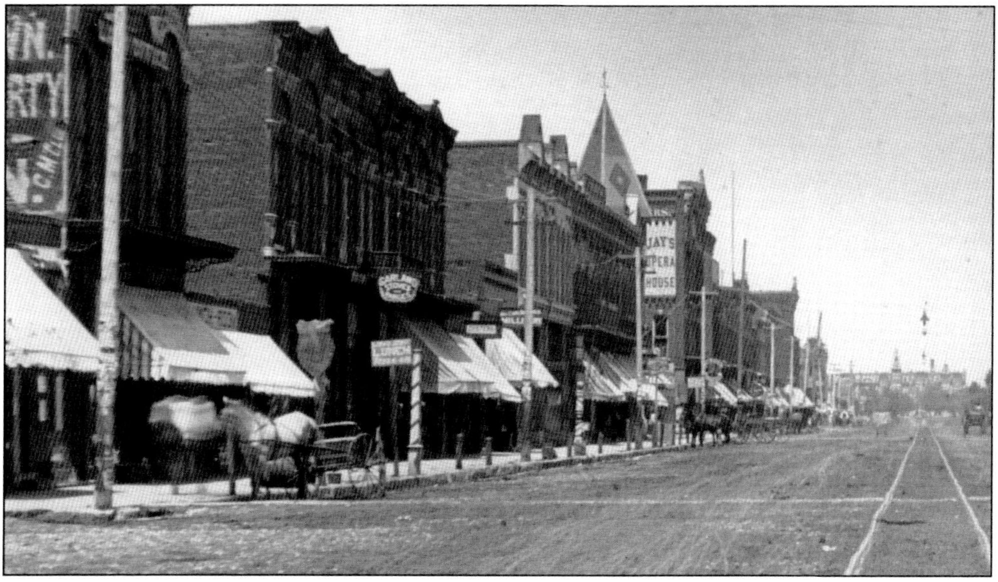

This view of the west side of Commercial Street between Third and Fourth Avenues in 1895 truly reflects the founding fathers' dream of a commercial center on the Plains. Two- and three-story brick buildings with enticing facades were bringing in customers daily to purchase their supplies. Toward the center is the impressive Emporia National Bank tower.

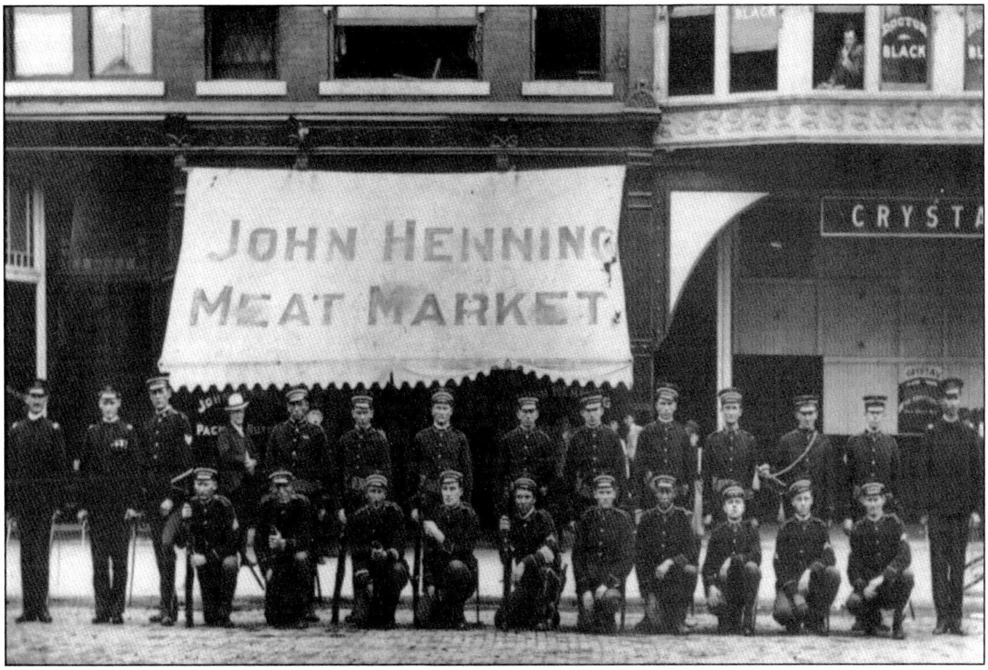

John Henning came to Emporia in 1874 and established one of the best meat markets in the city. He had previously worked six years in the Commissary Department in the government Indian Department. Because of his success, he was able to build a handsome brick residence at 627 Union Street that still stands today. The Henning Meat Market, seen here, was located at 612–614 Commercial Street next to Haynes Hardware store. The large awning serves as an advertisement for the market.

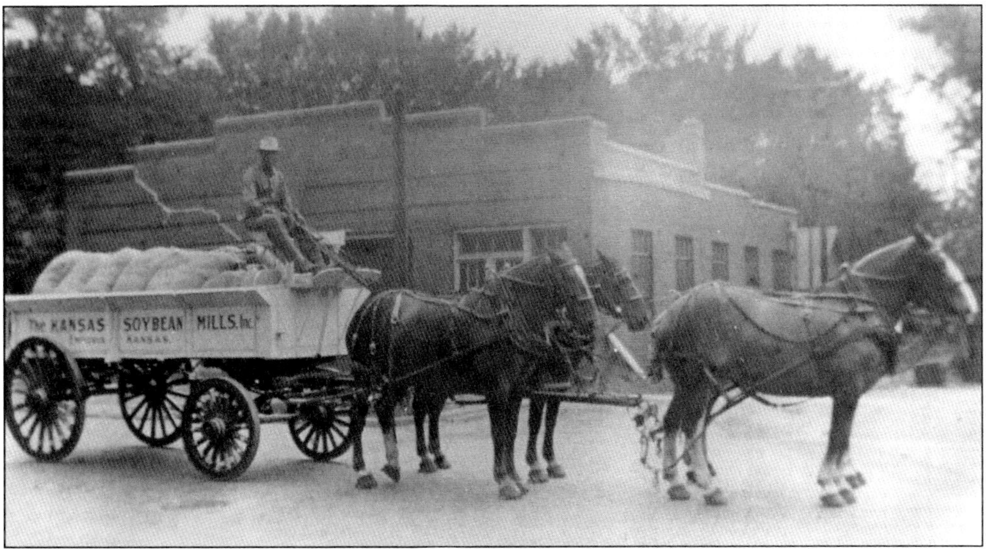

This image shows Bert Rich hauling a load of soybean meal to be milled at Emporia's soybean plant. Rich came to Emporia from Kentucky in 1878. For many years he worked on the railroad, laying and repairing track to nearby towns. Upon his death in 1975, he was regarded as one of the best African American construction contractors in the region. (Courtesy of the Walter M. Andersen Collection, Emporia State University Special Collections Archives.)

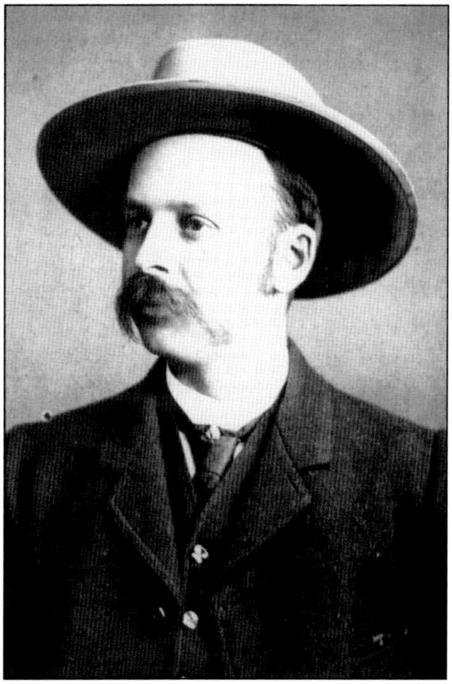

Architect Charles W. Squires came to Emporia in 1879 and designed many of the town's grand homes and public buildings of the Victorian era. Upon his death in 1934, the *Emporia Gazette* reported that he had designed more than 2,700 structures in Kansas. His friend William Allen White said of him, "Charley Squires put his mark on this town; the mark of his generation. He built with absolute verity to the inner spirit of his day."

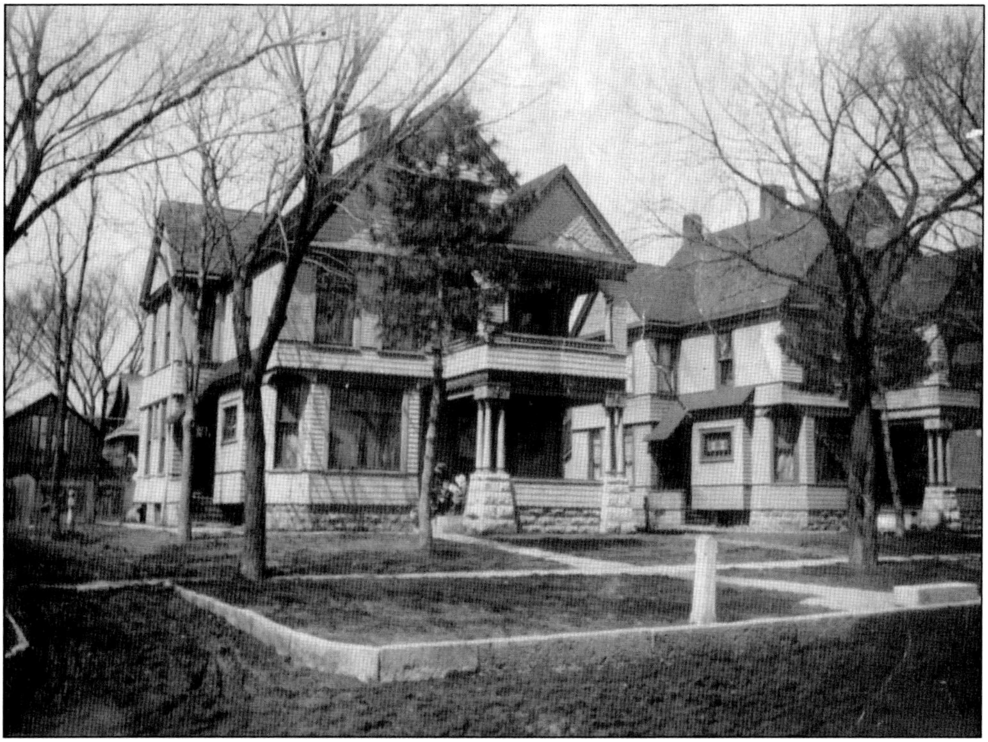

Squires built his own home at 613 Exchange Street in 1895 for his bride, Susan Howey. He lived there until his death in 1934. To the north of his house, he constructed one of similar style for L.A. Lowther, who was superintendent of Emporia schools for nearly 40 years. Also on the same block at 627 Exchange Street, he designed a home for Dr. William Meffert and his bride in 1906.

Col. Harrison Cory "H.C." Cross lived in Emporia for over 30 years and was the first city mayor. With several business partners, Cross organized the First National Bank of Emporia in 1872. He served as its president for 20 years. Ironically, when Cross died in 1894, his obituary described him as a "man of the highest personal character" when in fact, he had been using the depositors' money freely in bad investments that left the bank deeply in debt. His son C.S. was left to deal with the aftermath.

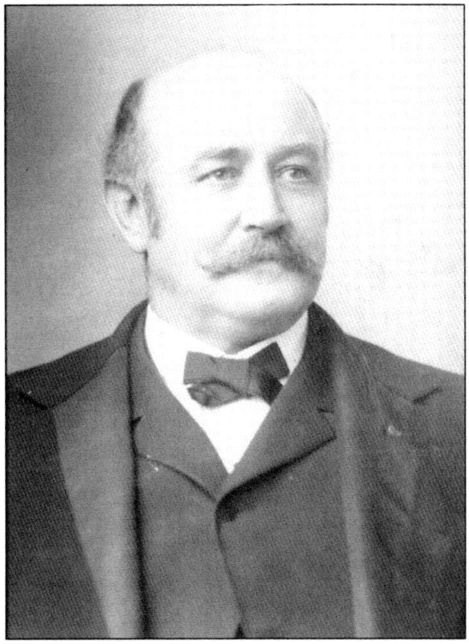

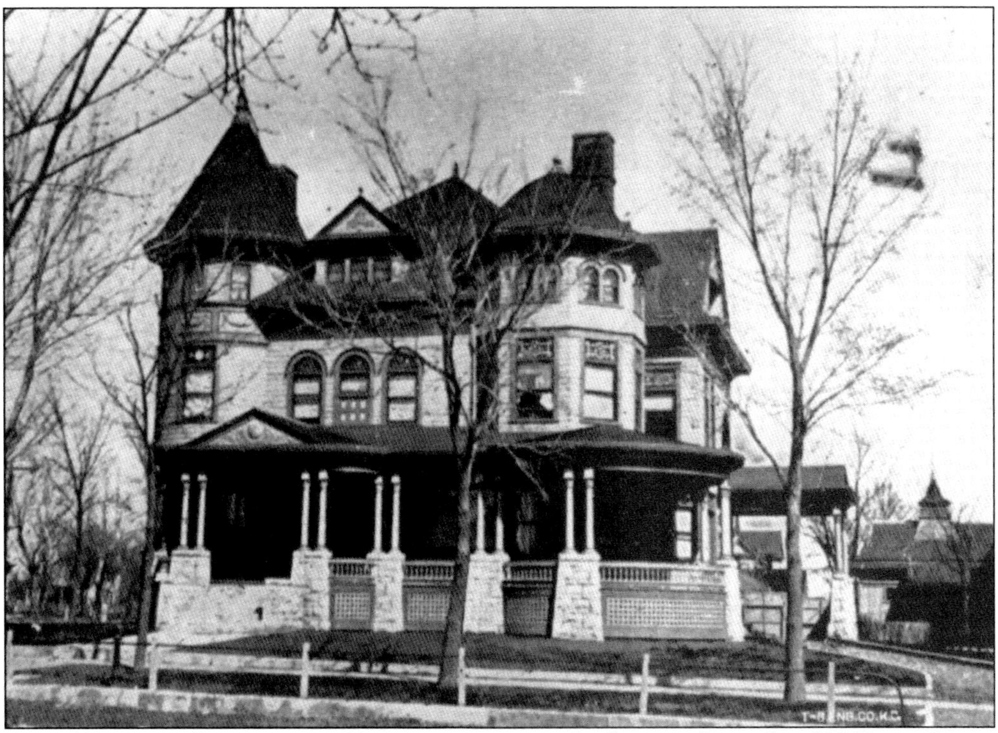

One of Emporia's few remaining Victorian mansions, this house is located at 526 Union Street. It was built by prominent Emporia businessman, banker, and developer H.C. Cross. Cross hired Charles Squires to design his elegant Queen Anne–style home. It was completed in 1894, and Cross only enjoyed his home a few months before his untimely death in 1895. Over the years, the house was used for a hospital, fraternity/sorority house, hotel, and boardinghouse. Today, it is undergoing a restoration as a business/residence.

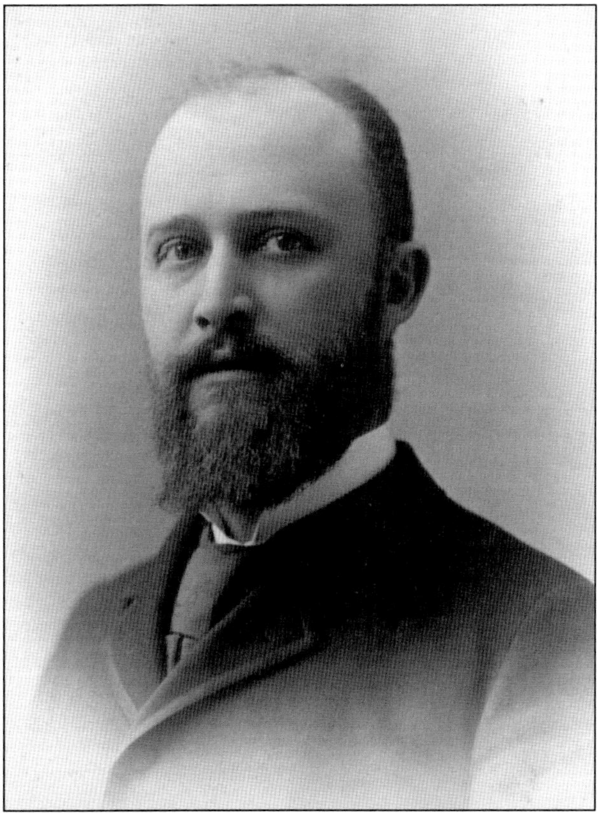

Charles Sumner "C.S." Cross, the son of H.C. Cross, became president of the First National Bank upon his father's retirement in 1891. In an attempt to keep the bank afloat following his father's poor investments, and to protect his father's reputation, Cross illegally floated a series of worthless bonds. After the bank examiners closed the bank on the morning of November 16, 1898, Cross shot and killed himself that afternoon at Sunny Slope, his famous farm where he bred Hereford cattle.

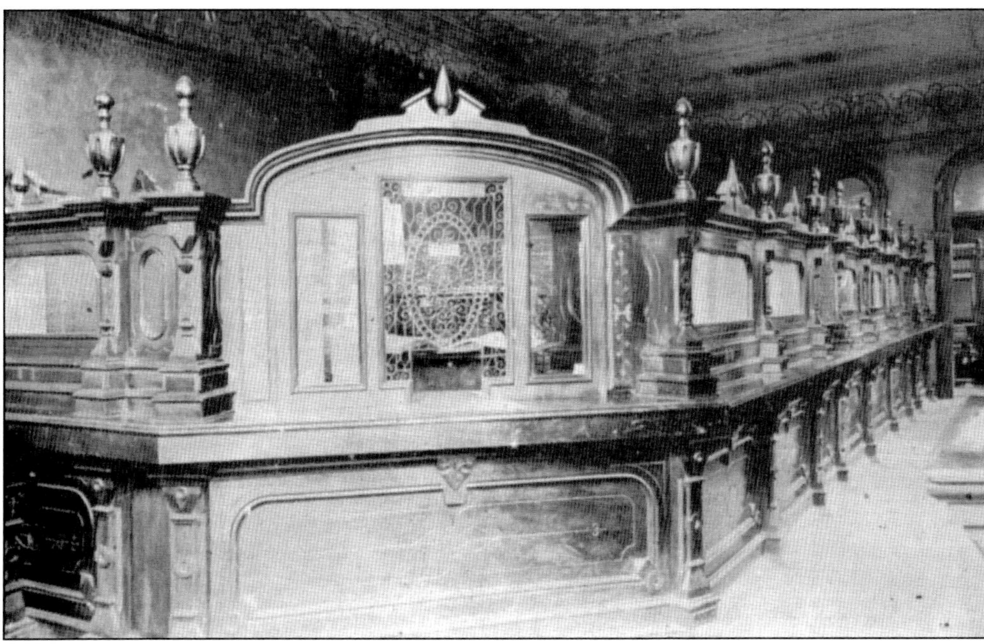

The ill-fated First National Bank was located at 529 Commercial Street. The site is where the second building in the town was erected. This image of the interior from the early 1890s shows the opulence of the building.

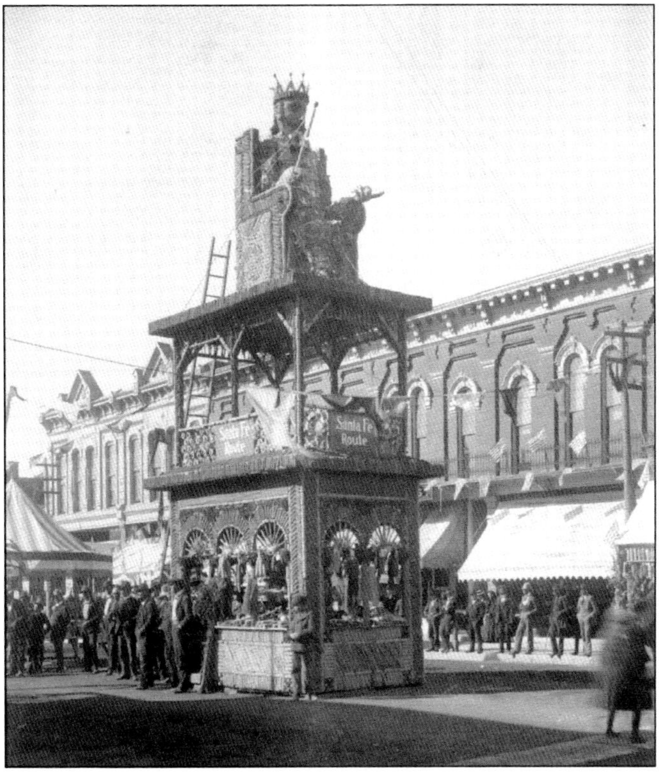

Following the closure of the First National Bank in 1898, the city of Emporia was in a state of fear and depression. To spark enthusiasm for the upcoming turn of the century, newspaper editor William Allen White organized and promoted the Emporia Street Fair held on September 28–29, 1899.

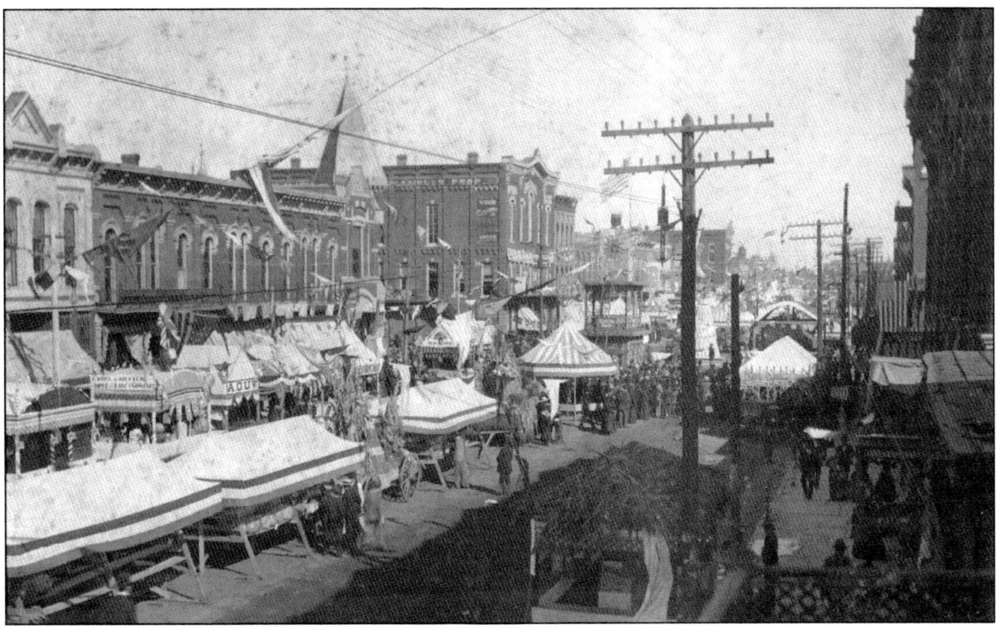

The year 1899 was very productive for agriculture, and people were ready for a celebration. For two days, booths featuring agricultural products lined Commercial Street. A parade filled with decorated floats thrilled everyone present. White also introduced the first car to the citizens of Emporia. Images of the parade depict the great detail and work that made the street fair a huge success.

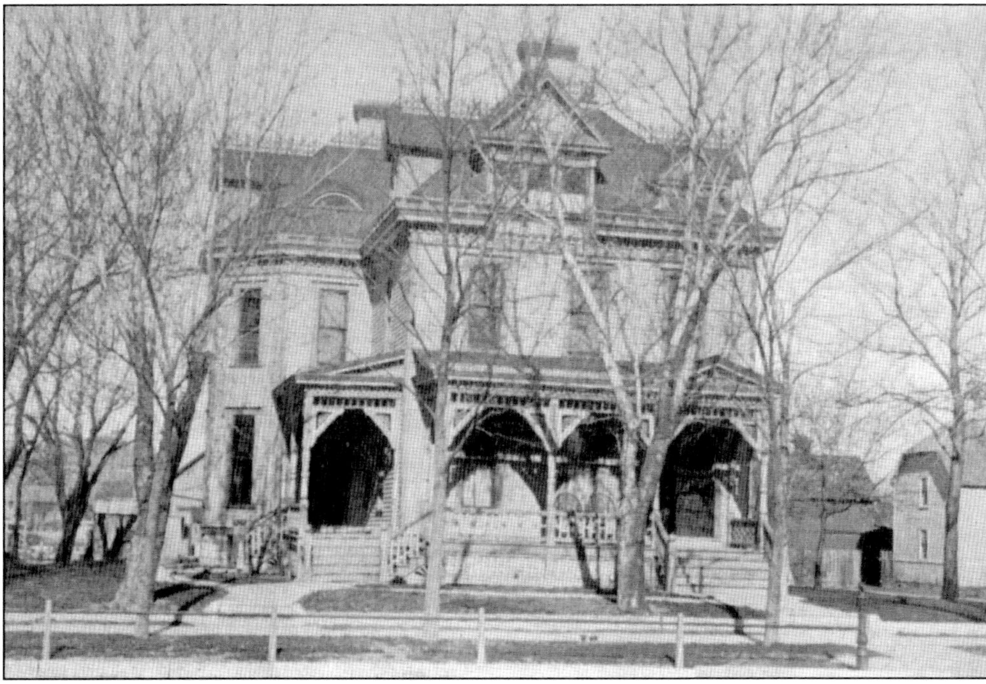

William Martindale brought his family to Emporia in 1866, moving from Greenwood County, where he had settled in 1857. Amassing great wealth through cattle business, farming, milling, and banking, he was able to build this large Victorian residence in the 800 block of Constitution Street. Martindale was also a member of the Kansas House of Representatives and the Kansas Senate in the late 1860s and served as a director of the First National Bank.

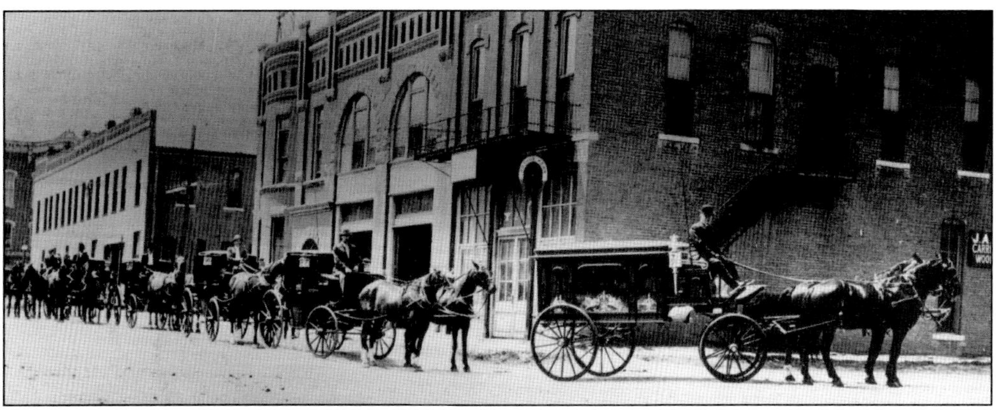

Pete Newton was a familiar name in Emporia for many years. He arrived in the area at the age of eight in 1880. By the turn of the century, he was operating one of the best baggage and hack delivery services in town. With the advent of the automobile, he gave up his horse-drawn business for the automobile business, selling Buicks for more than 30 years. This 1910 image shows Newton's horse-drawn hearse in front of the city building.

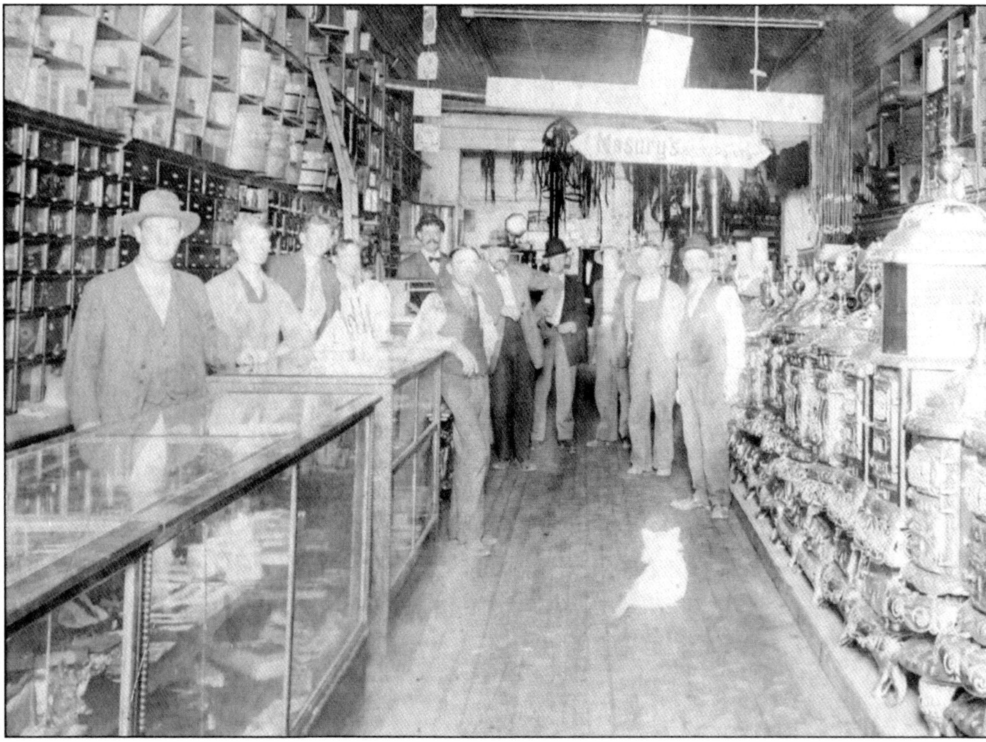

Peters Hardware was opened in the 400 block of Commercial Street in 1881. For over 20 years, George Peters operated the successful store, which specialized in stoves and tin ware, heavy and shelf hardware, and implements. This image shows the interior of his fine store around 1900.

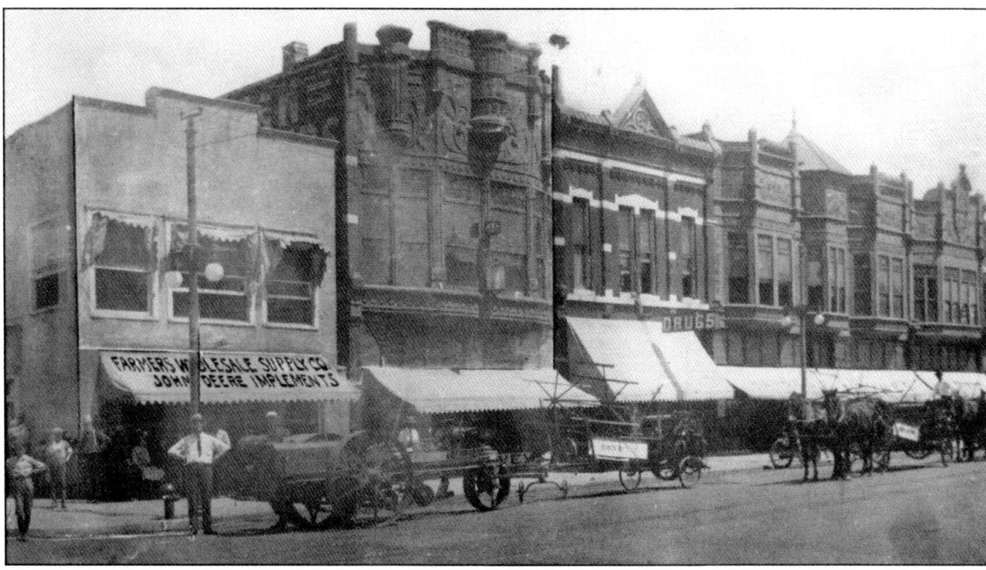

Surrounded by agricultural lands, Emporia was the place to purchase farming supplies and equipment. Displaying their John Deere grain binders like a parade in this 1918 image, the Farmer Wholesale Supply Company provided farmers an opportunity to make a purchase. The company was located on the southeast corner of Seventh Avenue and Commercial Street. The building at far right is the Haynes Hardware Company store.

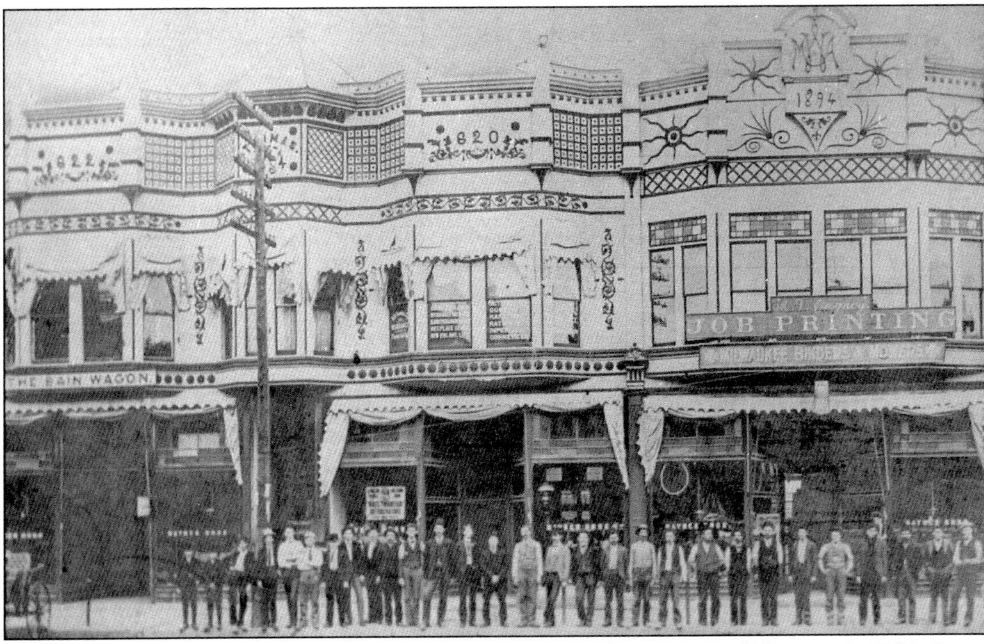

Haynes Hardware Store became part of the Emporia trade center on February 1, 1894. It was owned and operated by the four Haynes brothers: Nathan Biddie, John Quintus, William Everett, and Henry Shields. The store, in the middle of the 600 block on the east side of Commercial Street, had one of the most elaborate metal facades in the city. This image shows the employees gathered in front of the store at the turn of the century.

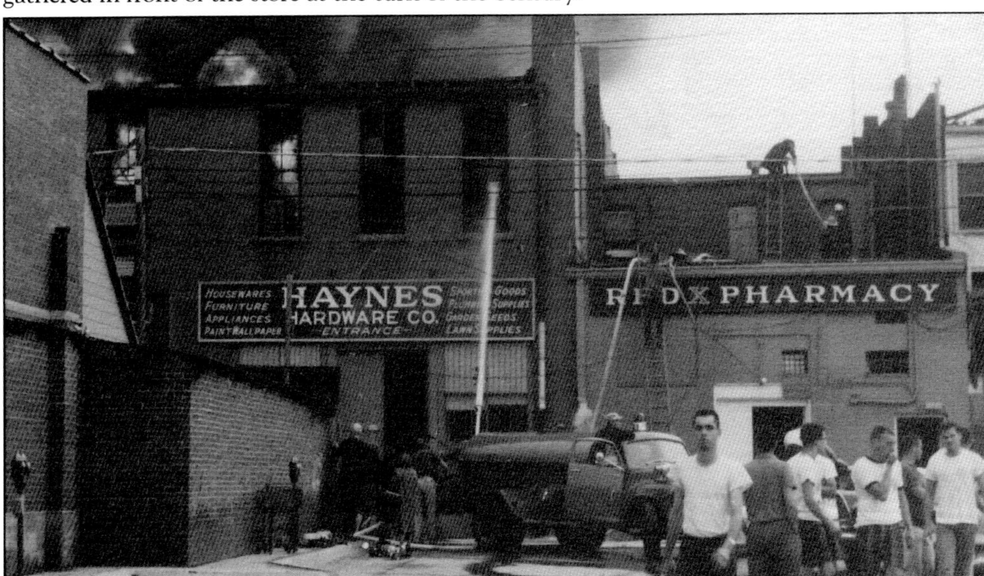

One of Emporia's most spectacular fires occurred on April 23, 1964, when the Haynes Hardware Company at 618–622 Commercial Street was destroyed. Dozens of volunteers, including men from both colleges, helped firemen fight the blaze. Red X Pharmacy sustained some minor damage but was open for business the next day. Damages were estimated at $250,000, but the store was rebuilt and open for business on November 30, 1964. (Courtesy of the Walter M. Andersen Collection, Emporia State University Special Collections Archives.)

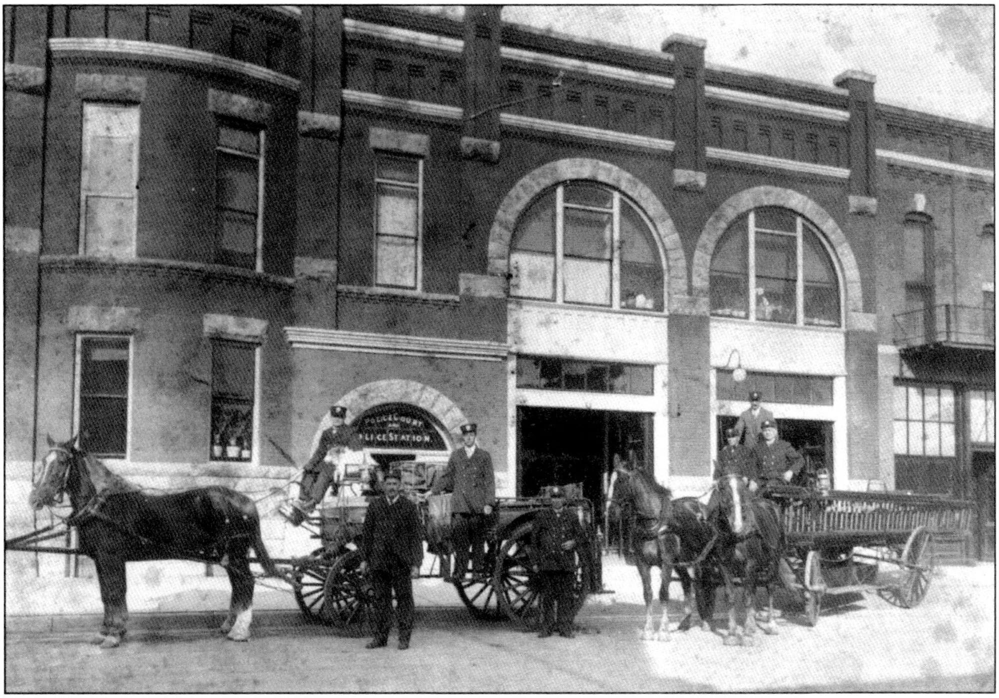

In the early 1900s, horses were still being used to transport fire equipment. This picture, taken around 1915, shows fire horses Joe and Prince (left) and Bob and John (right). Seated in the wagon on the left with the fire department's dog, Toto, is fireman C.C. "Shorty" Johnson. Standing from left to right are Chief Charley Stinson, Archie Walcott, and John Call. The hook and ladder wagon on the right features, from left to right, John Hays, Frank Deister, and Dave Thompson.

Jay's Opera House, located at the corner of Fifth Avenue and Commercial Street, was used for festivals, dances, lectures, and political gatherings. Originally built in 1880 by Maj. F.P. Bancroft, the third floor of the building was designed for theatrical use and was known as Bancroft's Hall. In 1879, the building was passed on to W.S. Jay and became known as Jay's Opera House. A clothing store was located on the first floor.

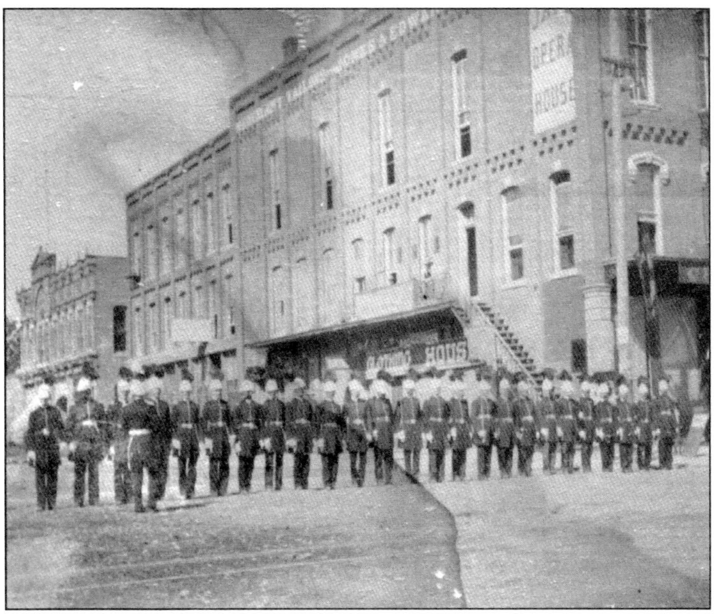

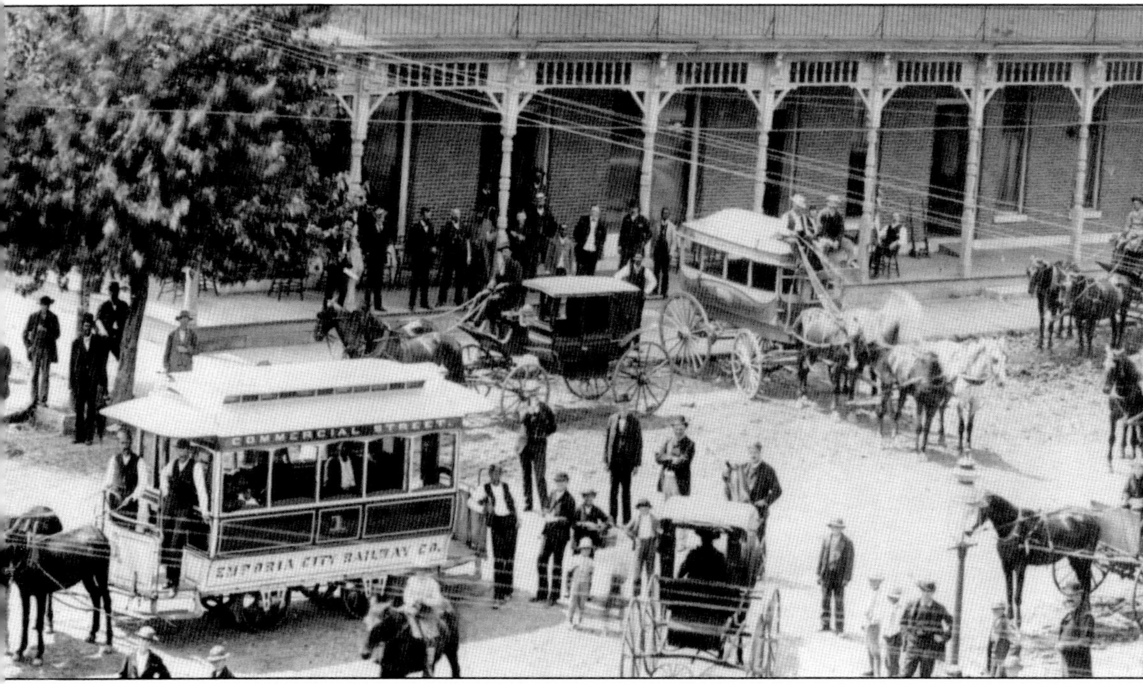

Beginning in March 1884, one of the more interesting modes of transportation to the Coolidge Hotel at the corner of Sixth Avenue and Merchant Street was Emporia's mule-drawn streetcars. According to a July 9, 1885, *Emporia Weekly News* article, the Emporia City Railway Company had run three and a half miles of track on which they ran five regular cars at 15 minutes per trip. One track ran to both the Katy and Santa Fe depots from the Coolidge Hotel, while the other track ran from the normal school to Soden's Grove. The cost of the fare was 5¢, or 4¢ if patrons purchased 25 tickets for a dollar. Patrons could also transfer from the northbound cars to the east-west cars for the price of one fare. Nine men were employed to operate the streetcars. (Courtesy of the Walter M. Andersen Collection, Emporia State University Special Collections Archives.)

The three-story *Emporia Republican* office was located on the southeast corner of Sixth Avenue and Merchant Street. C.V. Eskridge was the owner and proprietor from 1882 until his death in 1900. The daily paper was noted for carrying Associated Press wire service reports and engaging in correspondence with the smaller communities of southeast Kansas.

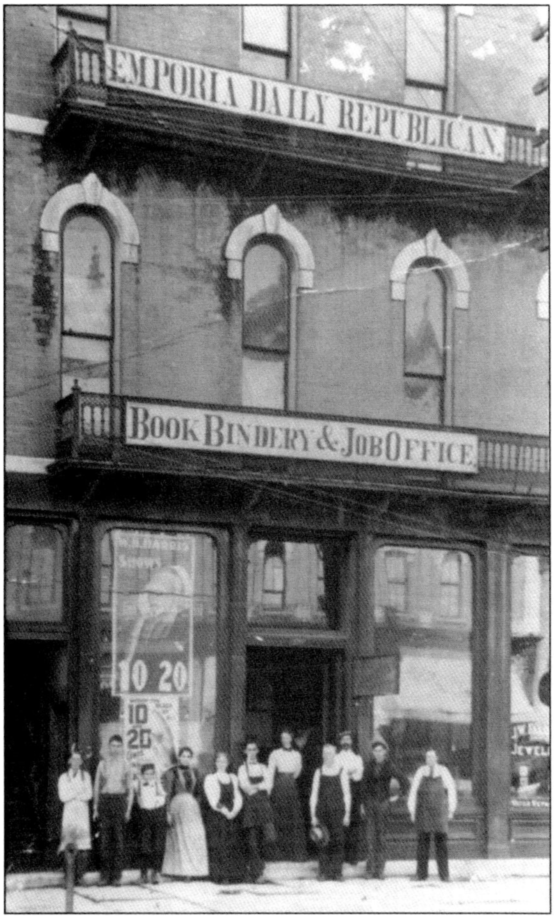

The *Emporia Democrat* was the only Democratic newspaper in Lyon County. W.F. Hetherington established the paper on March 1, 1879, and named it the *Kansas Sentinel*. In August 1882, J.M. McCown, a local lawyer, purchased the paper and renamed it the *Emporia Democrat*. The weekly paper was published from 1879 to 1889. In 1883, the *Emporia Democrat* office was located at the northwest corner of Fourth Avenue and Commercial Street.

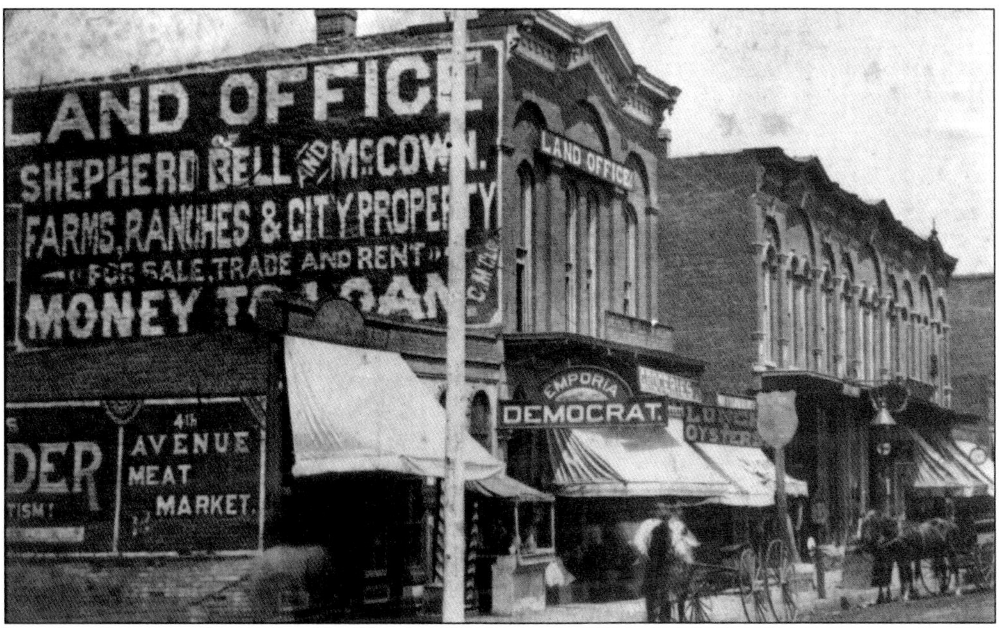

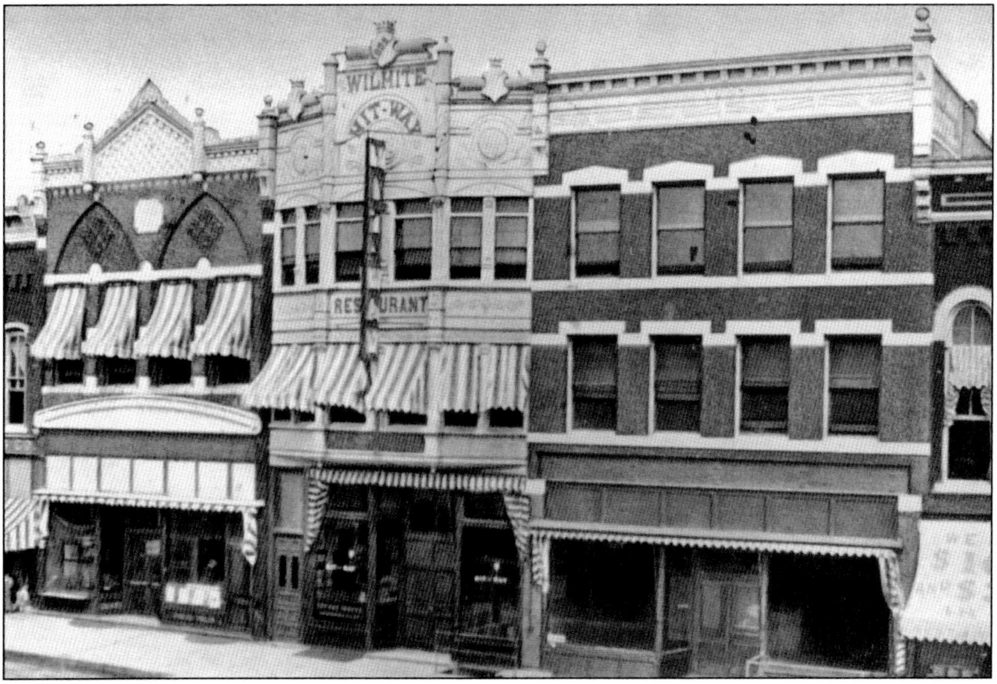

O.M. "Mit" Wilhite founded the Mit-Way Hotel at 510–514 Commercial Street in 1893. The three-story hotel had 75 elegantly furnished rooms with hot and cold water, bath, telephone, and electric lights. A newsstand, cigar store, billiard hall, barbershop, tailor, and telegraph services were also connected to the hotel. Wilhite and his family lived in rooms on the third floor until they moved into their new home on Wilman Court in 1918.

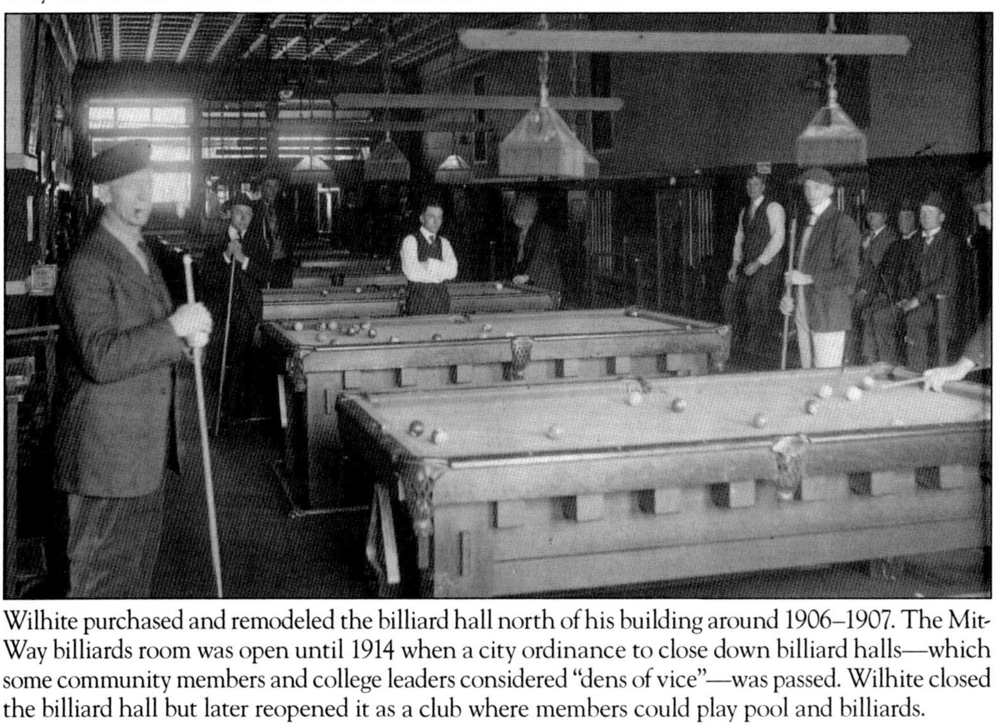

Wilhite purchased and remodeled the billiard hall north of his building around 1906–1907. The Mit-Way billiards room was open until 1914 when a city ordinance to close down billiard halls—which some community members and college leaders considered "dens of vice"—was passed. Wilhite closed the billiard hall but later reopened it as a club where members could play pool and billiards.

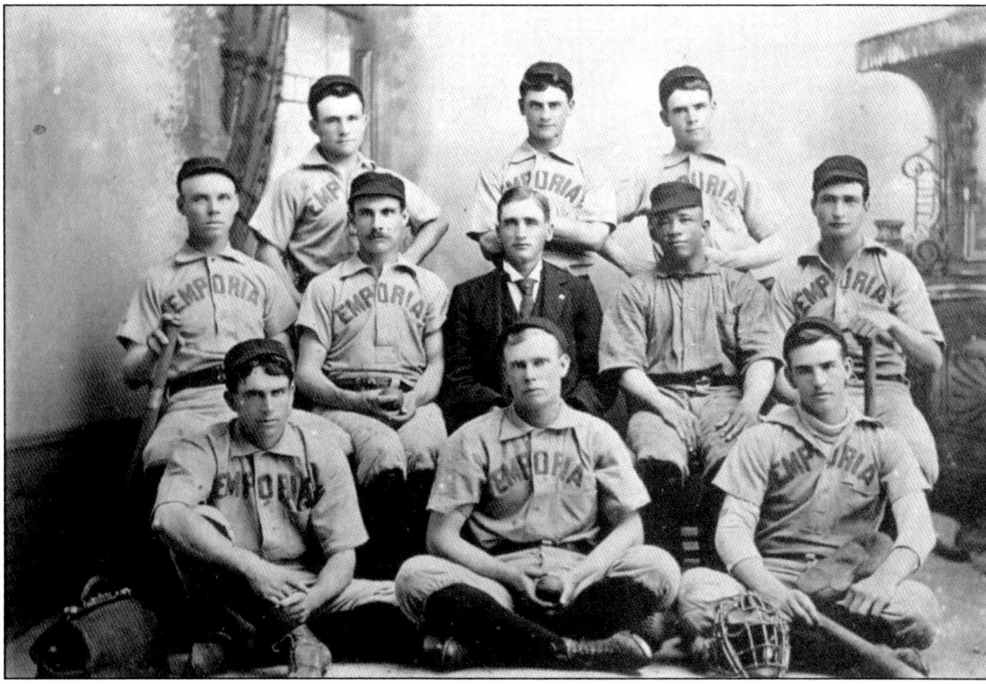

One of Emporia's biggest town boosters was O.M. "Mit" Wilhite, who was well known for promoting and supporting several clubs and organizations, especially baseball and the municipal bands. As a former baseball player in the 1880s, Wilhite donated a lot of his time and money to organizing and managing town baseball teams like the one pictured here (Wilhite is at center, wearing a suit).

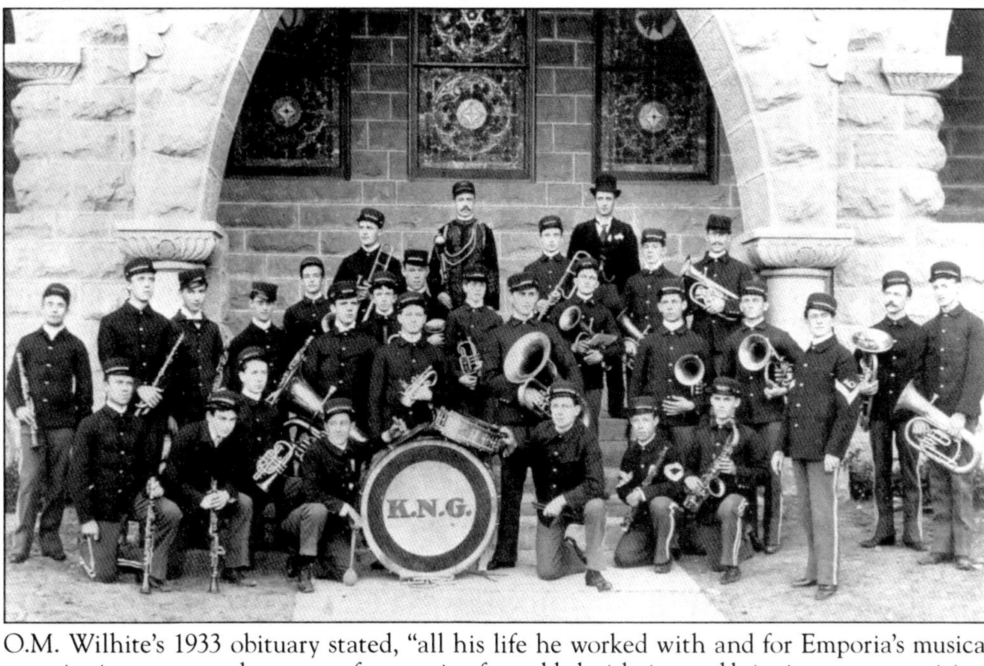

O.M. Wilhite's 1933 obituary stated, "all his life he worked with and for Emporia's musical organizations, even to the extent of promoting favorable legislation and bringing expert musicians to town." One of those musical organizations was Emporia's Kansas National Guard 161st Field Artillery and Municipal Band, pictured here in 1927. Wilhite is in the back without a uniform.

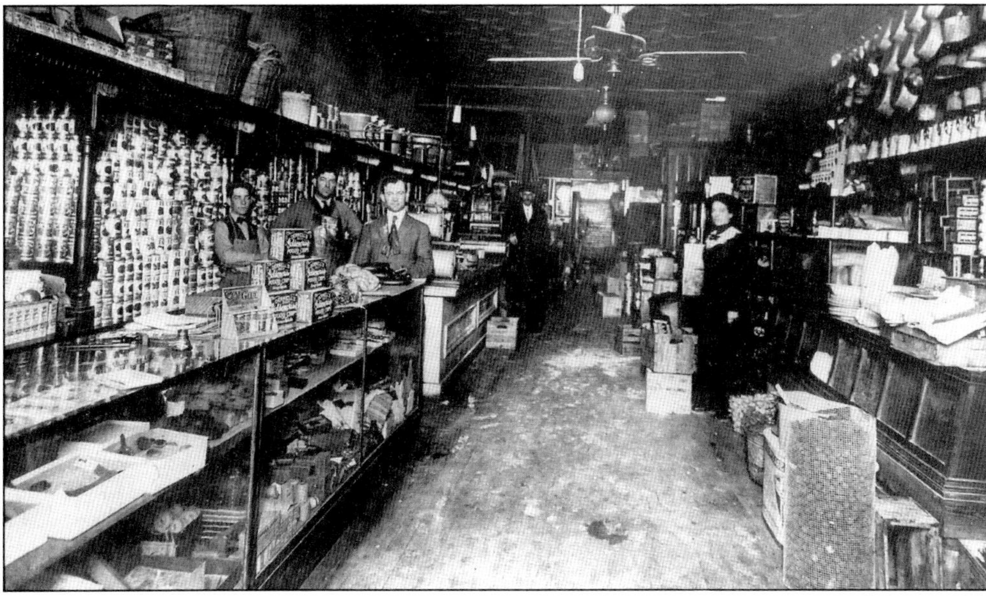

The Reeble family grocery stores were a staple in Emporia for 124 years. In 1883, Rudolph Reeble established the first store, located at 128 Commercial Street. His son Will, pictured above in the white collared shirt, quit school in 1895 to work in the store full time. After Rudolph's death in 1921, Will bought out his brother George's shares of the family business. Will opened a second store at Tenth Avenue and Commercial Street in 1933. His two sons, Bernard and Lester, formed a partnership with their father in 1945. Bernard managed North Reeble, and Lester, South Reeble. In 2007, the two stores were sold along with their family's Price Chopper store on West Highway 50.

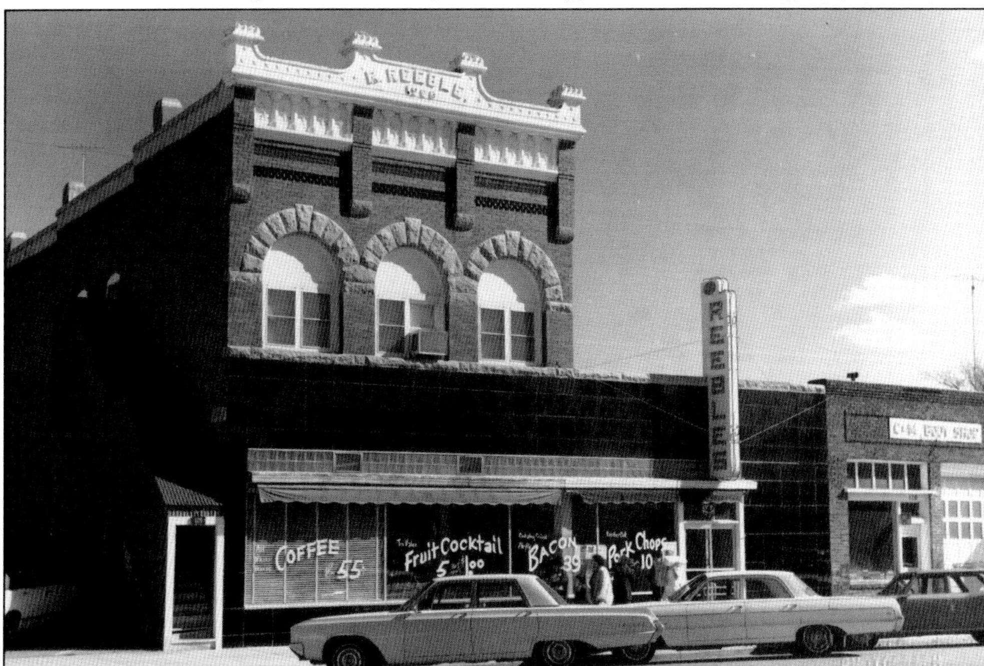

Rudolph Reeble built this two-story brick structure at 124 Commercial Street in 1906. A new addition was built onto the store in 1947.

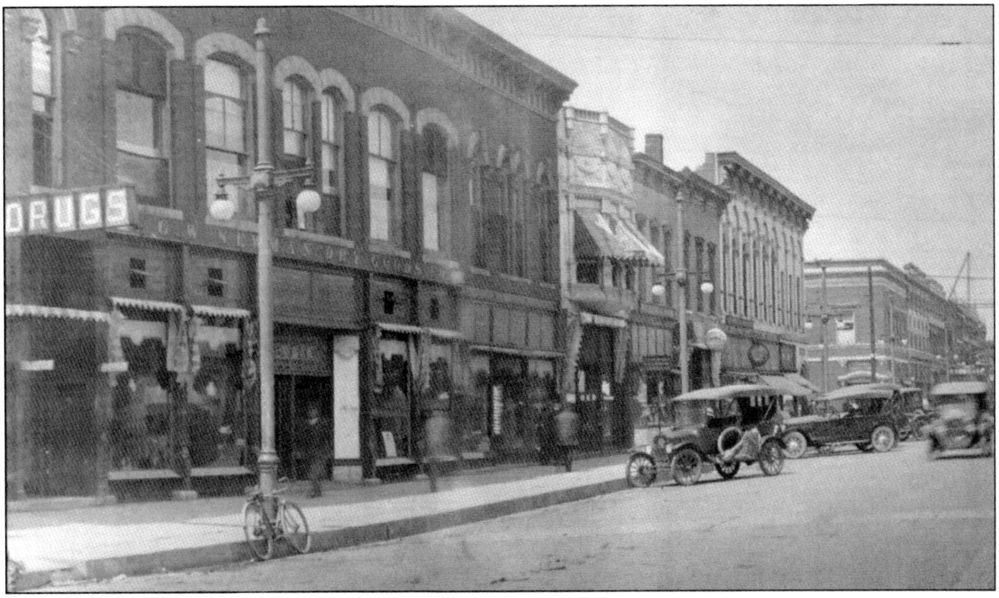

Known as Newman's Dry Goods, and later Newman's Department Store, this store opened for business in 1869. The owners were brothers G.W. and A.A. Newman. Later, another brother, F.C., joined the business. It was located in the 500 block of Commercial Street on the west side as part of Union Block. Over the years, the storefront was remodeled several times, changing its exterior appearance but retaining original architectural details in the interior. The store closed in 1999.

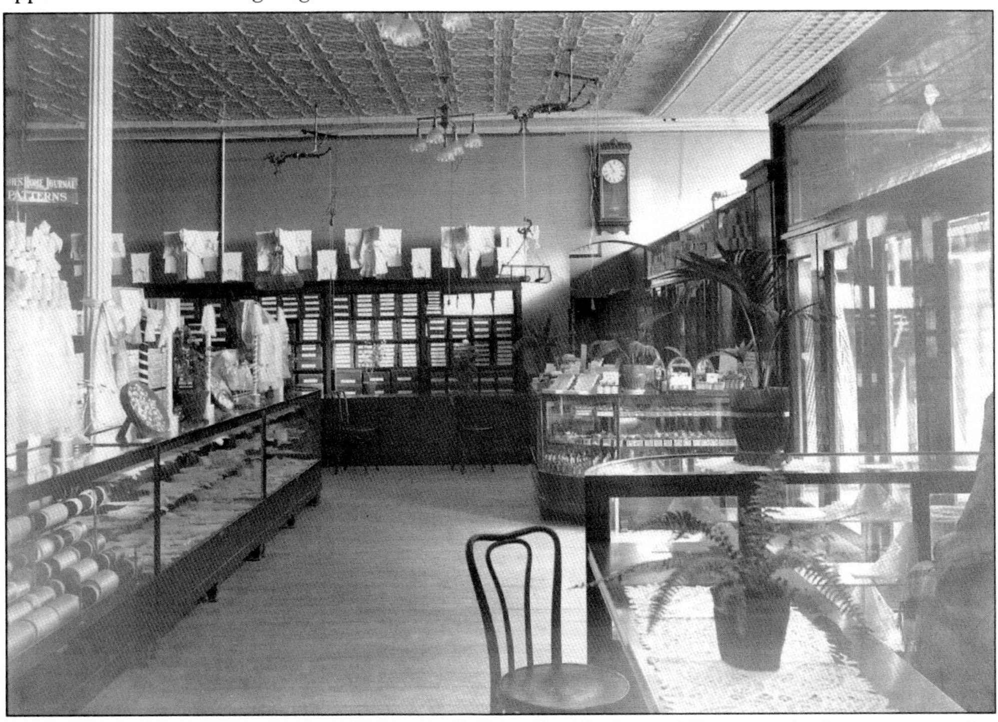

This image shows the interior of Newman's Dry Goods Store. The store had many specialty departments, and customers could spend hours viewing the goods, which were displayed in cases such as these throughout the three-story store.

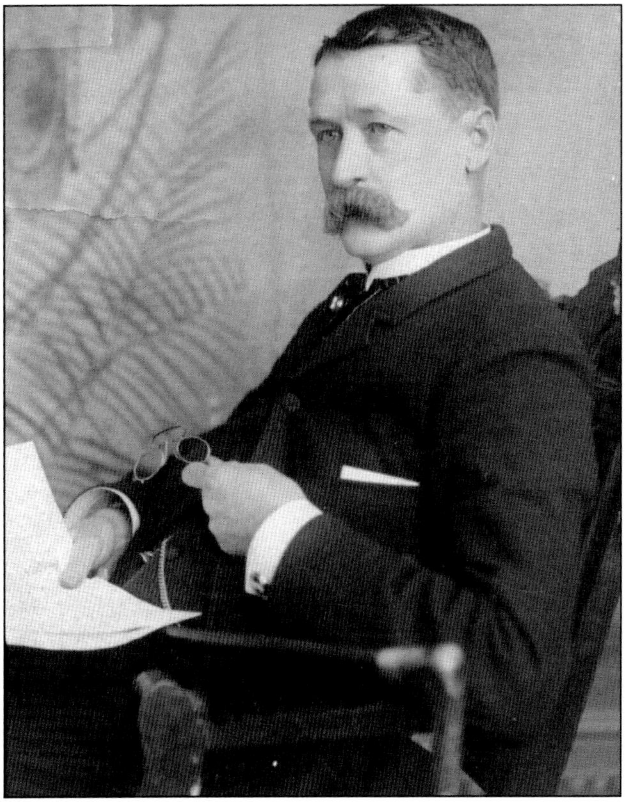

"Soldier, Philanthropist, the Children's Friend"—these words, engraved on Capt. Lemuel T. Heritage's tombstone, aptly describe Heritage's character. As a Civil War veteran, Heritage organized an annual reunion for his fellow soldiers on the anniversary of the Battle of Prairie Grove. His philanthropy was funded by money he made in the banking business. In 1867, Heritage helped organize the first bank in Lyon County, the bank of Swallow, Heritage, and Soden. It was later reorganized as the Emporia National Bank. Never married, Heritage left money to his church and the city library. He also left a $40,000 bequest to be used to help poor children in Emporia.

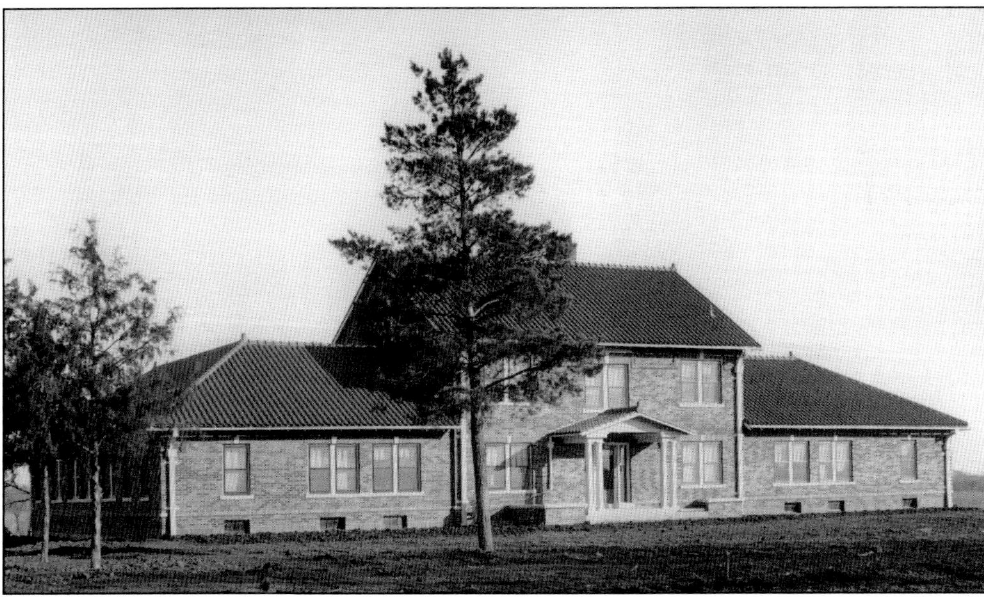

Prior to the 1970s, Lyon County took care of its poor and needy citizens at the county poor farm, located south of South Avenue on Prairie Street where the county road and bridge department is today. Pictured here is the new home that Lyon County built in 1926; it was named "the Heritage" in honor of Capt. L.T. Heritage, a philanthropist who had left his estate to the poor. (Courtesy of the Walter M. Andersen Collection, Emporia State University Special Collections Archives.)

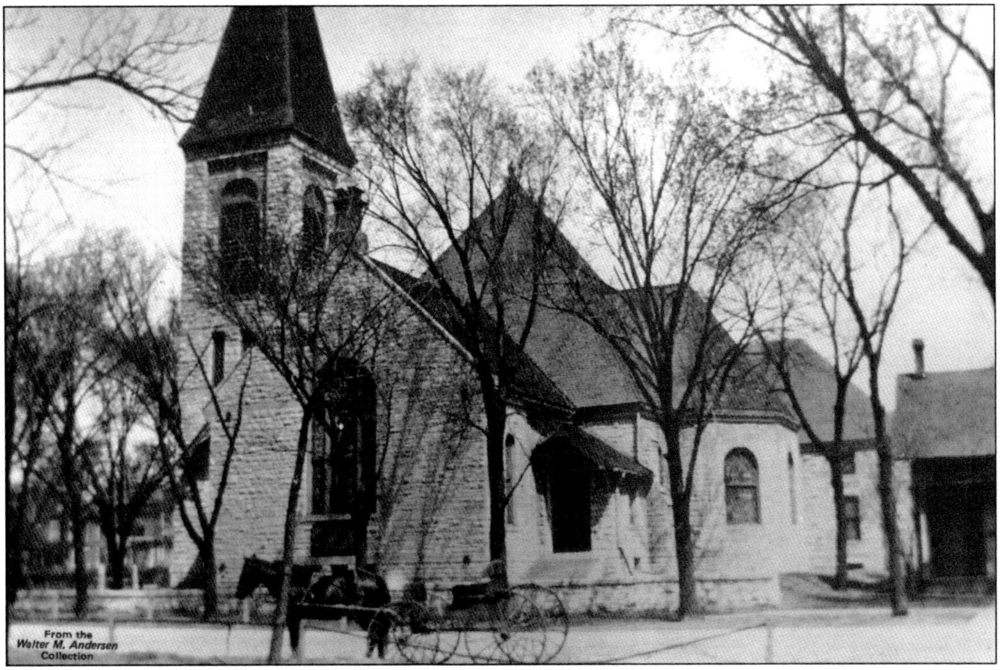

Rev. G.C. Morse organized the First Congregational Church in 1858. Their first church was built at the corner of Eighth Avenue and Mechanic Street on lots given to them by the town company. When they outgrew the building, the congregation raised money under the leadership of Rev. Richard Cordley to erect this Gothic-style church on the same site in 1881. The church cost over $12,000 to build. (Courtesy of the Walter M. Andersen Collection, Emporia State University Special Collections Archives.)

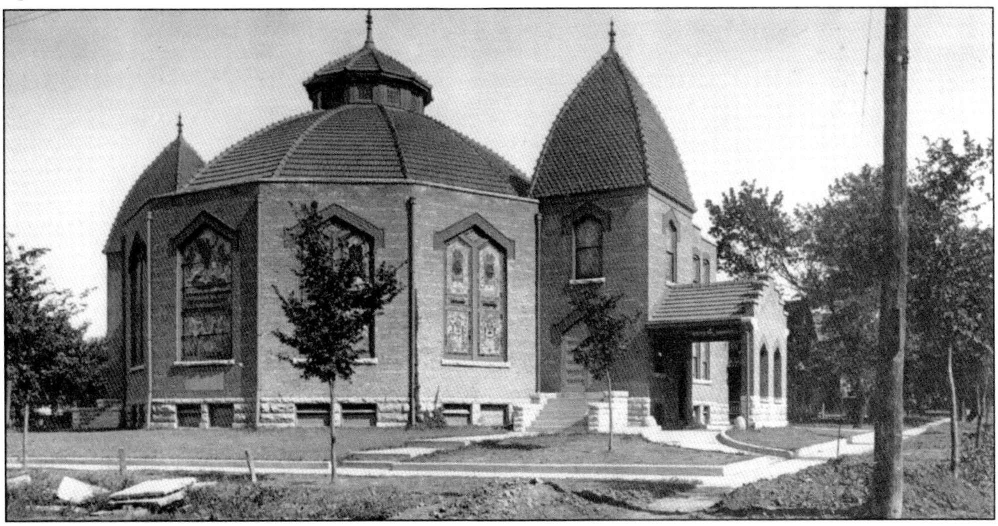

The First Christian Church was organized in 1856 and had the distinction of being the oldest church in the city and the oldest existing congregation of disciples in the state of Kansas. Its first church, located at Seventh Avenue and Exchange Street, was built under the leadership of Rev. Solomon Brown in 1859. The church pictured here was located at 701 Market Street and dedicated in 1883. It cost $9,500 to build. (Courtesy of the Walter M. Andersen Collection, Emporia State University Special Collections Archives.)

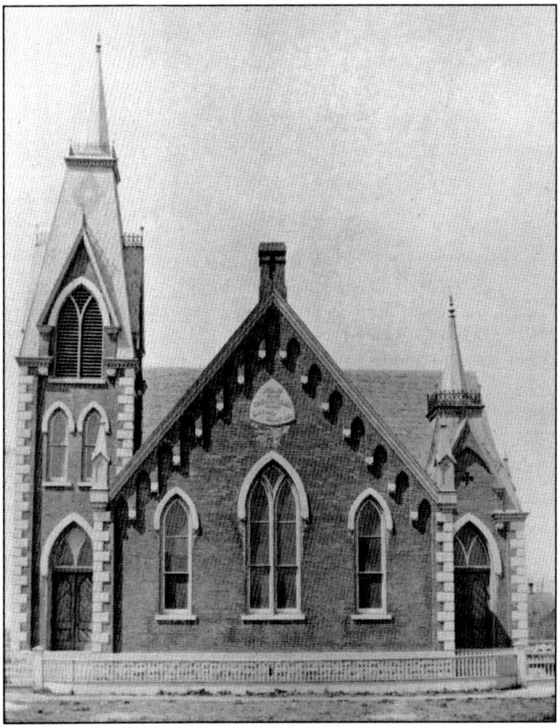

The Welsh Congregational Church, also known as Bethany Congregational, was organized in 1866 with 37 members. Rev. G.C. Morse served as pastor. One of several Welsh churches in the community, it was located at Second Avenue and Merchant Street on the northwest corner. It was constructed in 1867 and rebuilt in 1882. (Courtesy of the Walter M. Andersen Collection, Emporia State University Special Collections Archives.)

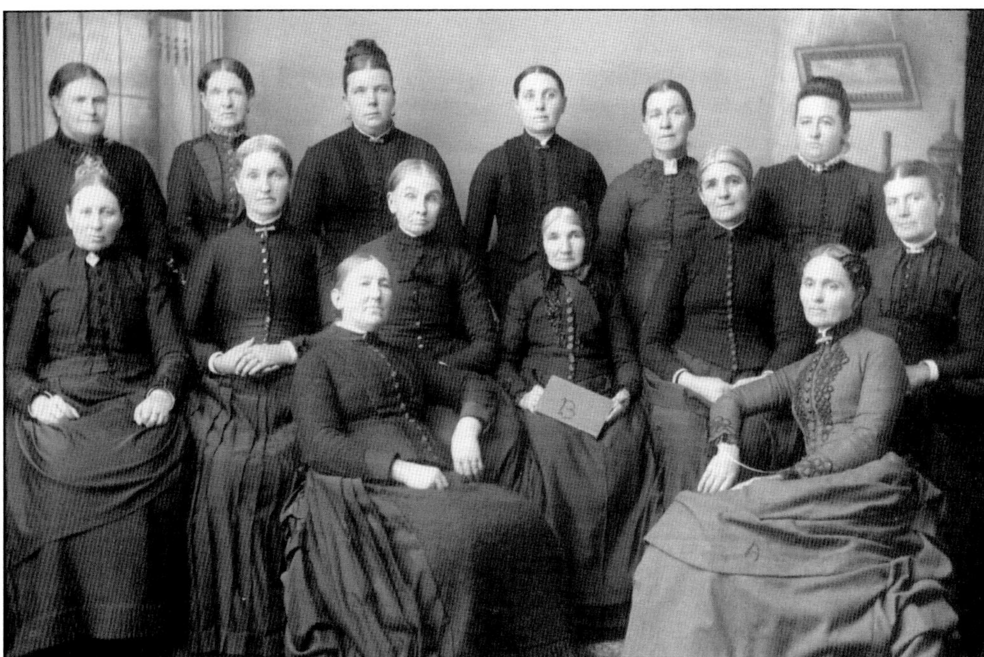

Since 1878, St. David's Day has been celebrated in Emporia. March 1 is the day set aside to remember the death of Wales's patron saint. It is recorded that David was instrumental in spreading Christianity throughout Wales in the fifth century. St. David's Day is always celebrated with a concert and traditional Welsh food. This image taken around 1883 shows the original St. David's Day Women's Society.

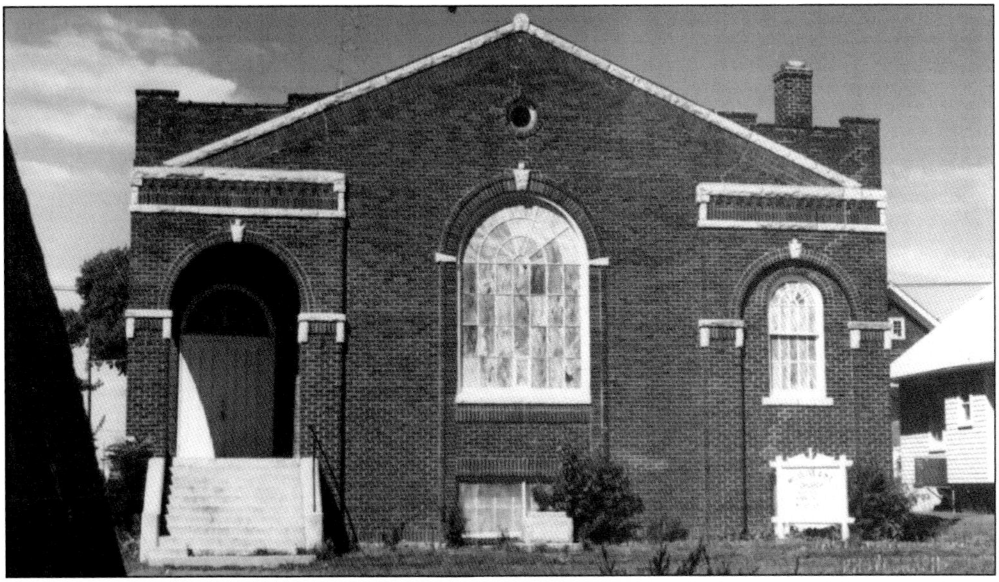

The Mount Olive AME Methodist Church has been located at Sixth Avenue and Congress Street since 1882. According to an *Emporia Weekly News* article on the status of Emporia's churches in 1883, it cost $4,000 to build. Membership in 1883 was 99, while the Sunday school enrollment was 115. T.J. Merritt was the pastor. (Courtesy of the Walter M. Andersen Collection, Emporia State University Special Collections Archives.)

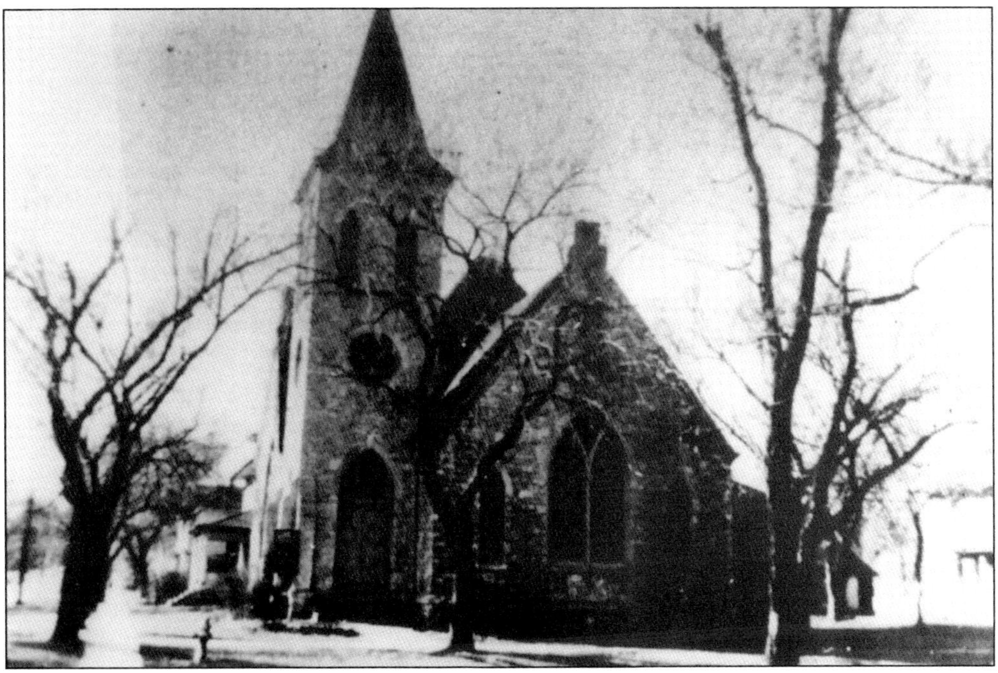

The St. Mark's Lutheran congregation built their first church in Emporia at 701 Constitution Street. The lots were purchased for $1,495.45 on November 16, 1885. The cornerstone was laid on April 10, 1888, and the building was dedicated on November 3, 1889. Rev. Frank D. Altman was pastor of the church during the construction. (Courtesy of the Walter M. Andersen Collection, Emporia State University Special Collections Archives.)

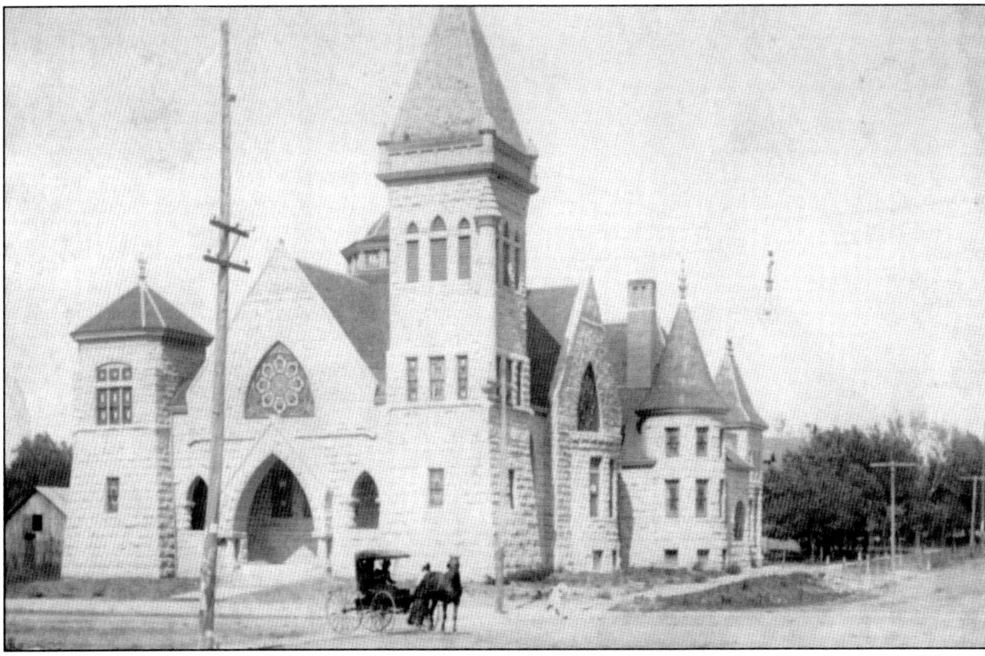

Among one of architect Charles Squires's grandest church designs is the First Presbyterian Church at 802 Commercial Street. The cornerstone was laid in 1895, and the structure was completed in 1897. The architecture reflects the Romanesque style popular in the 1890s, with towers, turrets, a dome, and stained-glass windows. It is one of Emporia's downtown landmarks.

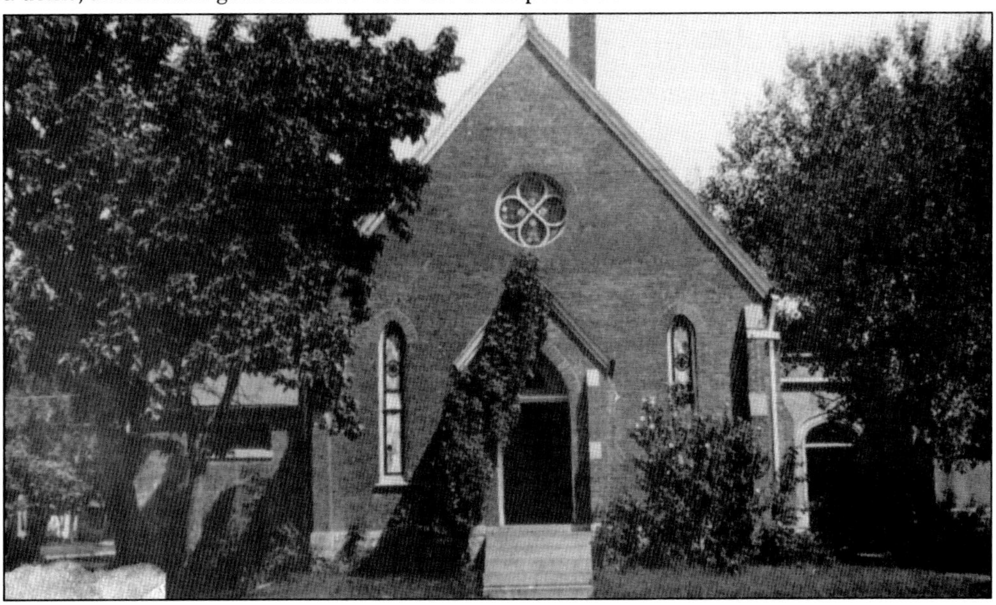

Organized in 1870 by Rev. L.R. Holden, St. Andrew's Episcopal Church has occupied the same corner of Eighth Avenue and Commercial Street since it began. One of the building projects in the 1920s expanded the church and then connected the parish house. Subsequent additions to the church involved removing two nearby houses and a filling station that stood between the Episcopal church and the Presbyterian church next door. (Courtesy of the Walter M. Andersen Collection, Emporia State University Special Collections Archives.)

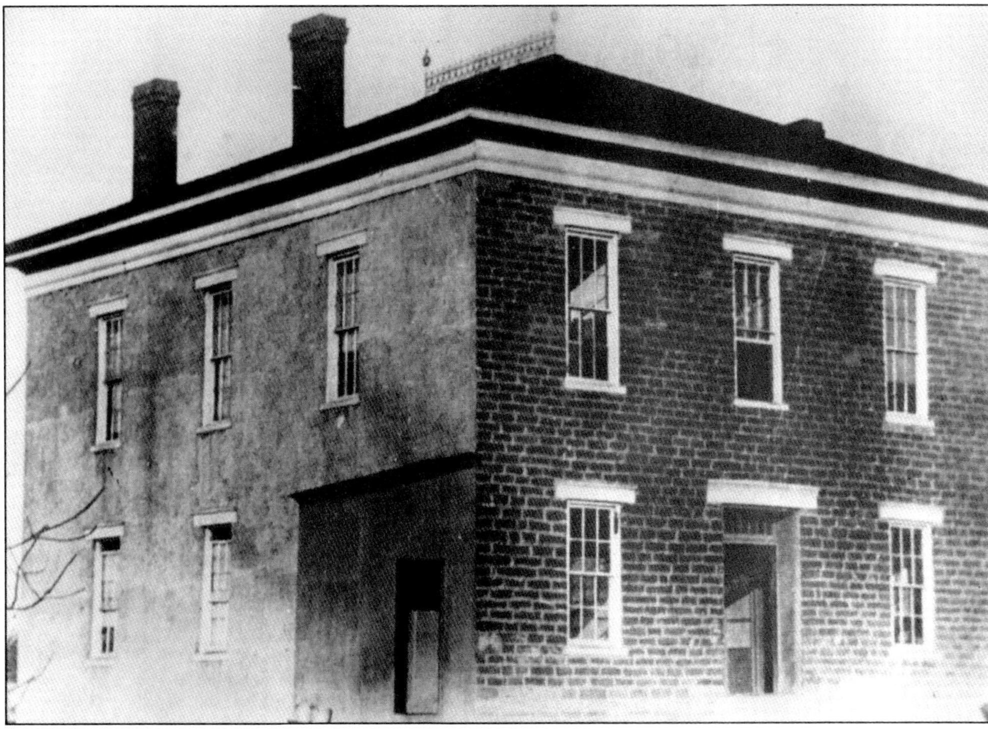

Completed in 1864, the Stone School was Emporia's first permanent school. Built with a $5,000 bond, it was the first school built in Kansas under the bond system and the largest district schoolhouse in the state. It stood on the northeast corner of the block between Sixth and Seventh Avenues and Constitution and Congress Streets. T.M. Gruel was the first principal, and Mary Jane Watson was his assistant.

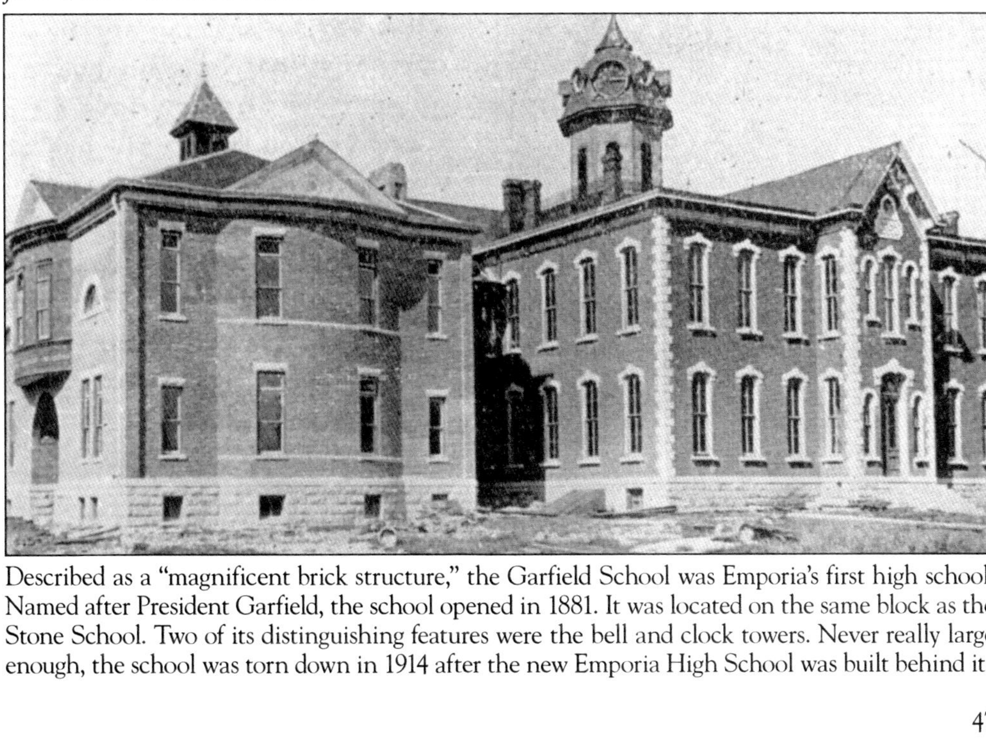

Described as a "magnificent brick structure," the Garfield School was Emporia's first high school. Named after President Garfield, the school opened in 1881. It was located on the same block as the Stone School. Two of its distinguishing features were the bell and clock towers. Never really large enough, the school was torn down in 1914 after the new Emporia High School was built behind it.

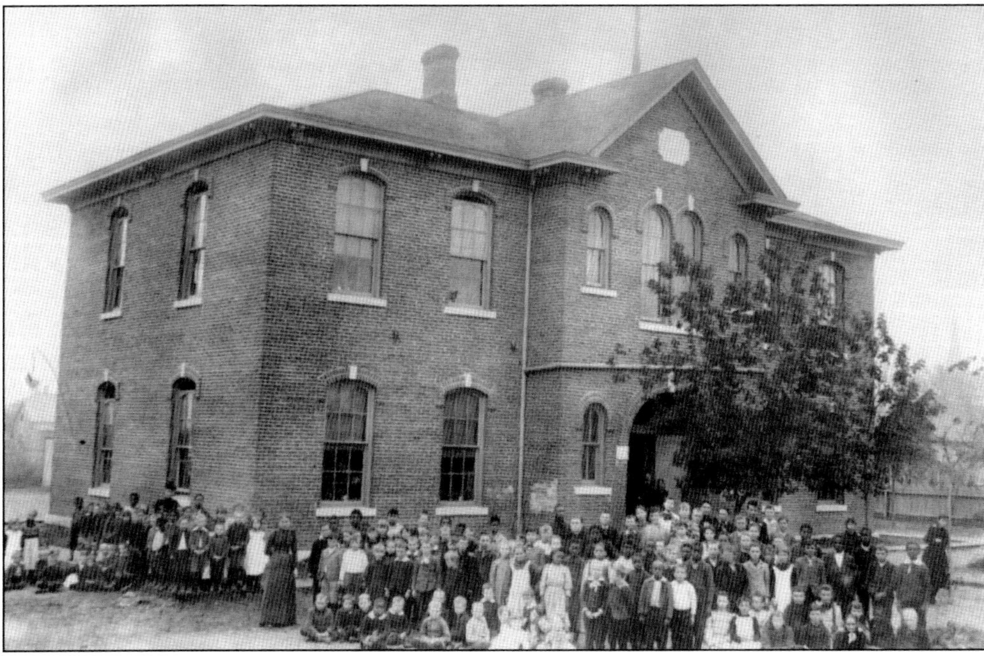

Sylvan Street School was located on the southwest corner of Sylvan Street and Eighth Avenue. Pictured here in 1893, it served as the Fourth Ward's school until the Century School was built in 1900.

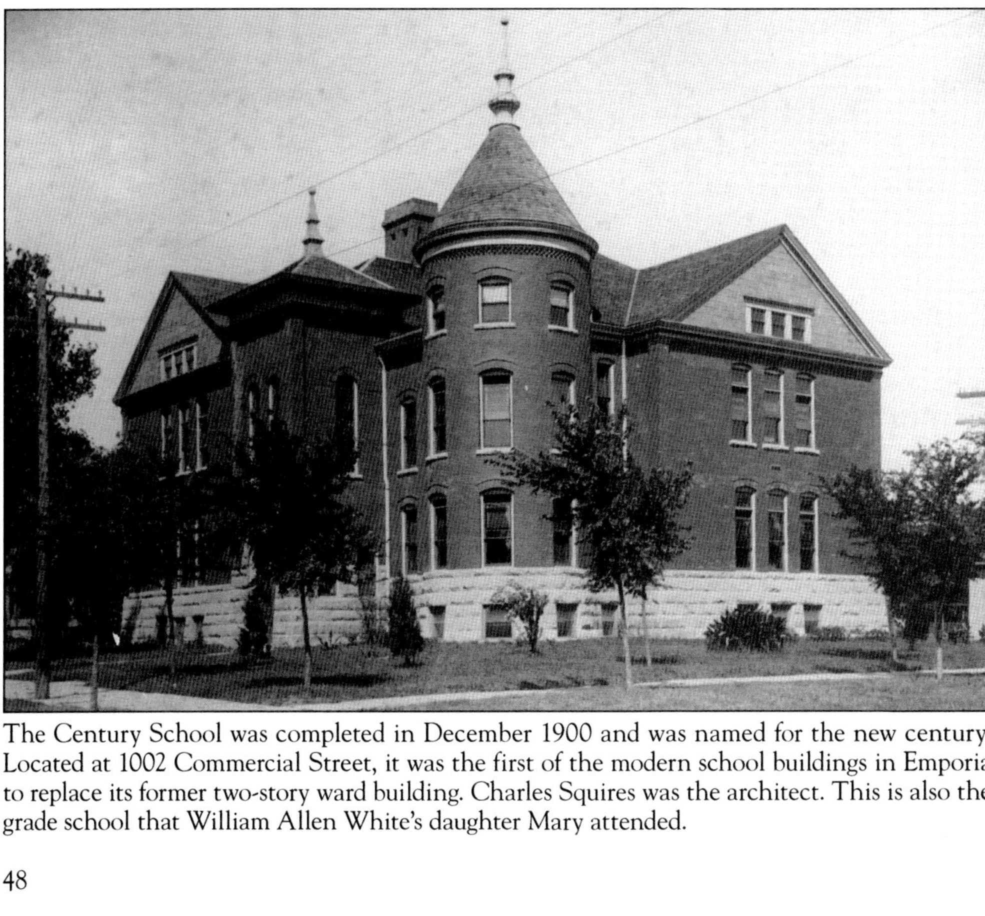

The Century School was completed in December 1900 and was named for the new century. Located at 1002 Commercial Street, it was the first of the modern school buildings in Emporia to replace its former two-story ward building. Charles Squires was the architect. This is also the grade school that William Allen White's daughter Mary attended.

Three

SMALL TOWN AMERICA COMES OF AGE

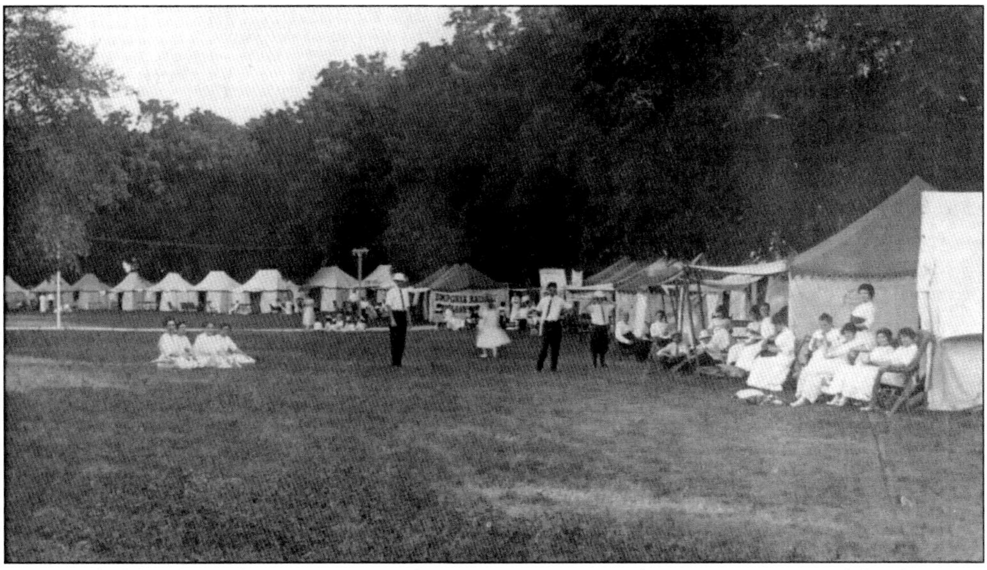

Emporia held its first Chautauqua in Soden's Grove in 1902. Chautauqua was an adult education movement in the late 19th and early 20th centuries that brought entertainment and culture for the whole community. An *Emporia Gazette* article described the 1913 Chautauqua as "a series of high-class entertainments, lectures, and musicales which are clean, wholesome, educational, and uplifting." Treating the event like a vacation, many Emporians and out-of-town visitors rented tents like the ones pictured above and camped out during the event, which lasted from seven to ten days. The camping area was nicknamed "Tent City." Tents were arranged in rows, and the avenues between rows were given names to help people locate friends and family. In 1913, a 10-by-14-foot family tent with two rooms cost $4.50 to rent. Families brought furniture from home to furnish the tents. Season tickets for the 1913 Chautauqua were $2 for adults and $1 for children. Individual admission prices for events were 25¢ for adults and 15¢ for children. The Chautauqua movement died down in the early 1930s.

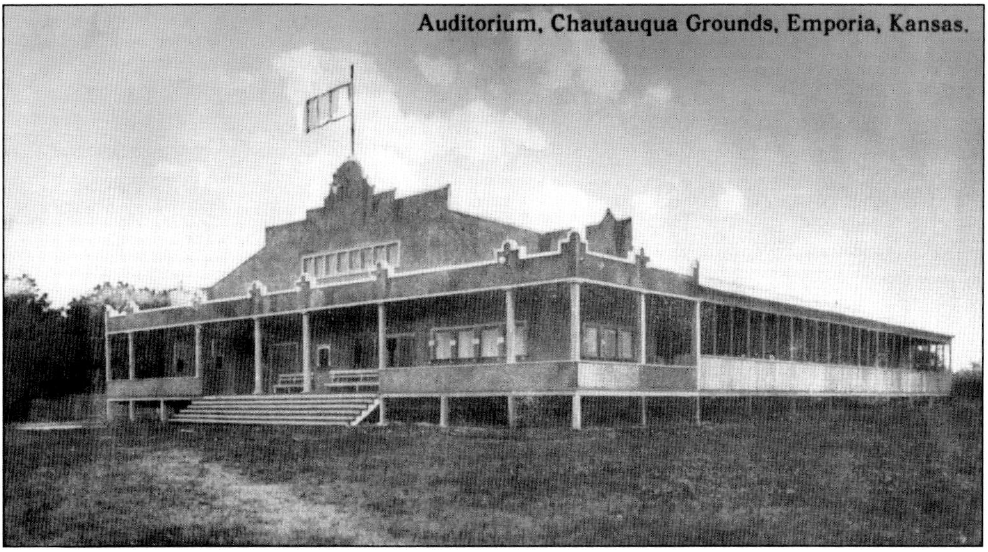

In anticipation of providing ample space for the large crowds that gathered throughout the year for the Chautauqua and other events, a pavilion with a seating capacity of 2,000 was built in 1914 on the north side of Soden's Grove. Features included a stage for the Chautauqua speakers and performers, a dance floor, and a skating pavilion.

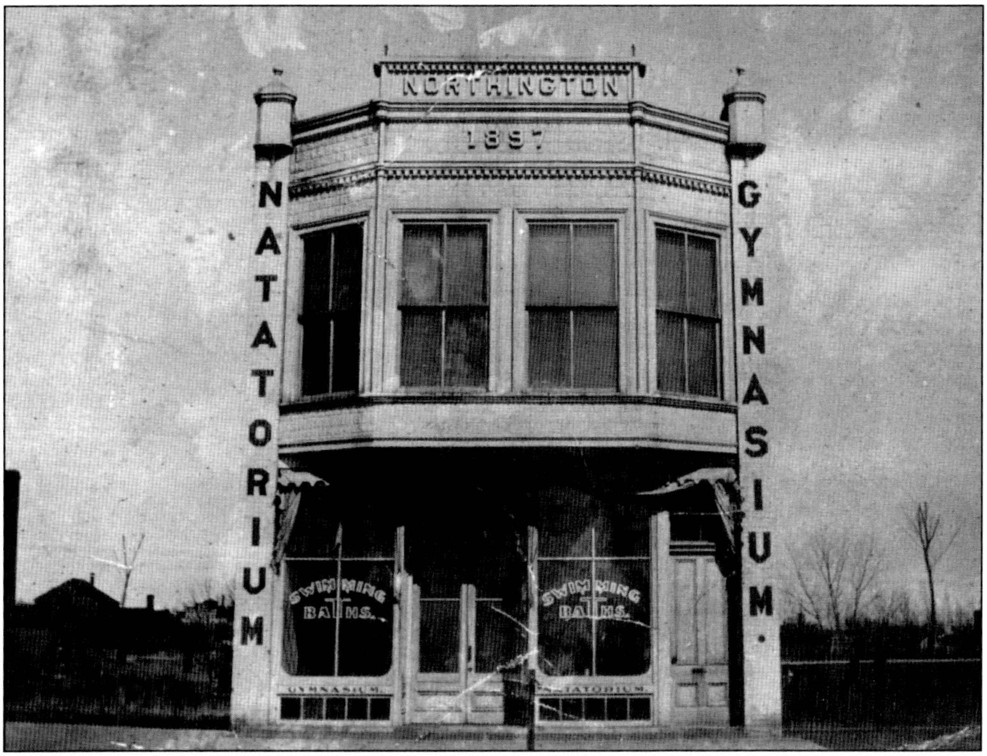

Dr. John Northington, a local dentist, built the natatorium and gymnasium at 212 Commercial Street in 1897. The facilities were for men only. When the building was razed in 1978, the swimming pool was still in existence but had been covered with a false floor by one of the previous owners. Northington was also noted for owning the first car in Emporia.

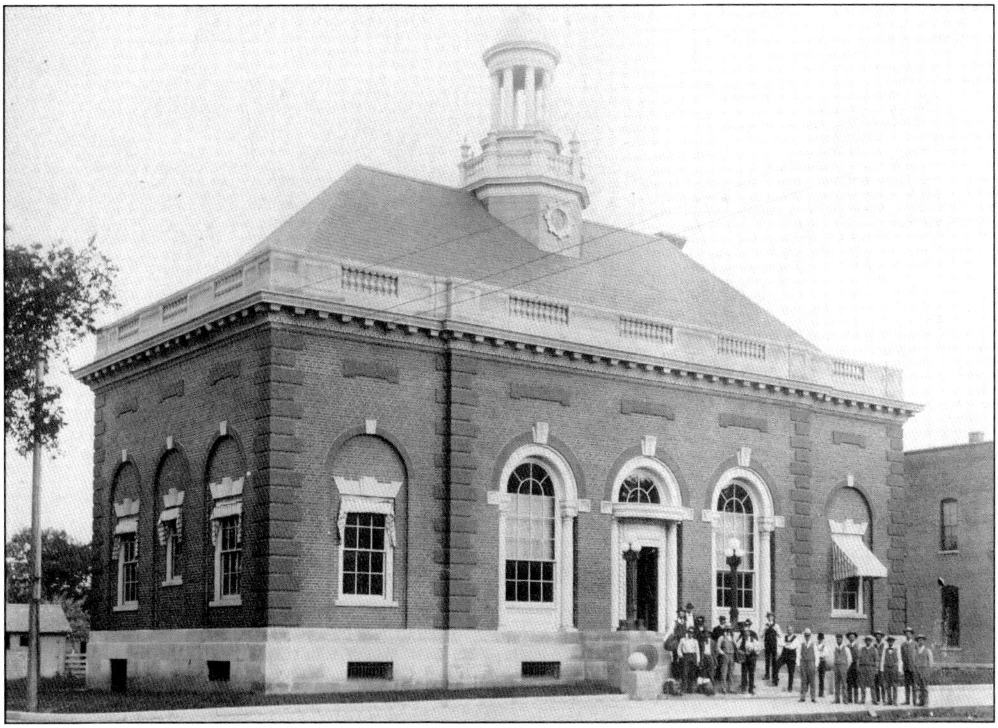

The Emporia Post Office, constructed in the Federal architectural style, was completed in 1903 at 501 Merchant Street. With the growing population, an addition was later built. The cupola on top of the building was struck by lightning twice. Following the second strike, it was not rebuilt. After the new post office was completed in 1959, the Unified School District No. 253 maintained its offices in the building for many years.

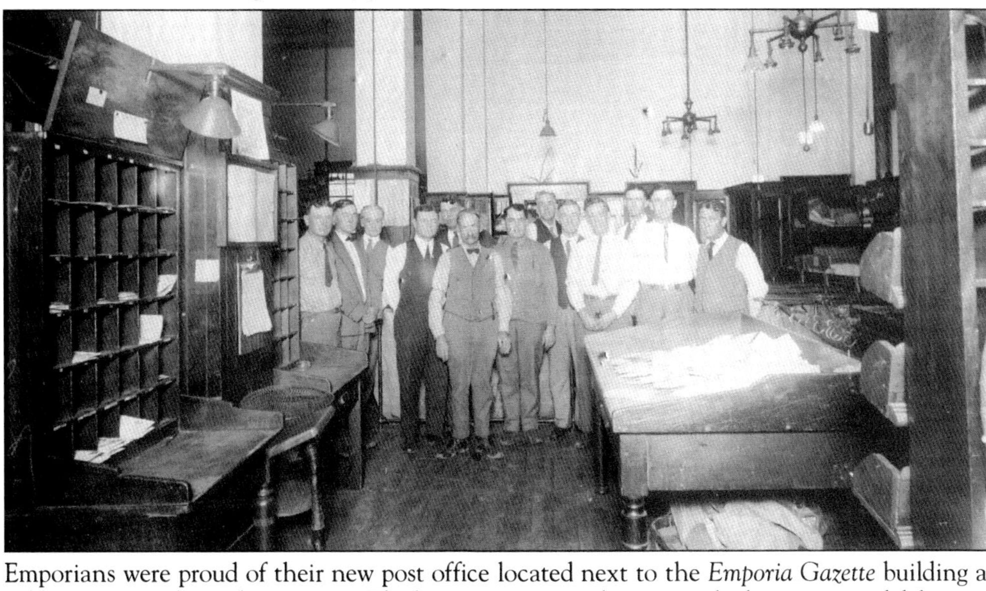

Emporians were proud of their new post office located next to the *Emporia Gazette* building at Fifth Avenue and Merchant Street. The large, spacious work areas made the sorting and delivering of the growing community's mail much easier. This image shows some of the postal employees posing in one of the sorting areas.

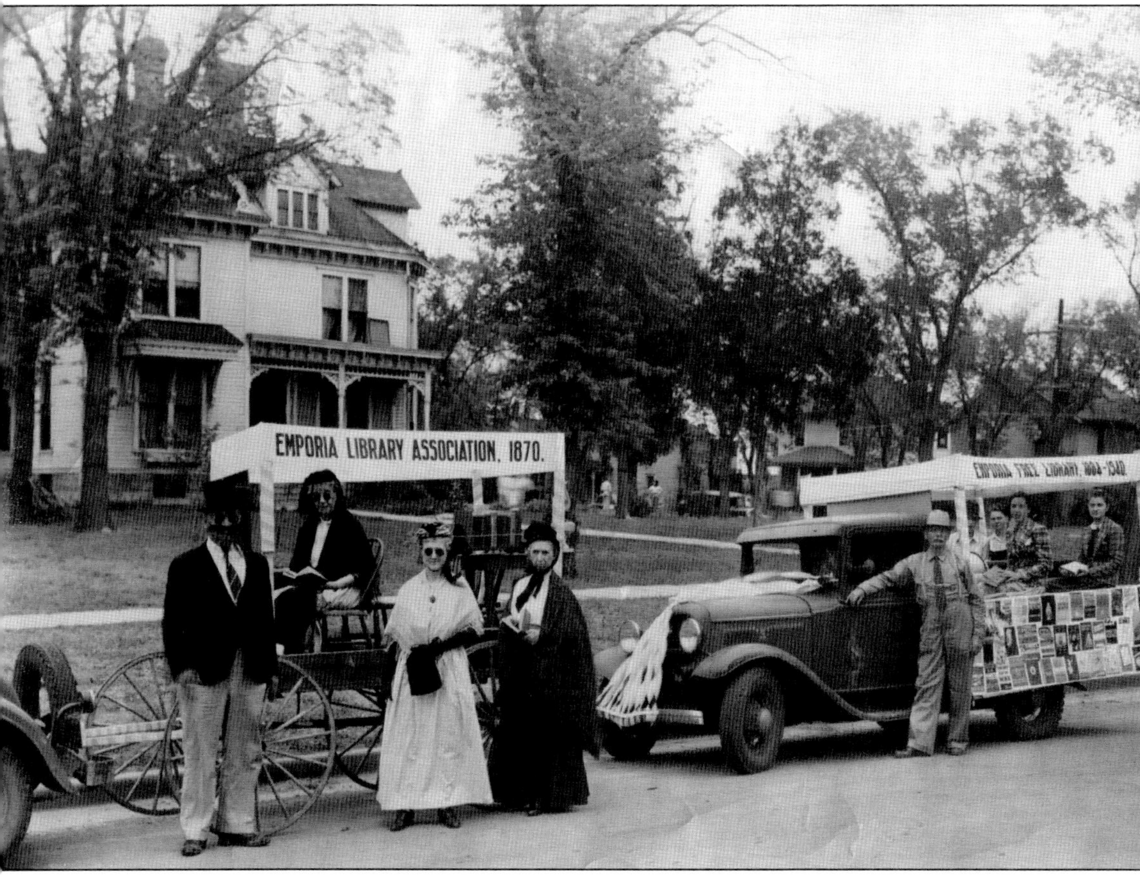

The parade floats pictured here represent the two groups who were responsible for organizing the first subscription and free libraries in Emporia. The Library Association of Emporia met in December 1869 to elect officers and set dues for its members to pay for rent, librarian's salary, and books. Annual dues were set at $3 for men and $2 for women. Money was also raised with lectures, stage shows, masked balls, and strawberry festivals. In 1884, a group of women interested in a free public library for Emporia met and formed a new association. Later that year, a city ordinance was passed establishing a free public library. In the 1890s, the library was housed in the Masonic building on West Fifth Avenue. In 1906, the new Carnegie Library at Sixth Avenue and Market Street was opened.

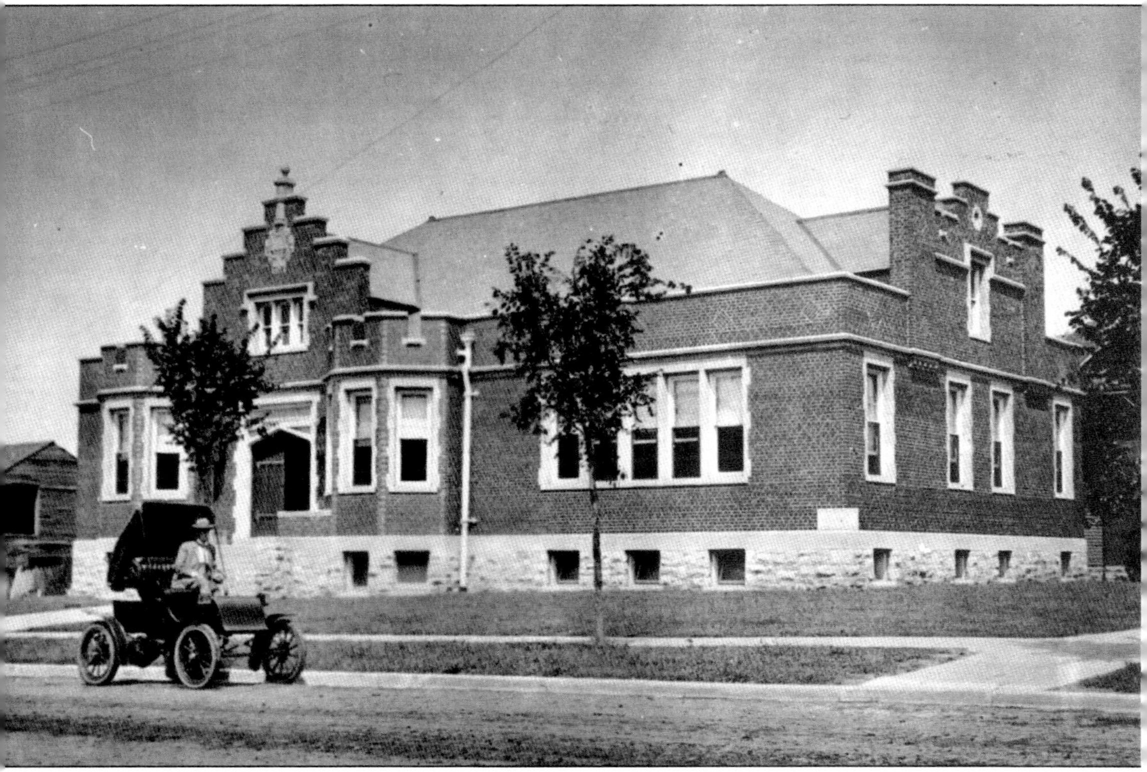

Thanks to Amanda Wicks, city librarian from 1893 to 1902, Emporia was able to acquire a gift of $20,000 from Andrew Carnegie to build a new city library (pictured here around 1908). Since Emporia had already received a gift from Carnegie to build the Anderson Library on the College of Emporia campus, Wicks's first application was denied. Undeterred, Wicks applied again and pointed out that the Anderson Library would house only college books and that the city's public library had no building. The gift was granted, and Carrie Plumb, wife of Preston Plumb, donated the land on the corner of Sixth Avenue and Market Street. When Capt. L.T. Heritage died in 1913, he bequeathed $12,000 to the city library—$2,000 to be spent at once on books, and the rest to be invested for future use.

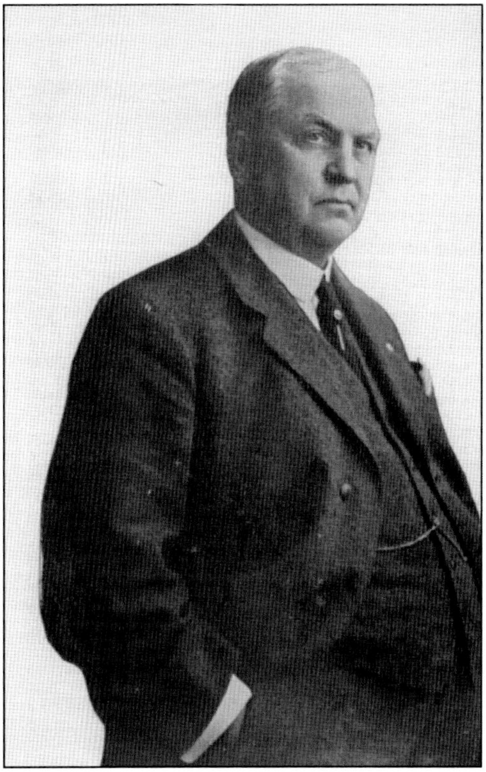

George W. and Nellie Newman were two of Emporia's most prominent and leading citizens. At age 19, Newman came to Emporia in 1869 from Maine with his brother A.A. Newman and founded Newman Brothers Dry Goods. After the departure of his brother, G.W. managed the store by himself until his other brother, F.C., joined him. At that time, the firm changed its name to G.W. Newman & Co. Newman, an exceptional businessman, was able to amass a handsome fortune.

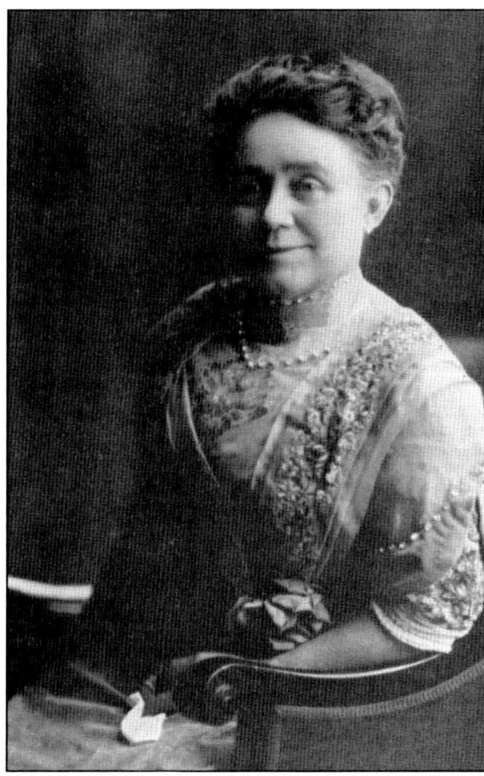

In 1873, G.W. Newman married Nellie A. Storrs, the daughter of Elizabeth Storrs, who had the distinction of being the first child to live in Emporia in 1857. The Newmans were instrumental for over 50 years in the development of Emporia. They were generous with their fortune; their most notable contribution was $50,000 to build the hospital that bears their name.

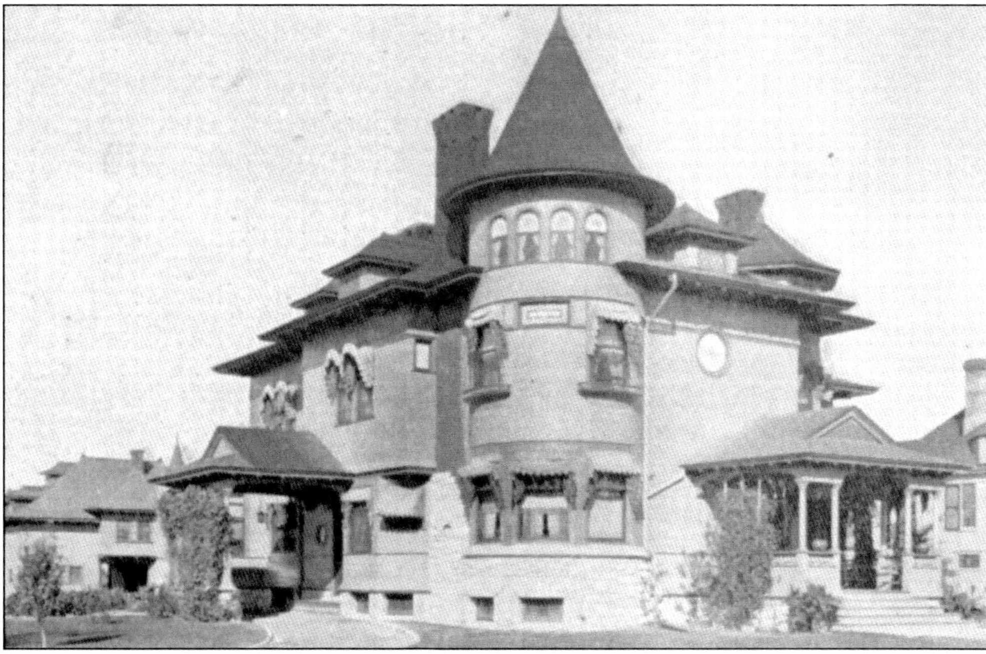

The Newmans built their handsome Queen Anne Victorian house at 318 West Twelfth Avenue in 1893. They lived there for many years. In 1948, the home was demolished for the construction of the First Congregational Church.

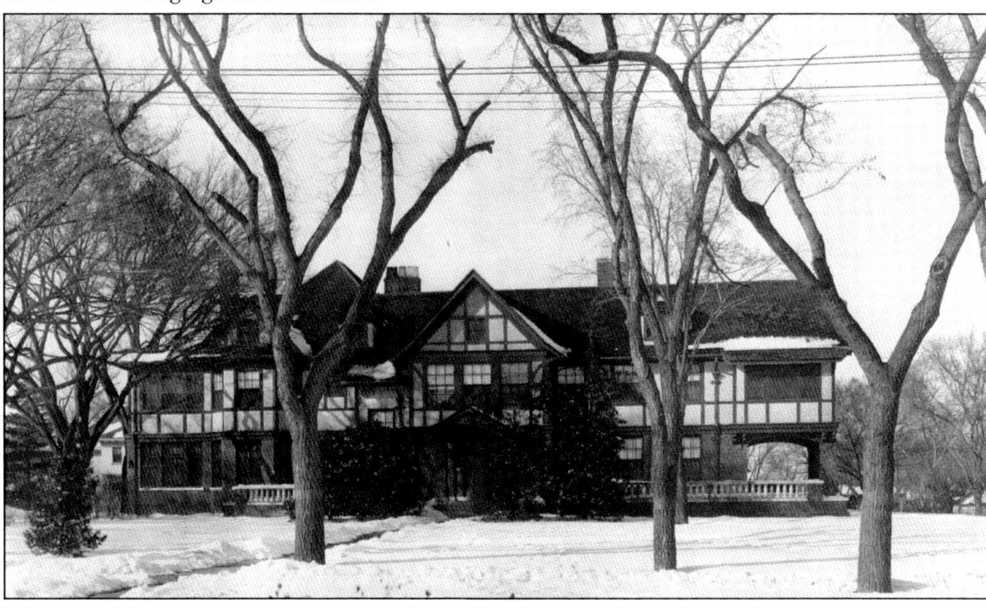

Many wealthy and prominent citizens built their homes along the north side of West Twelfth Avenue. The Selleck H. Warren home at 312 West Twelfth Avenue was built at a cost of $20,000 in 1920. It was occupied by the Warrens for only a short time and was then purchased by Warren Finney, who also lived there only a short time following his involvement in a Kansas bond scandal. In later years, the house served as a sorority home and the American Legion post, and today houses the Emporia State Federal Credit Union. (Courtesy of the Walter M. Andersen Collection, Emporia State University Special Collections Archives.)

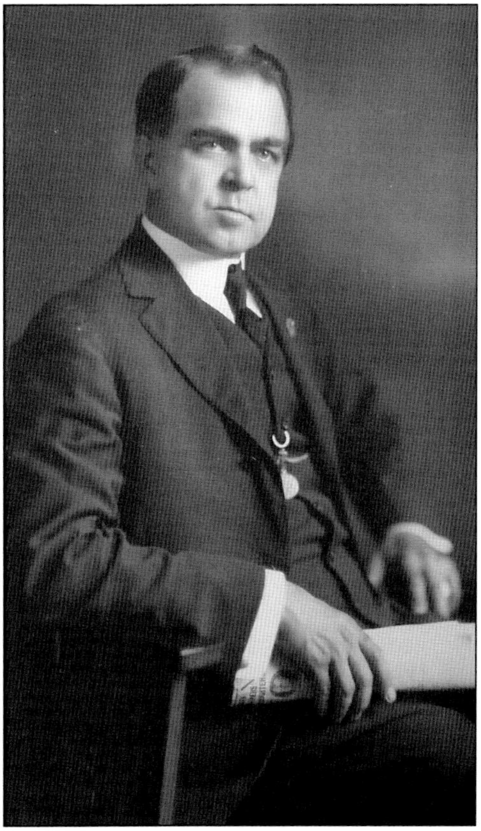

Albert H. Gufler was one of Emporia's leading businessmen and civic leaders for many years. Coming from the Theodore Poehler Mercantile Company branch in Lawrence, he came to Emporia to manage the branch established in 1900. Gufler was involved in the chamber of commerce and the development of the city in the early 1900s. He and his wife, Mary, and their seven children occupied the stately mansion on Twelfth Avenue.

Albert H. Gufler's mansion at 612 West Twelfth was designed by Emporia architect Henry Brinkman in 1915. The Neoclassical-style house completed in 1916 included a carriage house in the rear of the property. The Guflers lived in the home until 1946, when they sold it to the Kappa Sigma Epsilon Fraternity. In the late 1970s, the fraternity sold the house, and it is once again a private residence. (Courtesy of the James Roach family.)

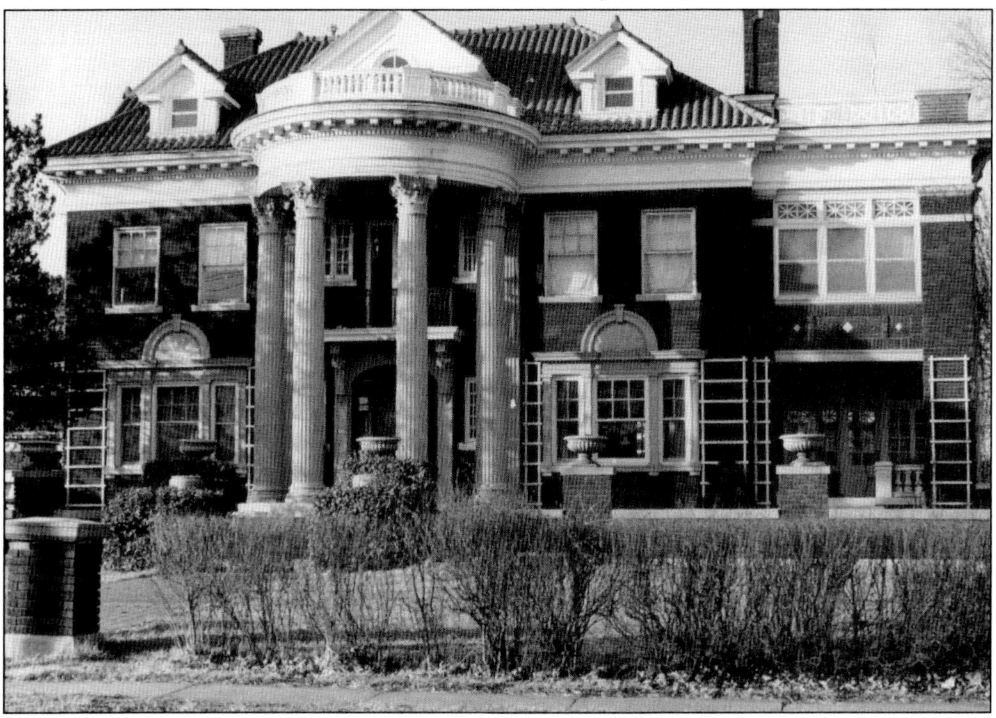

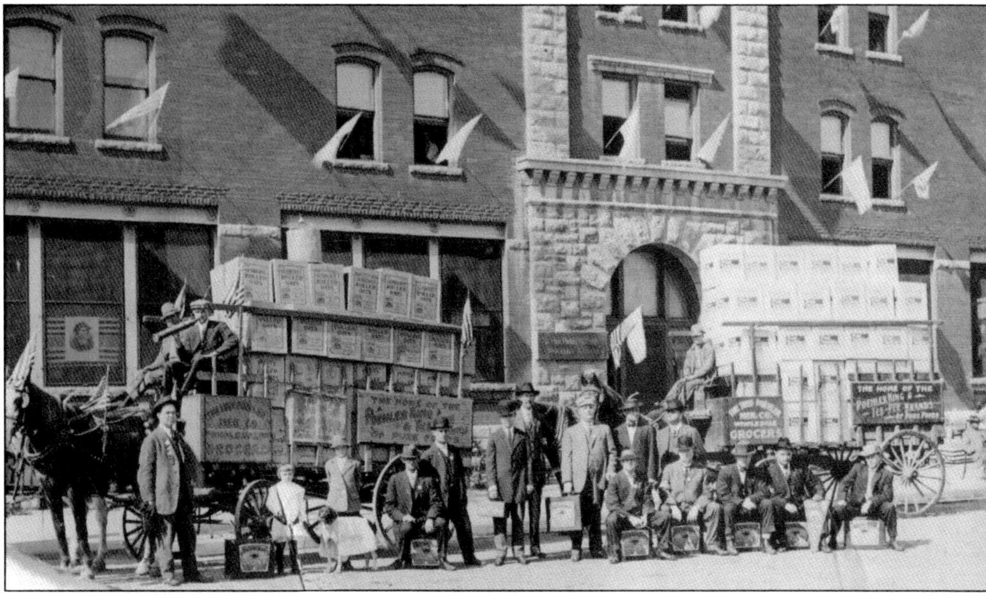

Following the Civil War, German immigrant Theodore Poehler settled in Lawrence, where he opened a wholesale and retail grocery business. Thanks to his successful business skills and management, he established three branch businesses at Emporia, Topeka, and McPherson. The Emporia branch opened in 1900 under the management of A.H. Gufler, who worked for Poehler in Lawrence. Gufler had the same business management skills as Poehler, and the company was one of the largest in Emporia. The Poehler offices and warehouse were located at 301 Commercial Street next to the railroad tracks. Pictured here are Poehler employees and salesmen standing in front of wagons loaded with boxes of whole grain oats in the early 1900s.

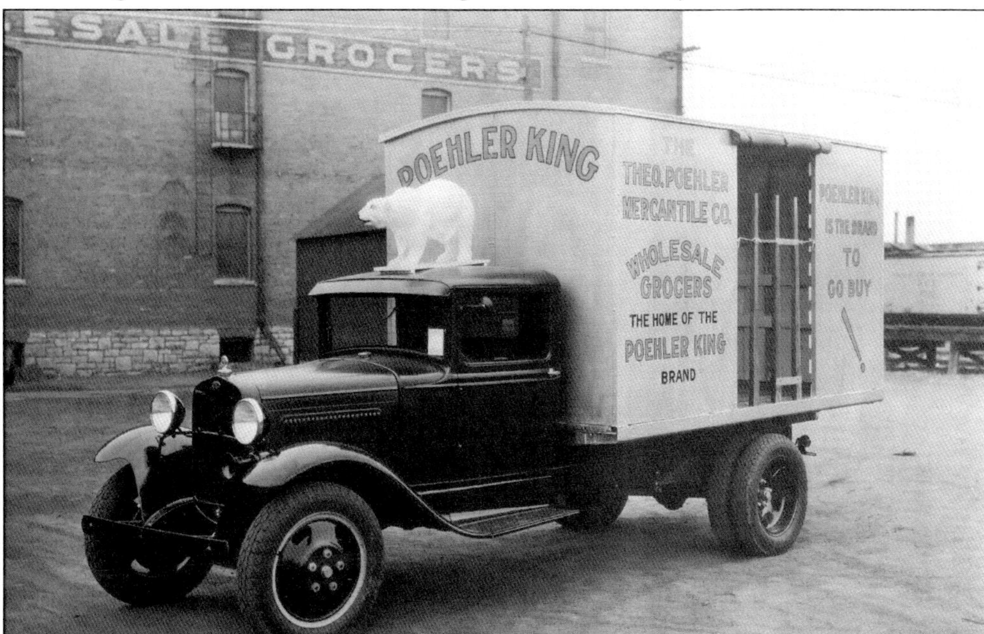

This image shows the transition from delivering products in wagons to trucks in the 1930s. The polar bear on top of the truck cab represents the Poehler trademark.

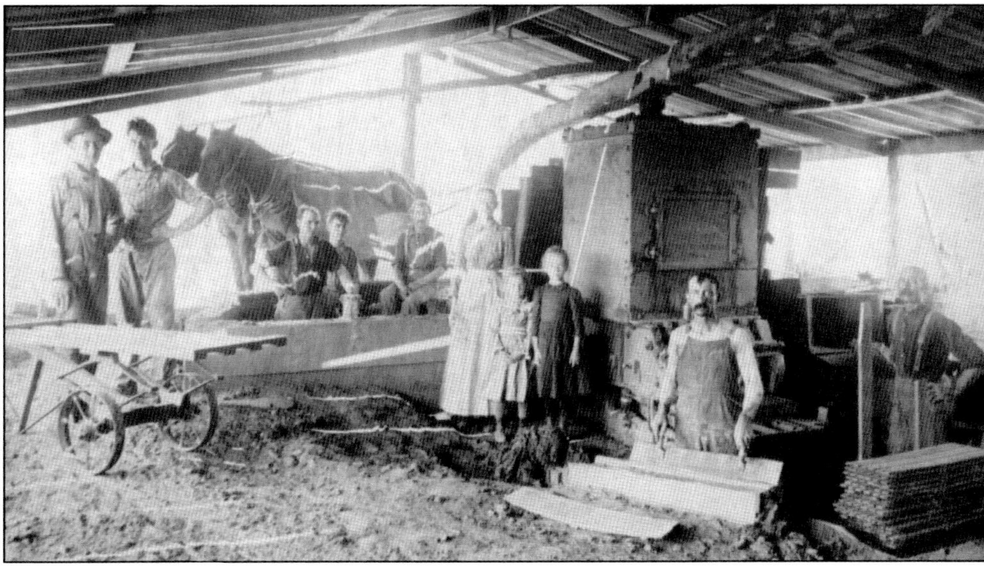

The Mechtley Brick Yard was located at West Logan Avenue and South Congress Street. There, James A. Mechtley produced many bricks for the buildings and streets of Emporia. Mechtley, who came to Emporia in the 1860s, helped build many of Emporia's early buildings. Although the brick factory no longer exists, Mechtley's sons and grandsons followed in his footsteps by becoming brick masons. This photograph was taken around 1900 in the brickyard. (Courtesy of the Walter M. Andersen Collection, Emporia State University Special Collections Archives.)

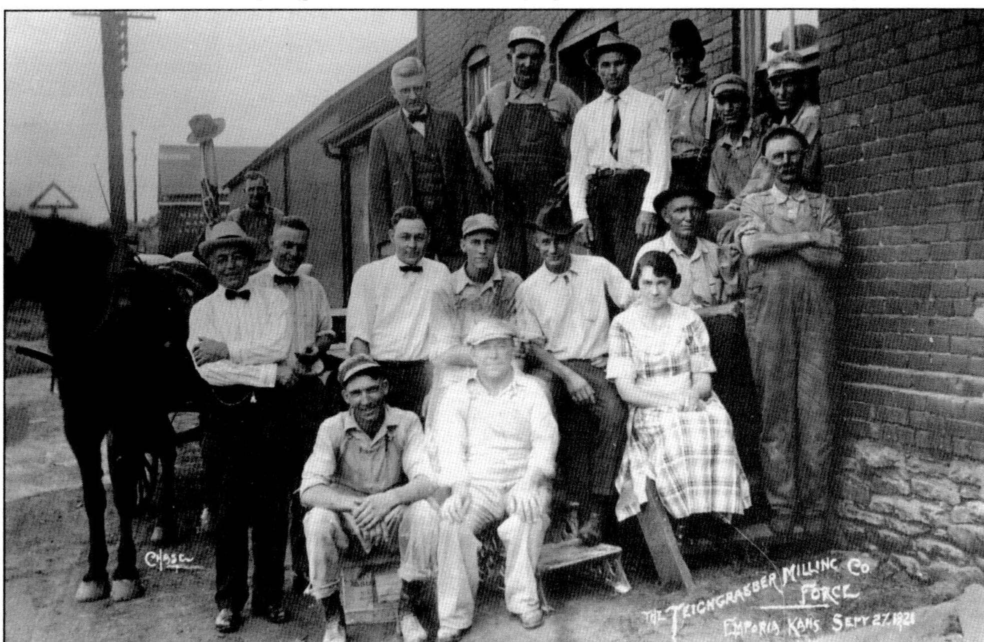

In 1911, Bernhard Teichgraeber came to Emporia and bought the City Mill and Elevator Company from John Kliver and the widow of his brother. The mill was located between Commercial and Mechanic Streets along the Santa Fe Railroad. During its peak years, it could produce 175 barrels of flour per day and 20 tons of corn feed. This 1921 image shows the mill's workforce. (Courtesy of the Walter M. Andersen Collection, Emporia State University Special Collections Archives.)

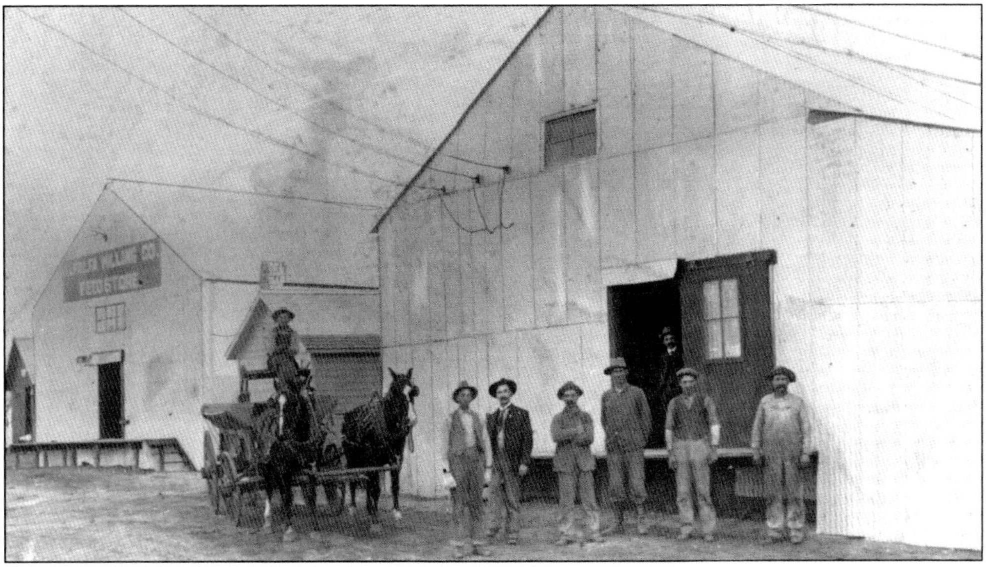

Among Emporia's various milling companies was the Eagle Alfalfa Milling Company, located at 813 East Sixth Avenue. This 1908 photograph shows some of the employees in front of mill barns owned by Walter Sponseller and Ulysses Wolfe. The company would produce feed products from alfalfa. In 1926, Wolfe became the sole proprietor, and the name was changed to Wolfe Alfalfa Milling Company. (Courtesy of the Walter M. Andersen Collection, Emporia State University Special Collections Archives.)

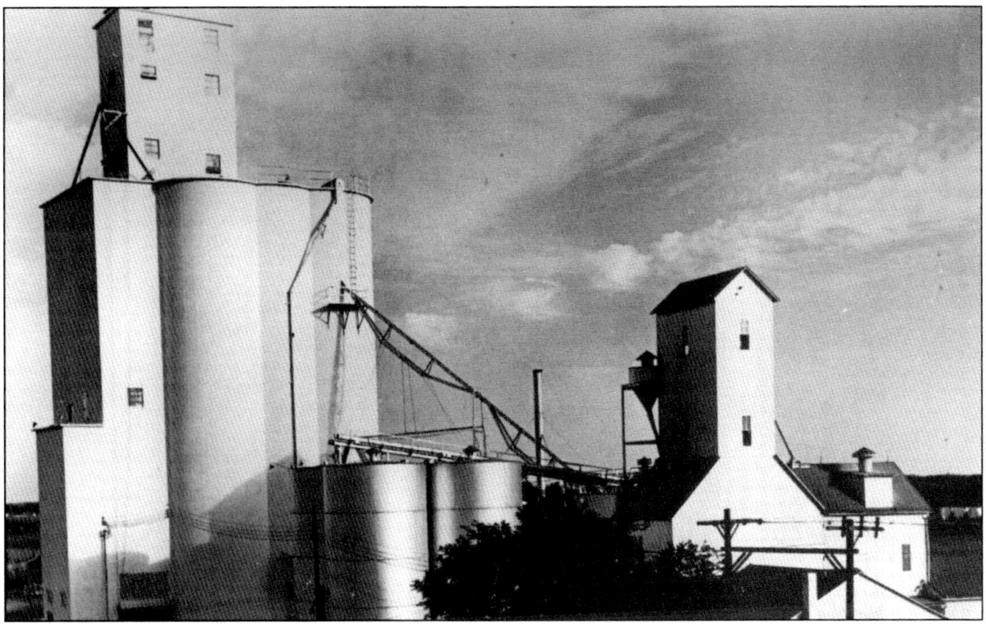

Although Kansas may be known as the wheat state, there is also a high production of soybeans. To accommodate the harvest, the Kansas Soybean Company established a mill in Emporia at Fifth Avenue and East Street near the old Katy Railroad tracks. This image shows the mill and elevator in 1935. Today, the old mill and elevator are dwarfed by the Bunge North American soybean plant. (Courtesy of the Walter M. Andersen Collection, Emporia State University Special Collections Archives.)

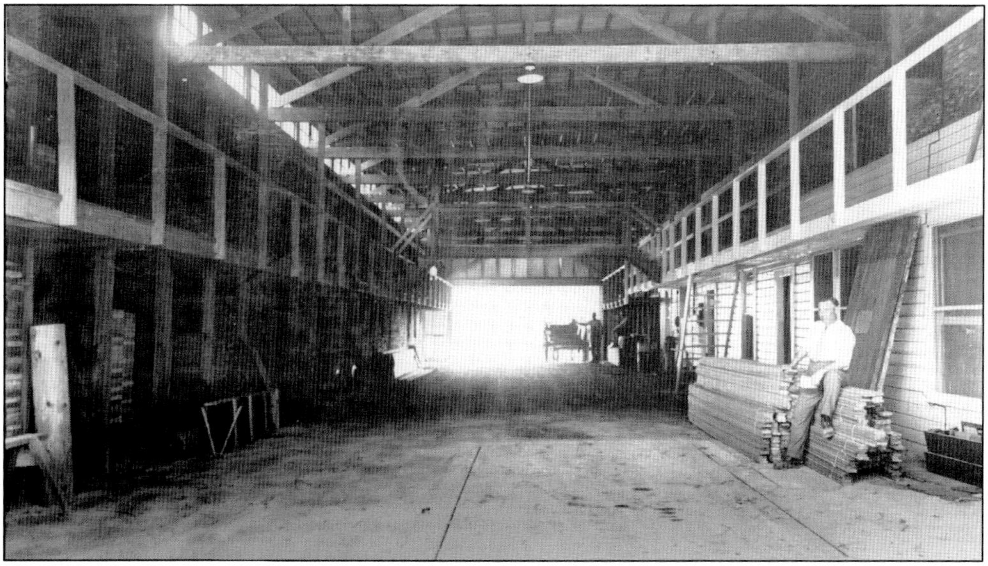

Fleming Lumber Company was one of Emporia's family-owned lumber companies from 1923 until 1998. The company was founded by Fred M. Fleming. The lumberyard located at 225 West Fifth Avenue was unique as the facade and yard employed a Tudor style that was common to many residences being built in the 1920s. This image shows the interior of lumberyard in 1928. Today, the building has been renovated into offices and storage units. (Courtesy of the Walter M. Andersen Collection, Emporia State University Special Collections Archives.)

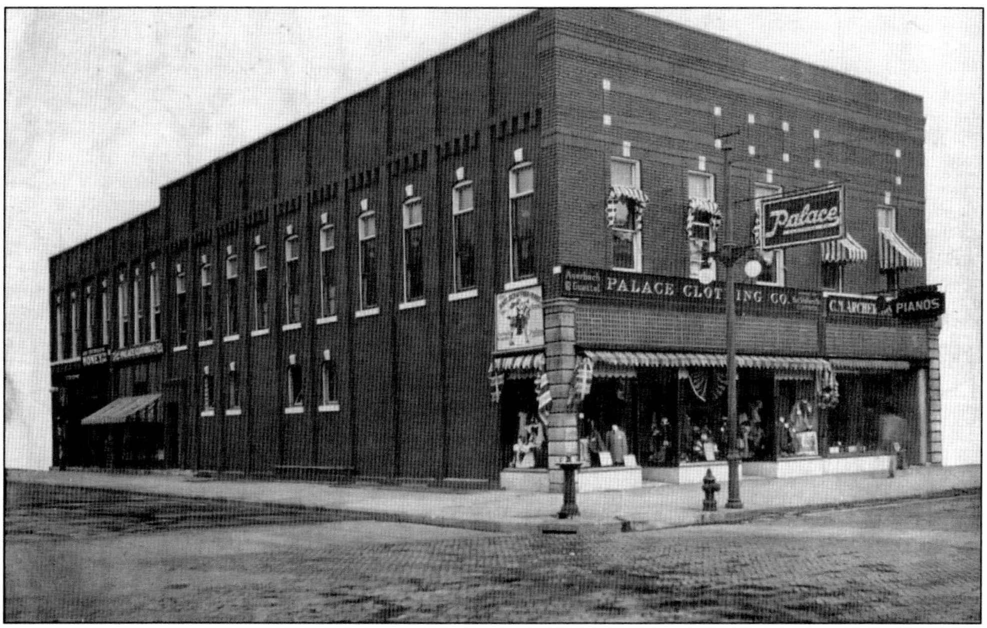

Throughout the years, this building on the northwest corner of Fifth Avenue and Commercial Street was home to many different businesses. It was erected as a three-story structure in 1870 by E.P. Bancroft. Most notably, it housed a clothing store, Jay's Opera House, a business college, a tobacco shop, and a paper warehouse. Palace Clothing Company acquired the building in 1910 and in 1940 did extensive remodeling by removing the third floor and refacing the building with buff brick inlaid with large *P*s for "Palace." This photograph was taken around 1912.

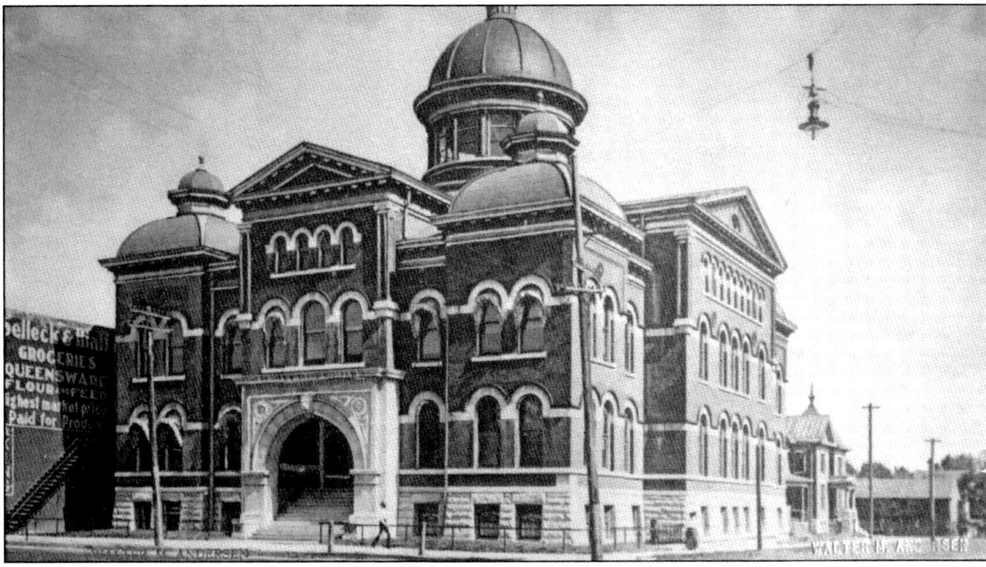

Architect Charles Squires certainly left his mark on Emporia when he designed the second Lyon County Courthouse. Constructed a block north from the first courthouse at Third Avenue and Commercial Street, the new building was located on the northeast corner of Fourth Avenue and Commercial Street. The imposing brick structure featured a central dome and a large stone arch entrance with the relief of a lion head and the date "1901." The structure was demolished in 1950 and replaced with a very modern-looking building. The stone arch was salvaged and is located on private property east of the city.

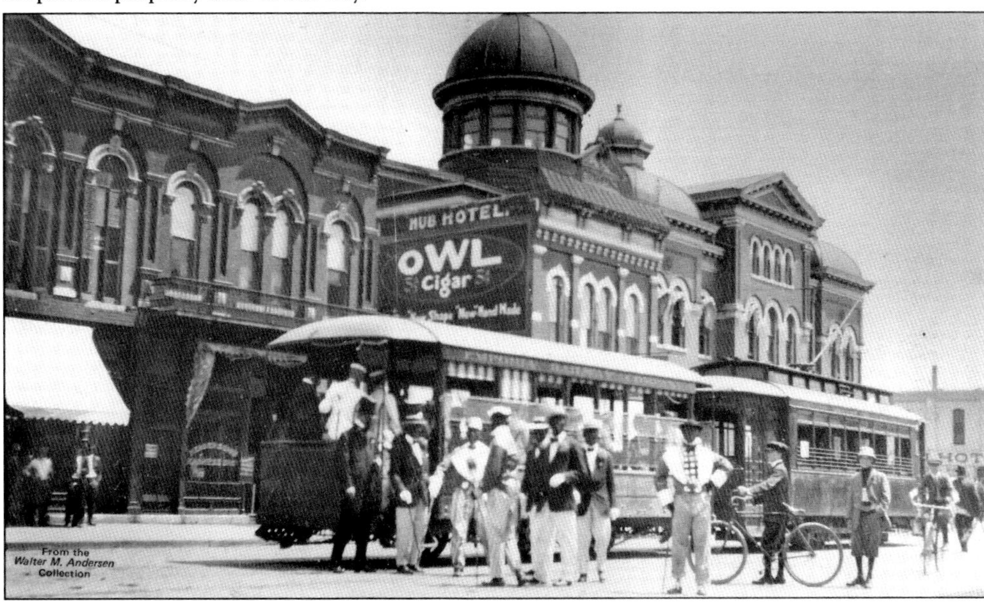

In May 1914, the Benevolent and Protective Order of the Elks sponsored Elks Field Day at Soden's Grove to raise money to send the Elks Band to a national convention. One of the highlights of the day was a performance by the Elks Minstrels, pictured here boarding the streetcars on Commercial Street to take them to Soden's Grove. According to an *Emporia Weekly Gazette* article, "the minstrels were decorated in gorgeous colors and kept the audience laughing for a solid hour. The jokes were witty and all the songs were well sung."

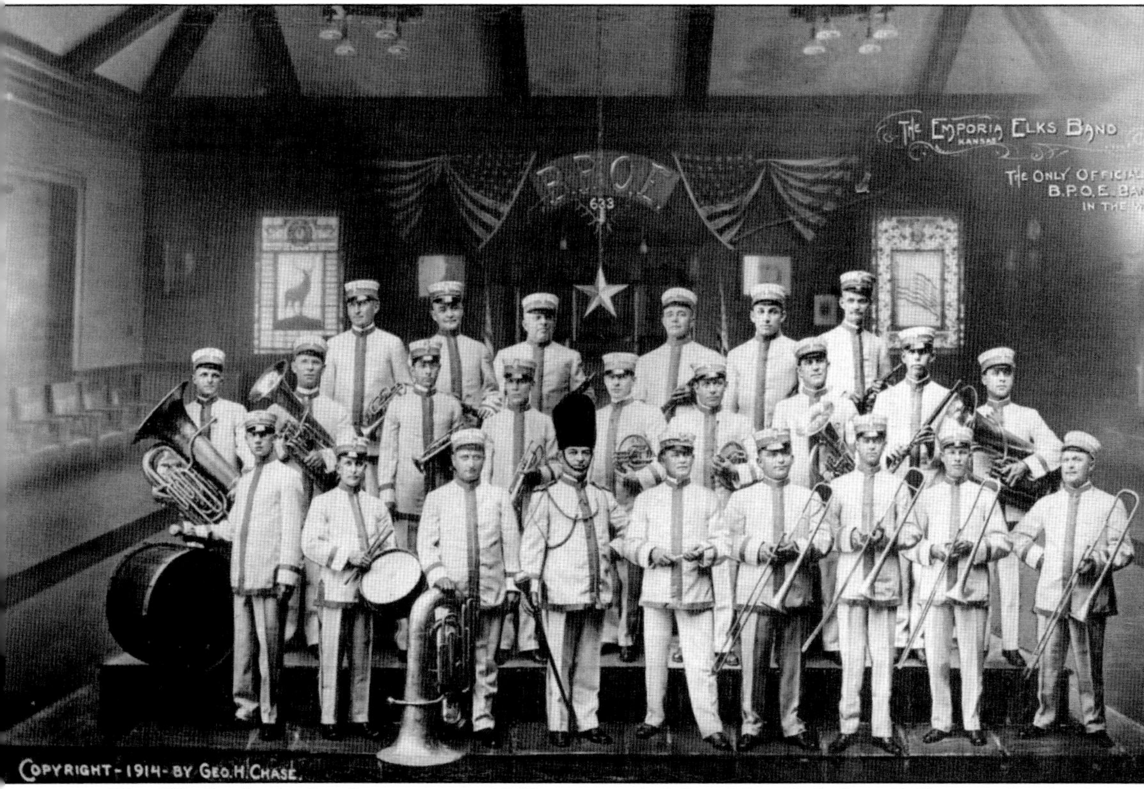

The Elks Lodge had its beginning in 1868 as a social club in New York City. Following the death of a member that left his wife and children without income, the club took on service roles and rituals and the name "Elk." The club soon evolved into a fraternal and charitable order with lodges across the country. The Elks Lodge was one of several lodges in Emporia. This image shows the Elks Band at a 1914 performance.

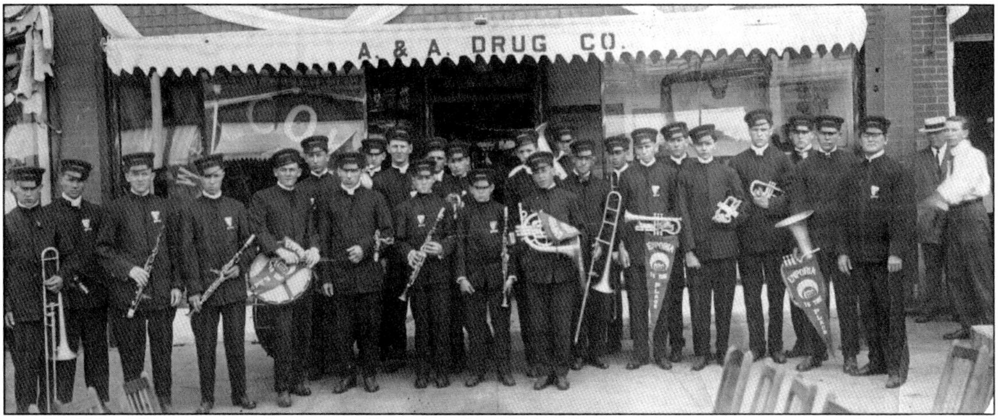

Marcellus C. Grady came to Emporia in the 1890s to teach music at the Kansas State Normal School. It is said that he did more for the advancement of band music than any other Emporia man. Not only did he lead the Emporia Municipal Band for many years, but he also developed a Kids Band and a Womens Band. As the kids grew, they would fill vacancies in the regular band. Pictured here is the 1914 Kids Band.

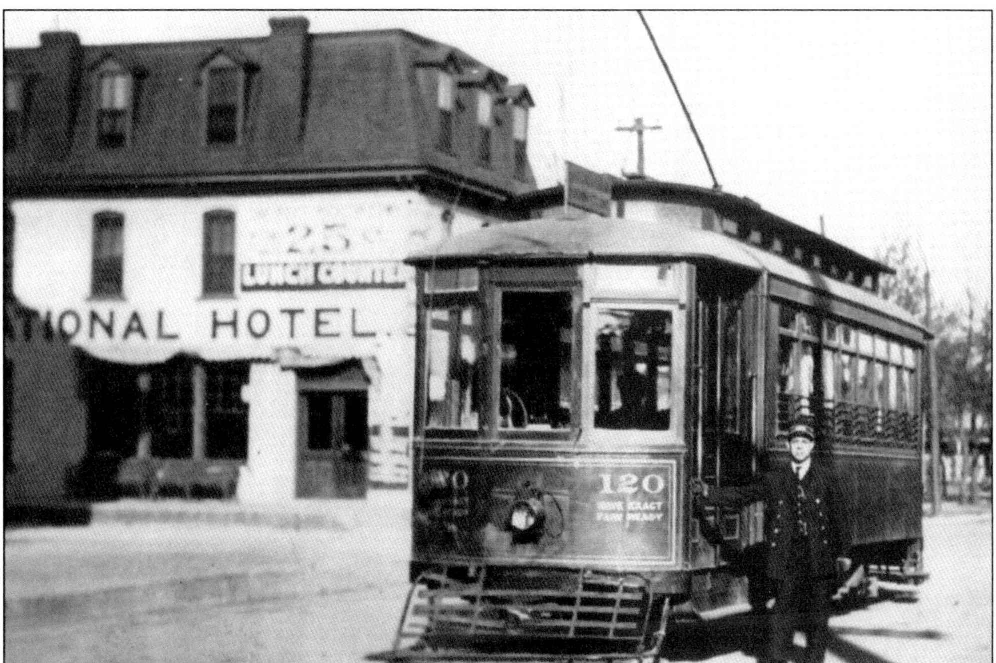

Advertised as the only first-class, up-to-date, steam-heated, electric-lighted hotel near the Santa Fe Railroad, the National Hotel, located at 309 Neosho Street, was a popular place for visitors to stay in Emporia. While staying at the National Hotel, pictured here around 1920, visitors could also conveniently ride street cars to other destinations in Emporia.

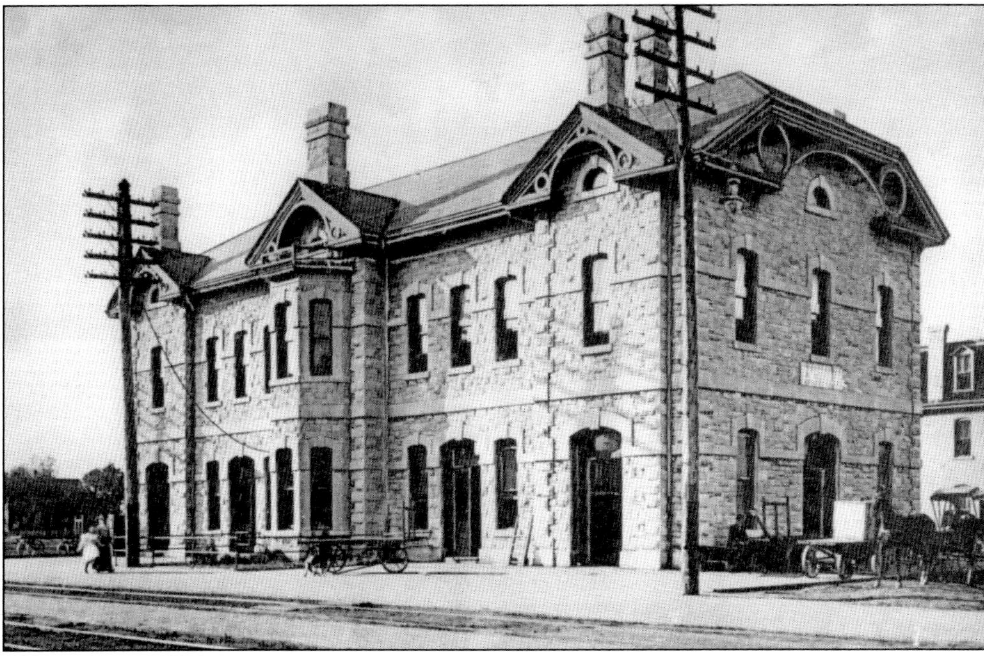

The first passenger train on the Atchison, Topeka & Santa Fe Railroad arrived in Emporia on September 14, 1870, to a large cheering crowd. Rail tracks had made their way to the city in July. Emporia would soon be one of the major hubs for the Santa Fe Railroad. Every westbound train from Kansas City would pass through Emporia before branching to other towns to the south and north. The large two-story stone depot and office building was built in 1883–1884. Tudor-style wings were added to the structure in 1924–1925. For over 100 years, Emporia served as the headquarters for the Eastern Division until consolidation with the Kansas City Division in 1986, when the operations moved to Kansas City. The depot was vacated, and in 1999, a fire of unknown cause destroyed the structure.

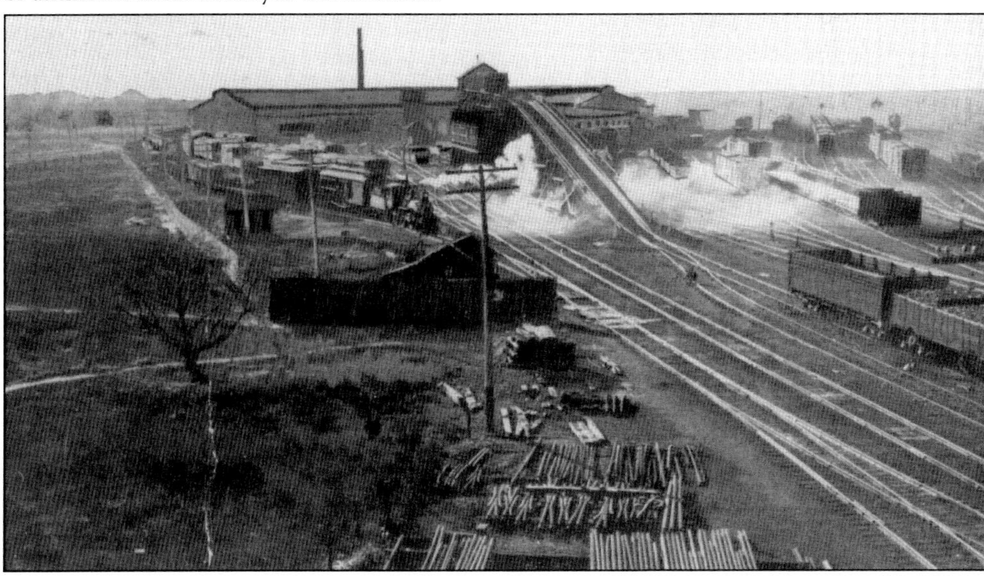

The large roundhouse seen here was located to the west of the depot. Other railroad buildings could be seen along the track for half a mile.

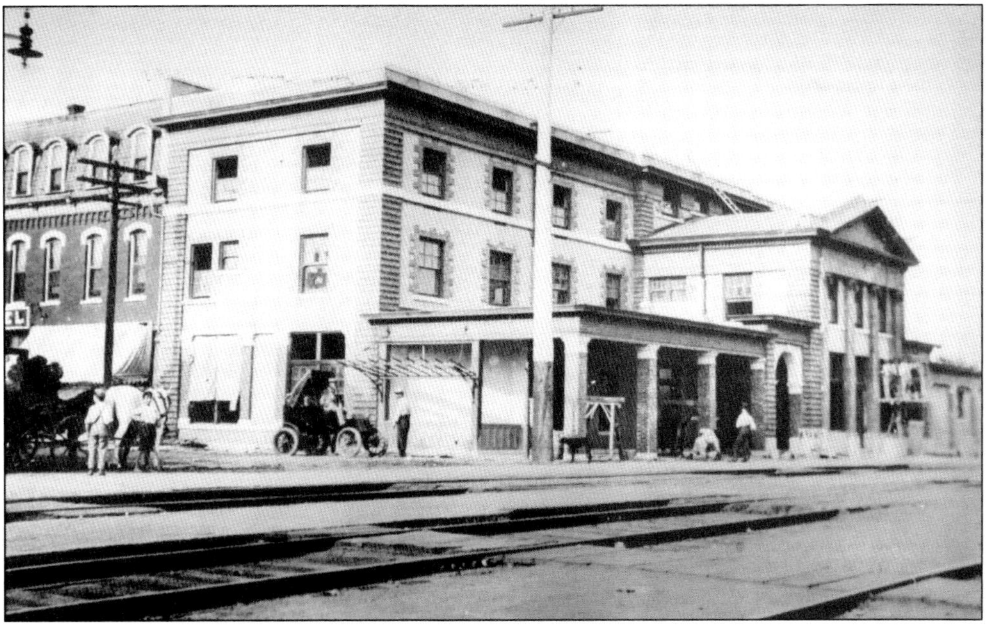

In 1876, Fred Harvey made a handshake deal with Charles Morse, the superintendent of the Atchison, Topeka & Santa Fe Railroad, to establish eating houses along the railroad for passengers to dine and rest while traveling. Soon, Harvey Houses were seen in most large cities along the route of the Santa Fe from Chicago to California. The Emporia Harvey House shown here was opened in 1880 and closed in 1937. This photograph was taken about 1908. The building was later demolished.

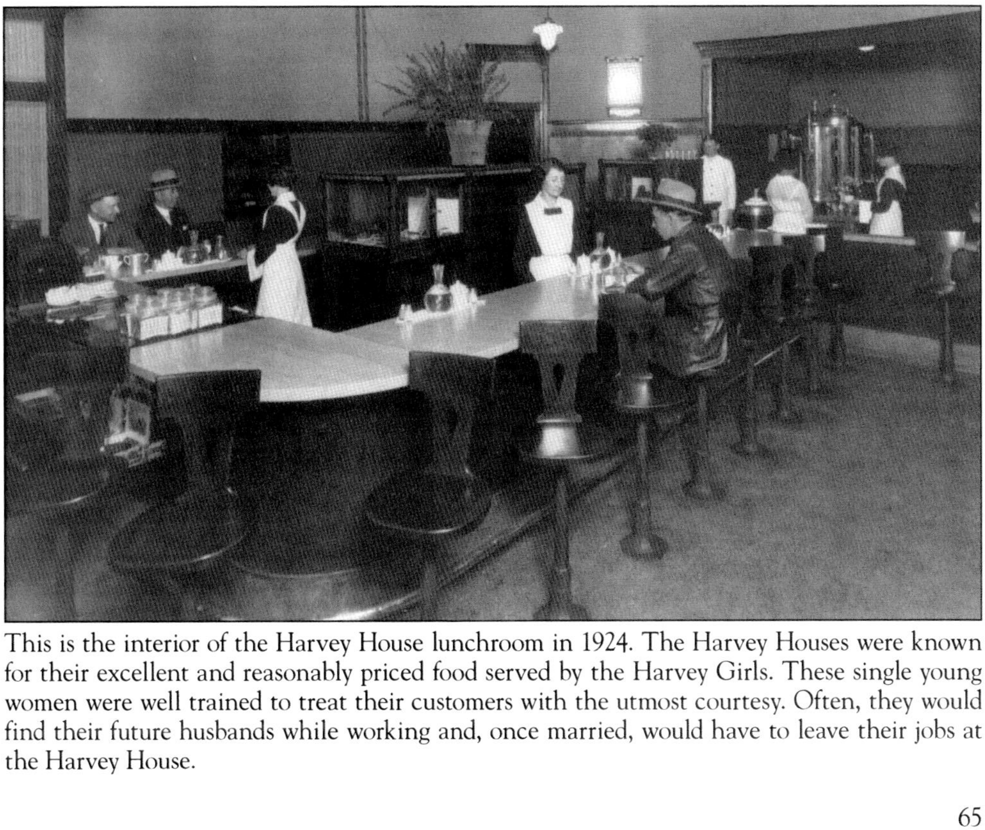

This is the interior of the Harvey House lunchroom in 1924. The Harvey Houses were known for their excellent and reasonably priced food served by the Harvey Girls. These single young women were well trained to treat their customers with the utmost courtesy. Often, they would find their future husbands while working and, once married, would have to leave their jobs at the Harvey House.

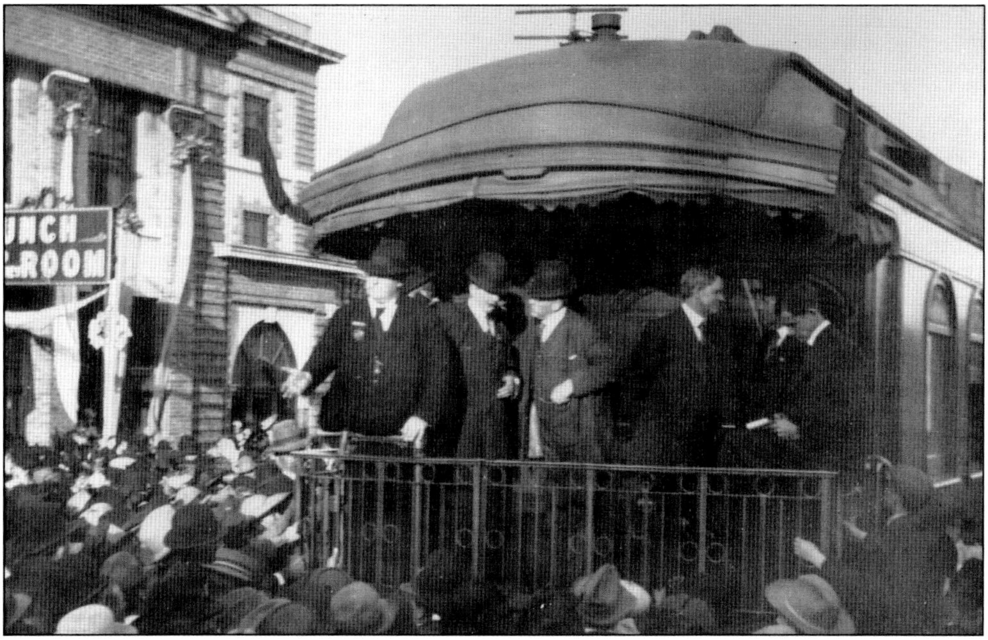

Being a major stop on the Santa Fe often brought politicians and celebrities to Emporia for a short visit. William Allen White was also friendly with many politicians, writers, and other dignitaries of the early 20th century. Among his political friends was Pres. William Howard Taft. This image shows Taft's arrival on the train in 1912.

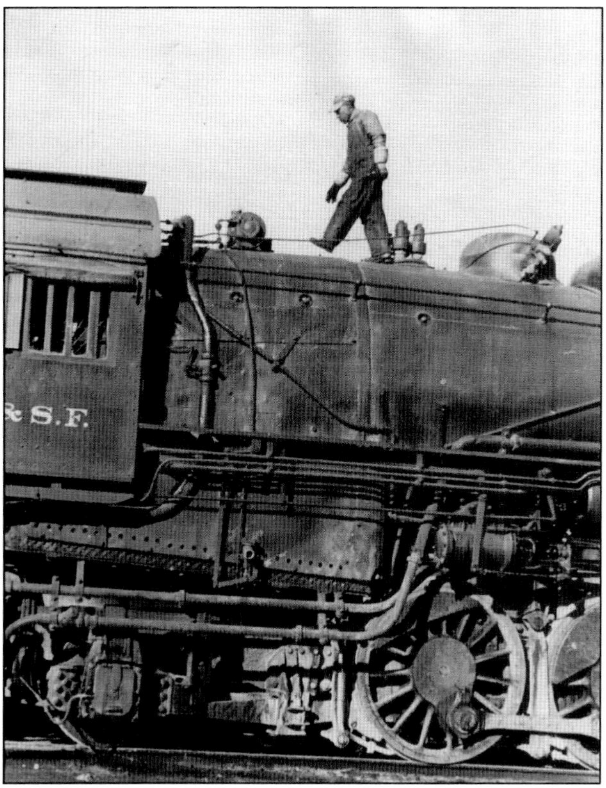

Many African Americans worked for the railroad. This image shows Lee Carter walking the engine to make sure everything is functioning correctly. A need for railroad workers also brought immigrants from Mexico, who settled in homes on the south side of Emporia.

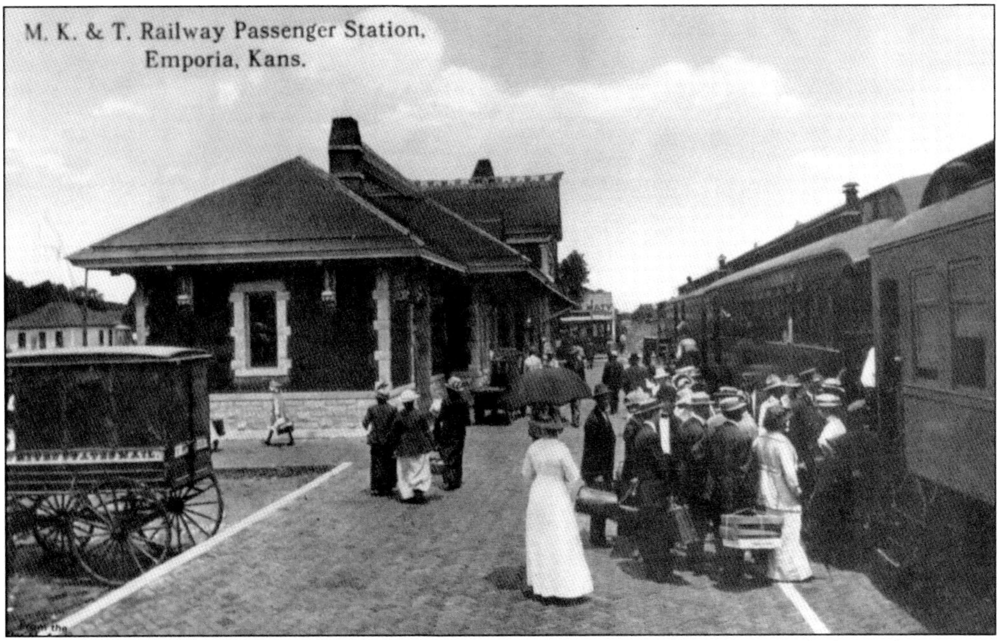

The Missouri, Kansas & Texas Railroad started in Junction City and moved south through Emporia and down into Texas. After receiving a land grant, the railroad company began laying track in 1869. This image shows the depot for the Katy, which was located on the west side of the tracks at Sixth Avenue and East Street.

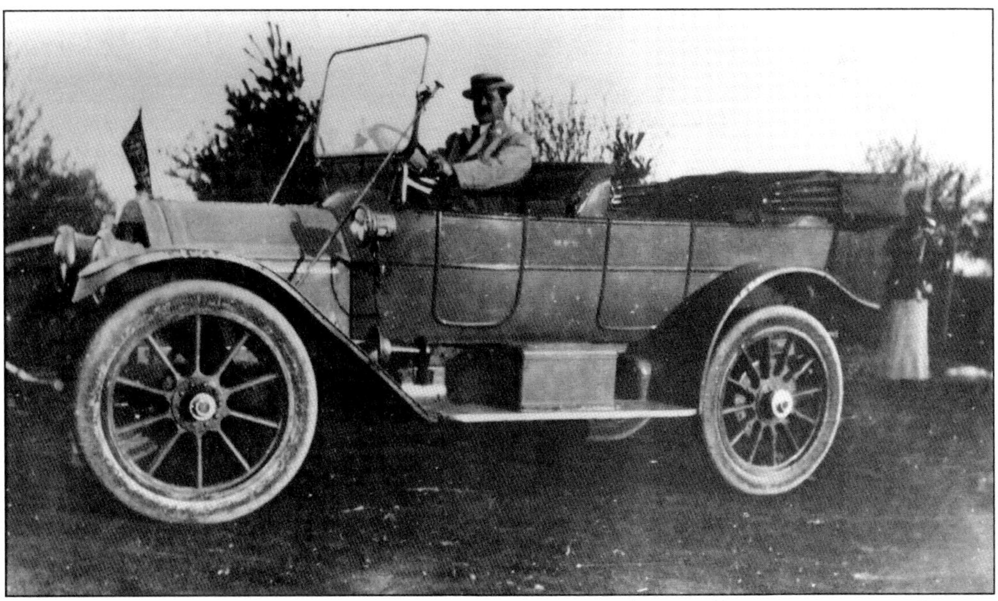

Sitting proudly in his touring car, ready to see the countryside, is William S. Kretsinger. Born in the nearby community of Lebo, Kretsinger was a well-known attorney for many years in Emporia. He married Rose Good in 1914. Their home at 911 Market Street was the workshop where she designed many prize-winning quilts. (Courtesy of the Walter M. Andersen Collection, Emporia State University Special Collections Archives.)

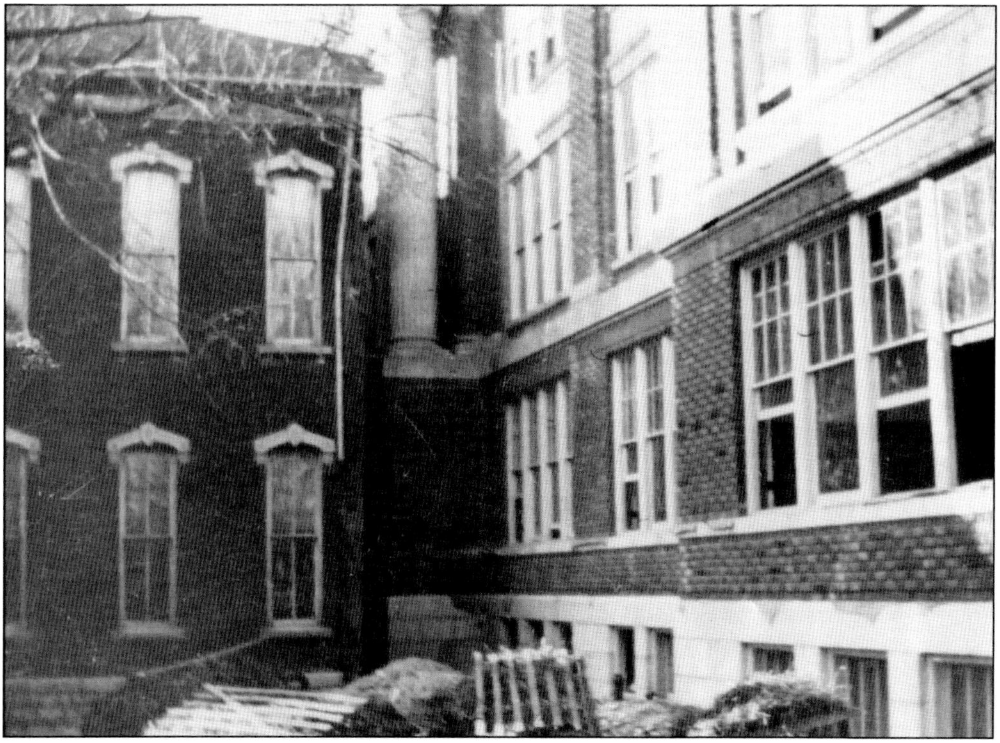

From 1912 to 1914, building crews erected the new high school directly behind Garfield School while classes were still being conducted at Garfield. On April 17, 1914, a farewell service was held to say good-bye to the old Garfield building that had served the community for 34 years. High school boys who helped carry furniture, equipment, and books from Garfield into the new school after school hours were given half a course credit.

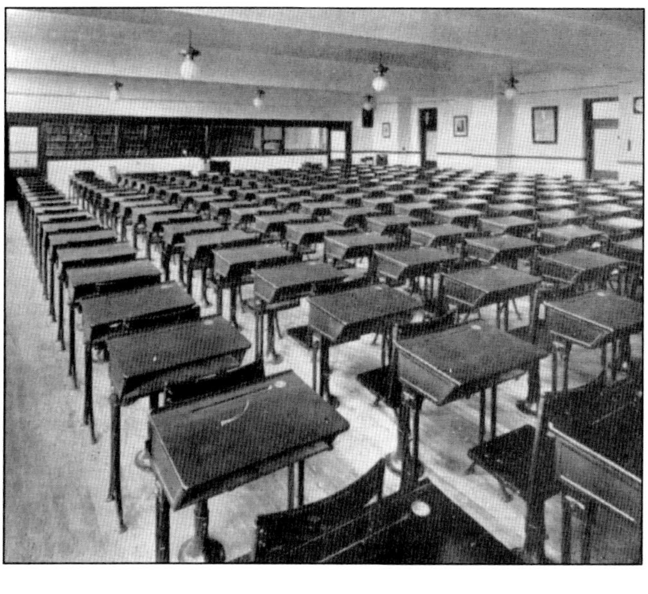

The large study hall located on the second floor seated 200 students. It was just one of the many large classrooms built for the new Emporia Senior High located at 216 West Sixth Avenue. The school cost approximately $150,000 to build and equip. William Mallis of J.H. Felt & Company Architects supervised the construction of the building by Johnson & Son Construction Company from Sedalia, Missouri. The first day of classes was April 21, 1914.

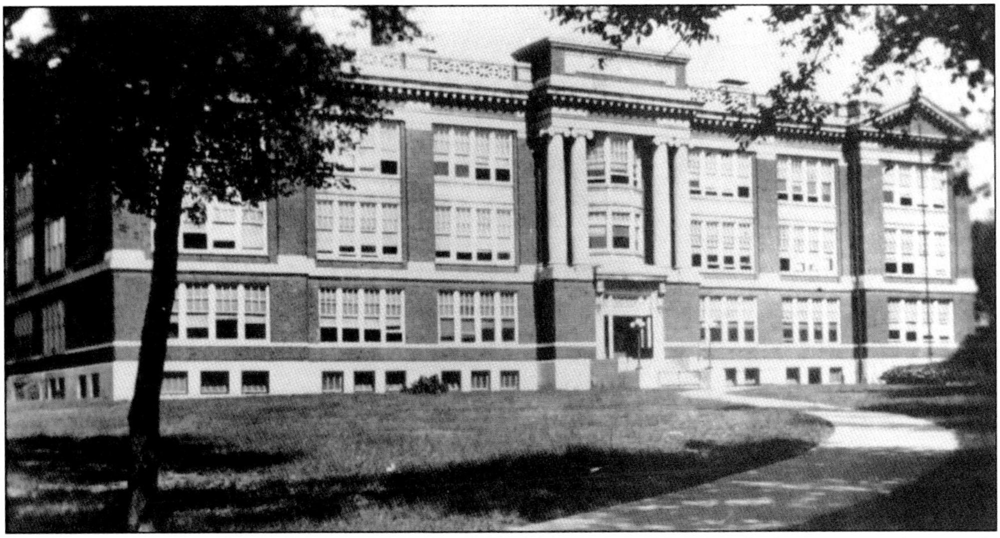

For almost 100 years, the Emporia Senior High building at 216 West Sixth Avenue saw thousands of students pass through its doors. From 1914 to 1925 the facility served grades nine through twelve, but after the junior high school was built in 1925, EHS served students in grades 10 through 12 until a new high school was built at 3302 West Eighteenth Avenue. In 1976, the building was renamed Lowther North Intermediate School, and served sixth graders until they were moved to Emporia Middle School in January 2012. In that year, the building was purchased by the Emporia High School Historic Building Group, which is building the 83-room Breckenridge Hotel and Convention Center.

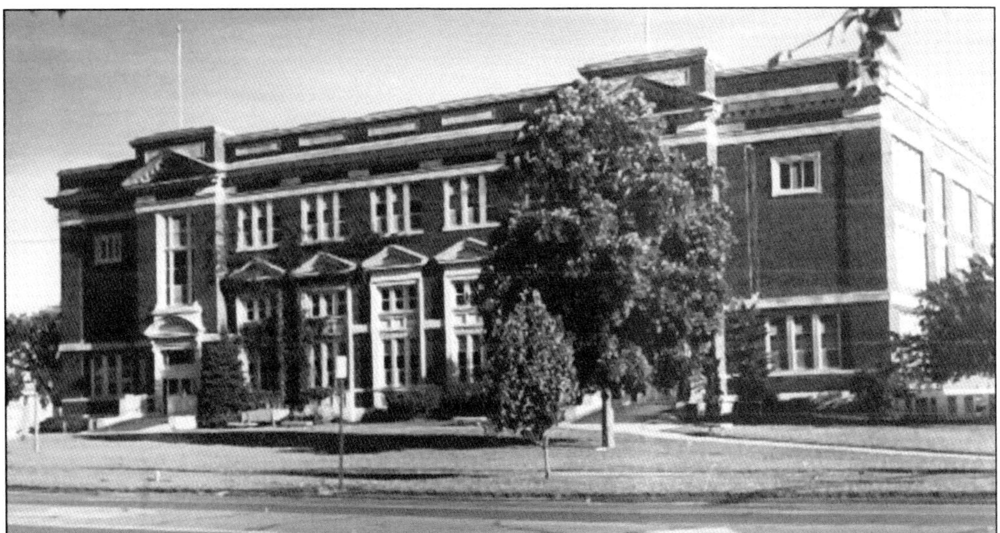

Lowther Junior High School was built in 1925 and named after L.A. Lowther, Emporia superintendent of schools from 1896 to 1935. Located across the street from Emporia High School, the junior high served students in grades seven through nine. When a new middle school was built in 1994, the fifth graders were housed in the newly named Lowther South Intermediate School. In 2011, the fifth graders were sent back to their neighborhood elementary schools, and the building was sold to the Lowther Building Fund, a nonprofit group that has turned the building into the Emporia Humanitarian Center.

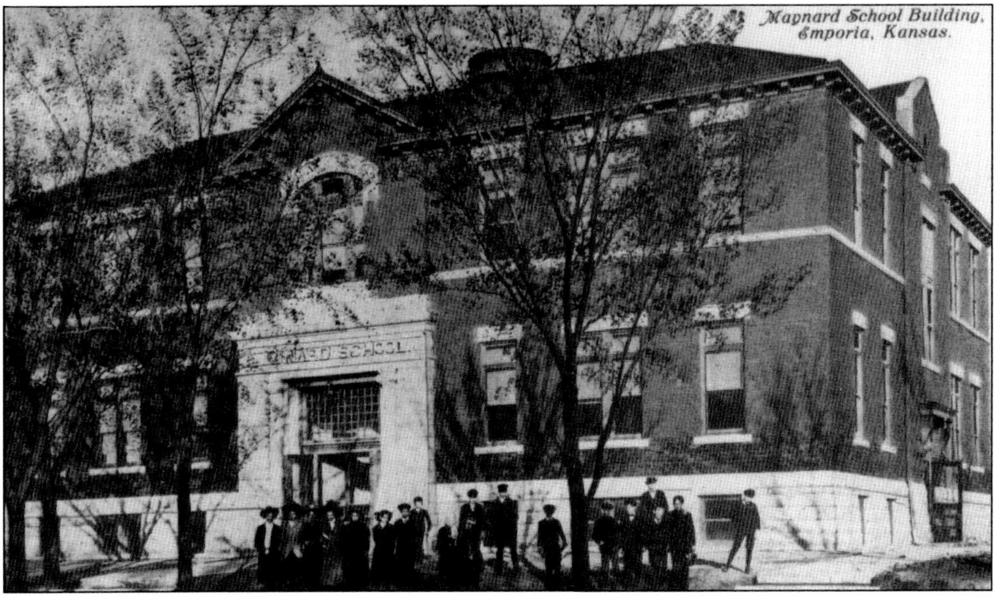

Maynard School was built in 1908 on the east side of Congress Street between First and South Avenues to replace the Third Ward's original school built in 1881. The school was named after Mary Maynard, a longtime teacher in the Emporia district who left her estate to the school district. Architect Henry Brinkman designed the building. This building was replaced in 1951 with the building at First Avenue and Constitution Street that currently serves as the Maynard Early Childhood Center. (Courtesy of the Walter M. Andersen Collection, Emporia State University Special Collections Archives.)

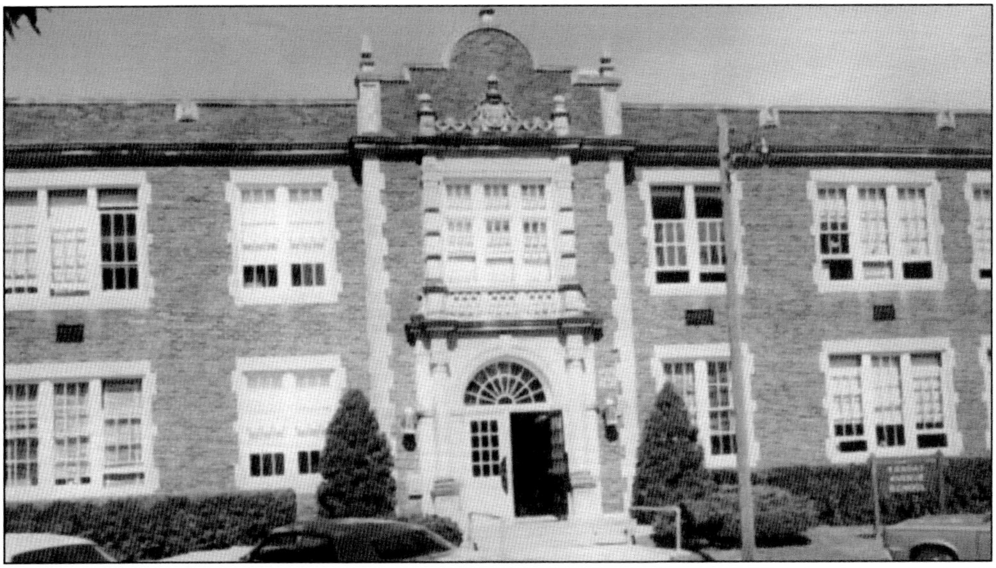

Kansas Avenue School, located at 315 South Market Street, was built in 1927 to replace the "old" Kansas Avenue School that was built in 1886. While the new school was being built, the students were sent to Riverside, Maynard, and Union Schools. In addition to being strictly fireproof, some of its special features included a specially designed kindergarten room and a combination gymnasium and auditorium. Today, the school is home to Turning Point Academy. (Courtesy of the Walter M. Andersen Collection, Emporia State University Special Collections Archives.)

O.W. Miller established the Emporia Business College in 1881. The courses were described as being practical and low cost, and students were assured of receiving good positions with promising advancements. For more than 20 years, the college was located in the second story of the Watson-Ballweg Lumber Company at Sixth Avenue and Mechanic Street until it moved in 1928 to the second floor of the Burnap Brothers' plumbing establishment at 724 1/2 Commercial Street. (Courtesy of the Walter M. Andersen Collection, Emporia State University Special Collections Archives.)

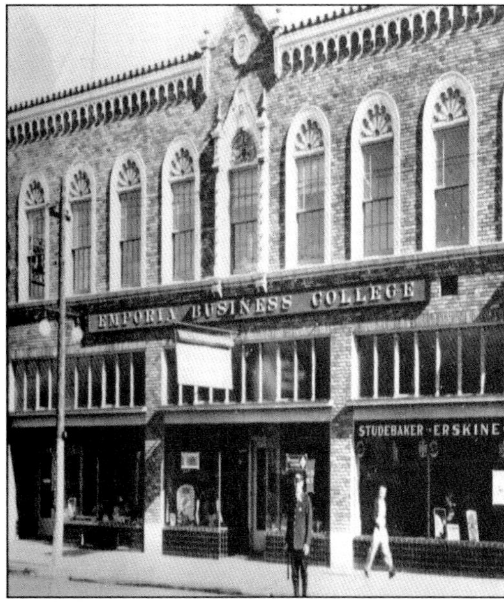

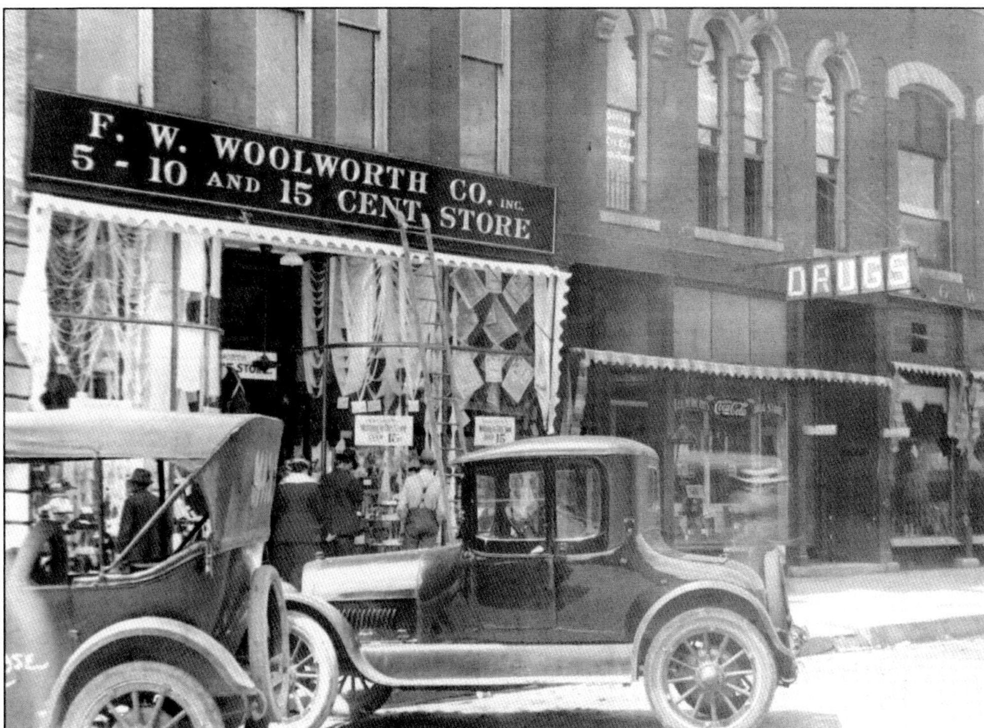

Ever since opening its first store in 1879, F.W. Woolworth five-and-dime stores were famous for their cheap merchandise and for being the first stores to put their discounted merchandise out for the shopping public to handle, select, and purchase. The F.W. Woolworth store opened in Emporia in May 1918 at 609 Commercial Street. While on Commercial Street, the store expanded twice to the north, with the second expansion adding a 32-seat lunch counter and checkout counters at the front to provide fast service. Woolworth left the downtown area when the Flint Hills Mall was built. Today, Graves Drugstore occupies the Woolworth space.

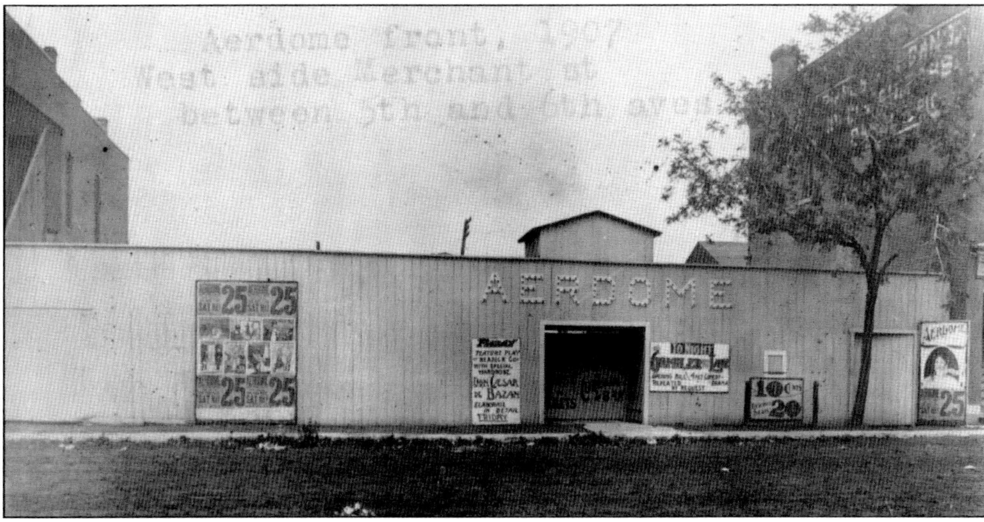

Once described by its creator as a predecessor to the Starlight Theater in Kansas City, the Aerdome was an outdoor theater that featured plays and vaudeville acts for 10¢ a show, or 20¢ for a seat close to the stage. In 1906, Frank Corbett built the first aerdome, pictured here, north of the *Gazette* building. In 1908, Corbett moved the building across the street to 514 Merchant Street.

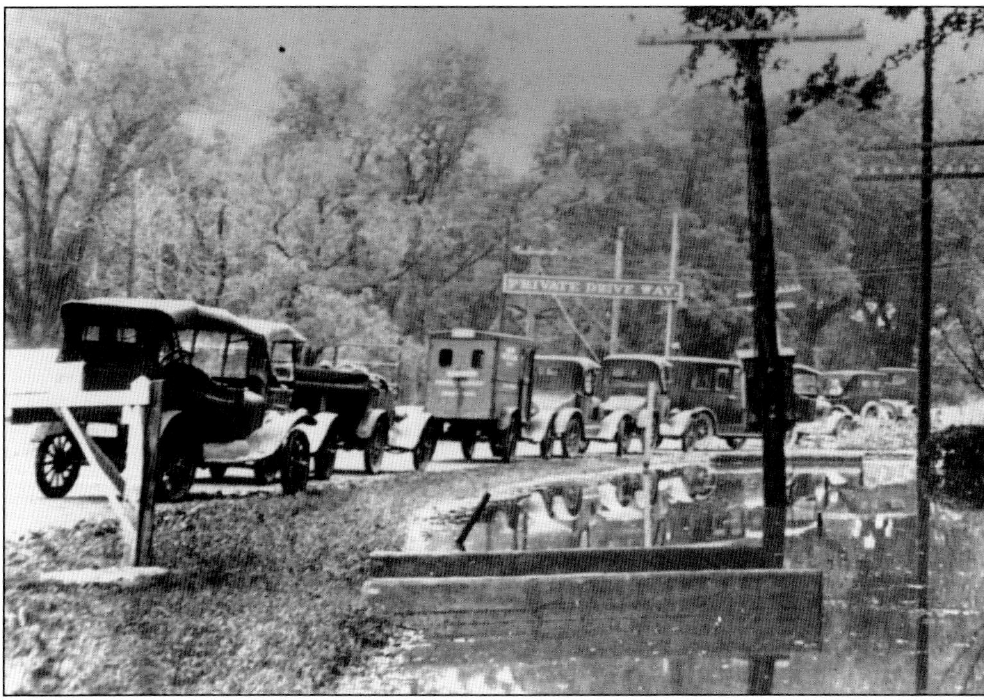

Driving down to Soden's Grove to view the floodwaters has been an Emporia pastime for many years. According to a 1926 news article, 47 floods were on the record books since records first started being kept in 1857. This averaged out to one flood every 18 months. One particularly bad year was 1923, when both the Neosho and Cottonwood Rivers went out of their banks. An engineer's report also predicted the great flood of 1951 when it stated that floods as destructive as one that had occurred in 1904 could be expected every 50 years. (Courtesy of the Walter M. Andersen Collection, Emporia State University Special Collections Archives.)

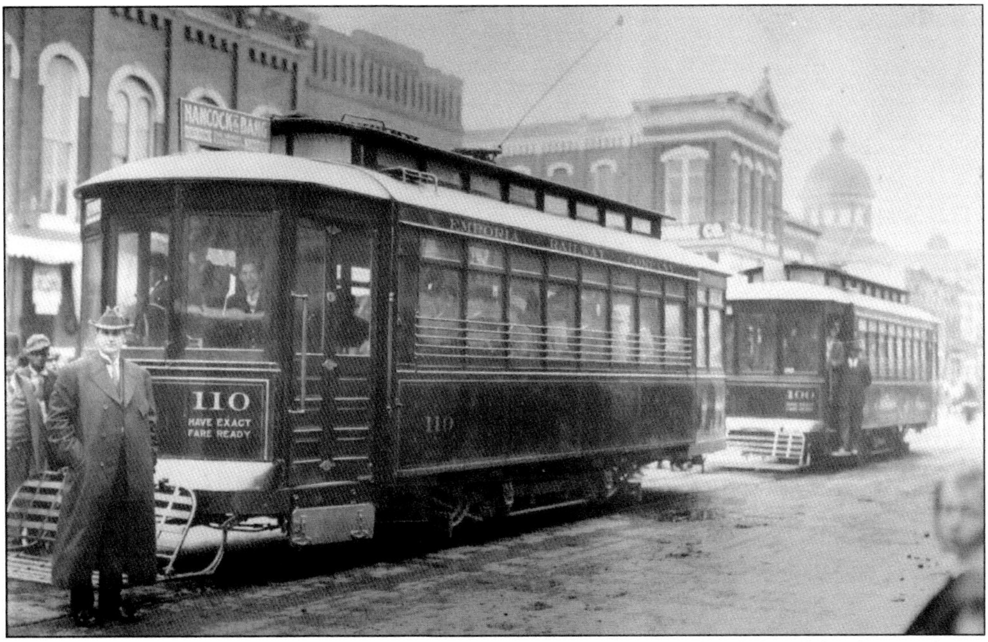

Mit Wilhite, standing in front of street car 110, was one of the civic leaders behind the drive to bring streetcars to Emporia. On October 26, 1911, the Emporia Railway and Light Company put the first streetcars into service. The cars ran from 6:30 a.m. to 11:00 p.m. For a nickel, patrons could ride the streetcars on the Commercial Street route that went as far west as the College of Emporia on Twelfth Avenue, or along the Sixth Avenue route that went to the Santa Fe and Katy depots.

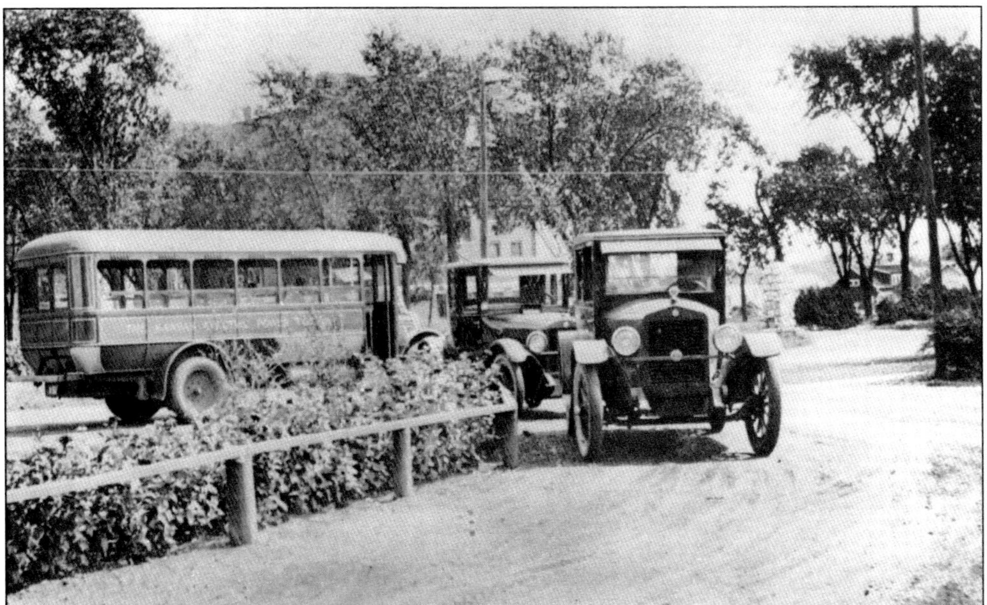

When the streetcars failed to be profitable, their owner, the Kansas Electric Power Company, was required to replace them with city buses. In this c. 1925 photograph, a city bus is delivering passengers to Newman Memorial Hospital. Cash fares cost 10¢, or books of 20 tickets could be purchased for $1.

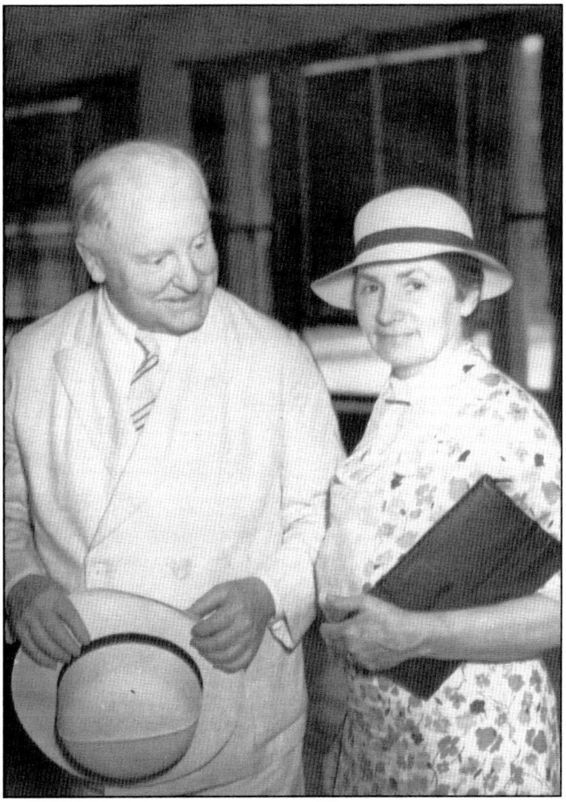

One of Emporia's early "power couples" was William Allen and Sallie Lindsey White. Known as the "sage of Emporia," White achieved national success and fame through his editorials, articles, books, and politics. In addition to helping her husband run the paper and entertaining famous guests, Sallie was also active in community affairs. The Whites were married for over 50 years; he died in 1944, and she in 1950.

If walls could talk, Red Rocks, the Whites' home at 927 Exchange Street, would have many interesting stories to tell about the presidents, authors, reformers, and numerous other visitors who enjoyed the Whites' famous hospitality. The Whites purchased the home in 1901, as pictured here, and then renovated it during the early 1920s. Today, Red Rocks is a state historic site where visitors are invited to tour the house and gardens and learn more about the legacy of the White family.

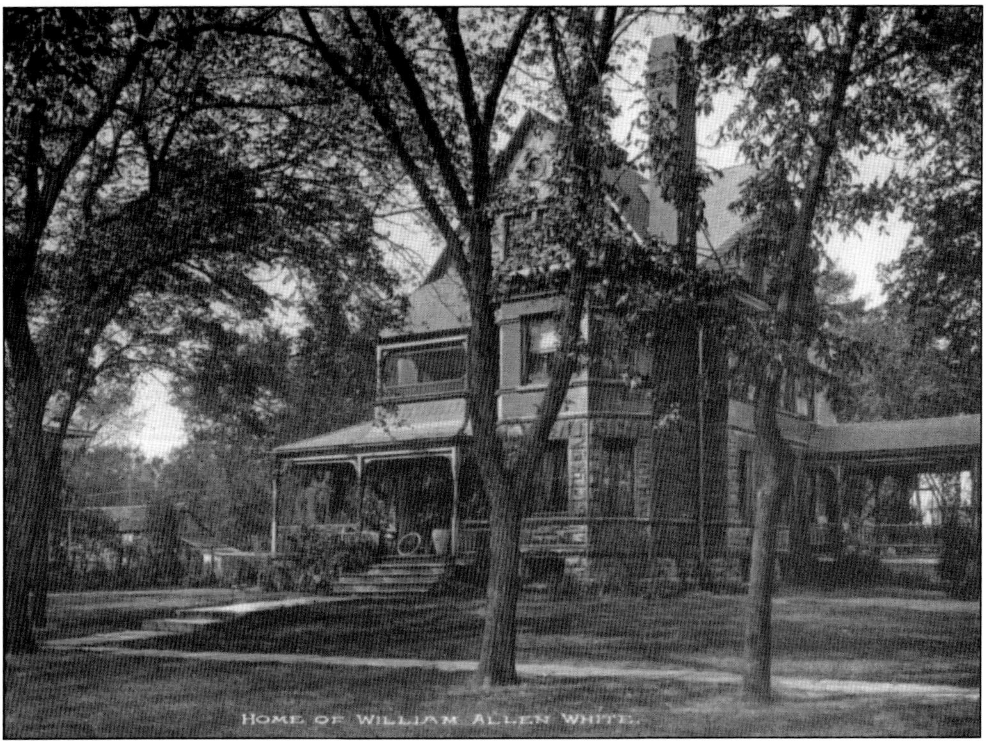

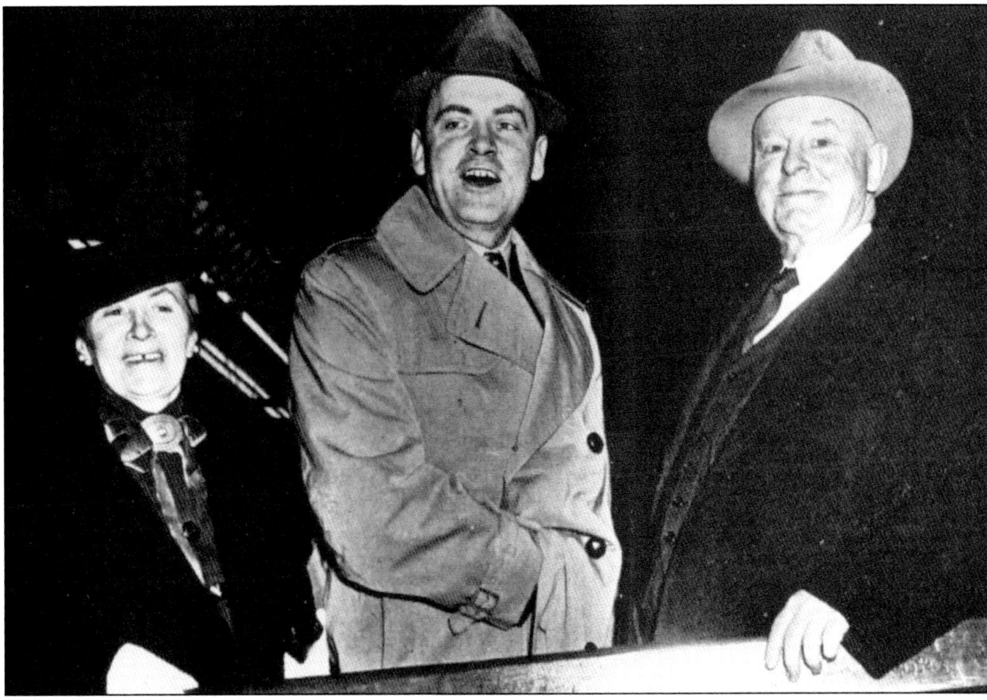

In this photograph, William Allen and Sallie White greet their son William Lindsey White (center) upon his 1939 return home from his work as a war correspondent. Born in 1900, William Lindsey White followed in his father's footsteps as an award-winning journalist and author. He married Kathrine Klinkenberg, and they adopted a daughter, Barbara. After his father's death in 1944, he and his wife took over the operations of the *Emporia Gazette*. (Courtesy of the Walter M. Andersen Collection, Emporia State University Special Collections Archives.)

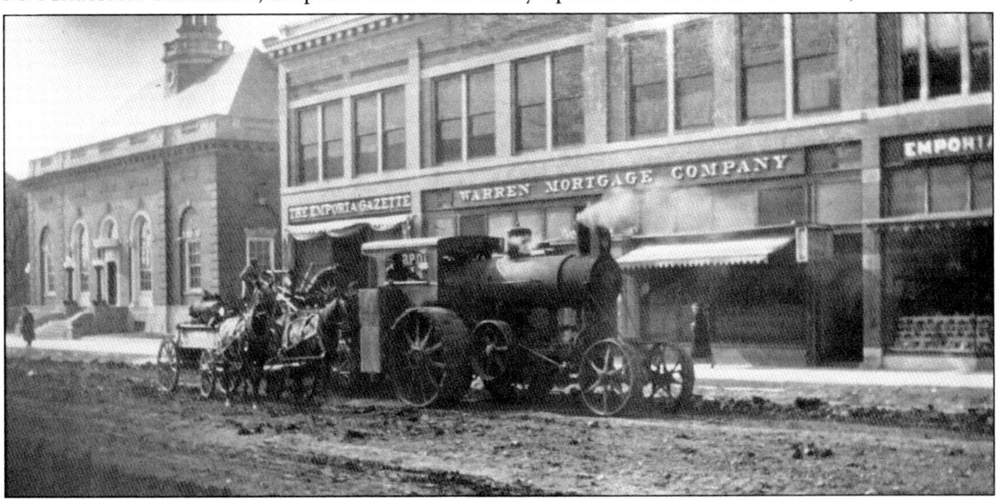

For more than a century, the *Emporia Gazette* has been housed in the building at 517 Merchant Street, pictured here during a street-paving project in 1913. William Allen White purchased the paper in 1895 for $3,000. Since White's death in 1944, the paper has remained in the family, run first by William Lindsey and Kathrine White, and then by their daughter Barbara White Walker and her husband, David. Presently, the paper is run by the Walkers' son Chris and his wife, Ashley.

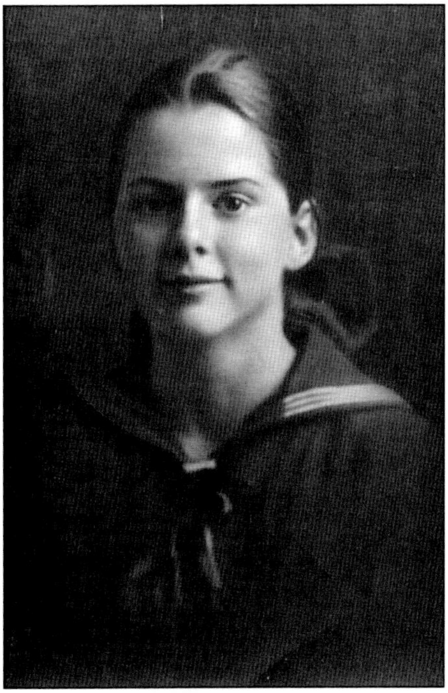

Mary Katherine White, daughter of William Allen and Sallie White, was born on June 18, 1904. She loved horses, books, music, and helping others less fortunate. A tragic horse accident cut her life short on May 13, 1921. White's life and spirit were captured in the eulogy her parents wrote the day after her funeral. It became her father's most famous editorial and later was used as the basis for a television movie about her life.

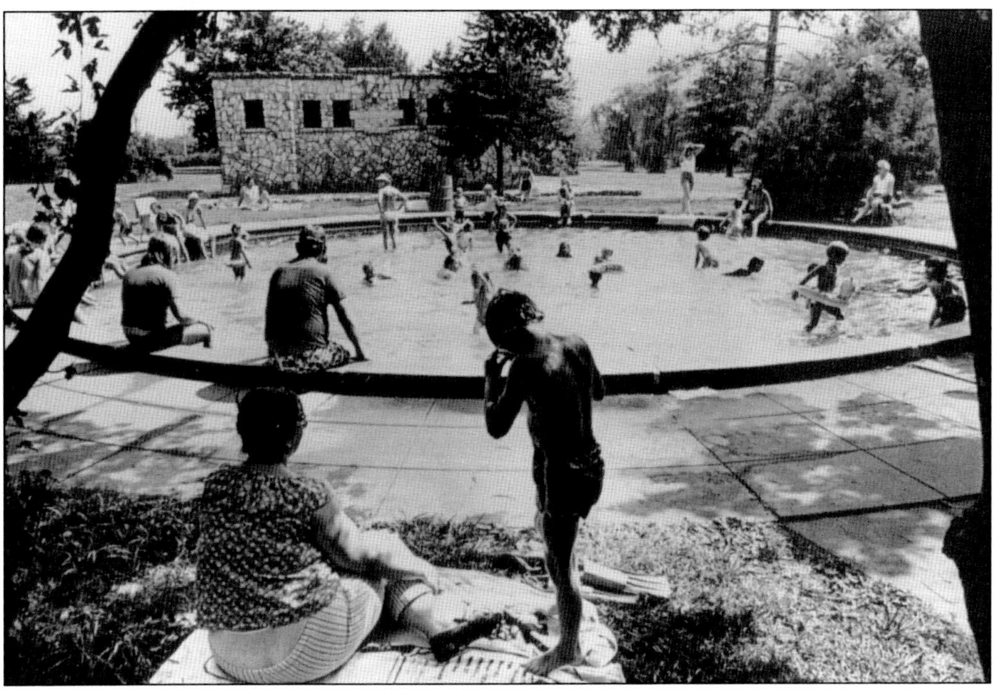

In 1926, William Allen and Sallie White donated 50 acres for a park to commemorate their daughter Mary. The park was named Peter Pan because her father had described her as "a Peter Pan who refused to grow up." The wading pool pictured here was dedicated on June 6, 1931. It was a gift to the children of Emporia from philanthropists Frank and Isabel Reed of Neosho, Missouri. (Courtesy of the Walter M. Andersen Collection, Emporia State University Special Collections Archives.)

Four

CITY ON THE MOVE

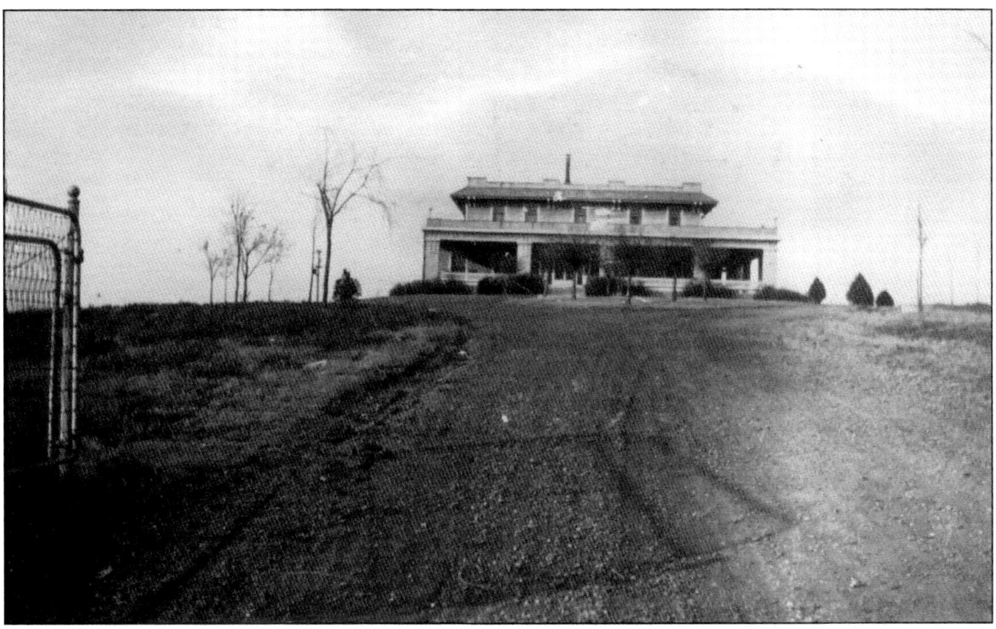

The founding members of the Emporia Country Club selected the land on the hill at the head of Rural Street with its commanding view of the Neosho Valley as the setting for their $15,000 two-story clubhouse and future outdoor activities that included golf, tennis, boating, fishing, and hunting. The clubhouse was formally opened on December 31, 1911. The first caretakers were Robert Peebles and his wife, who were from Scotland.

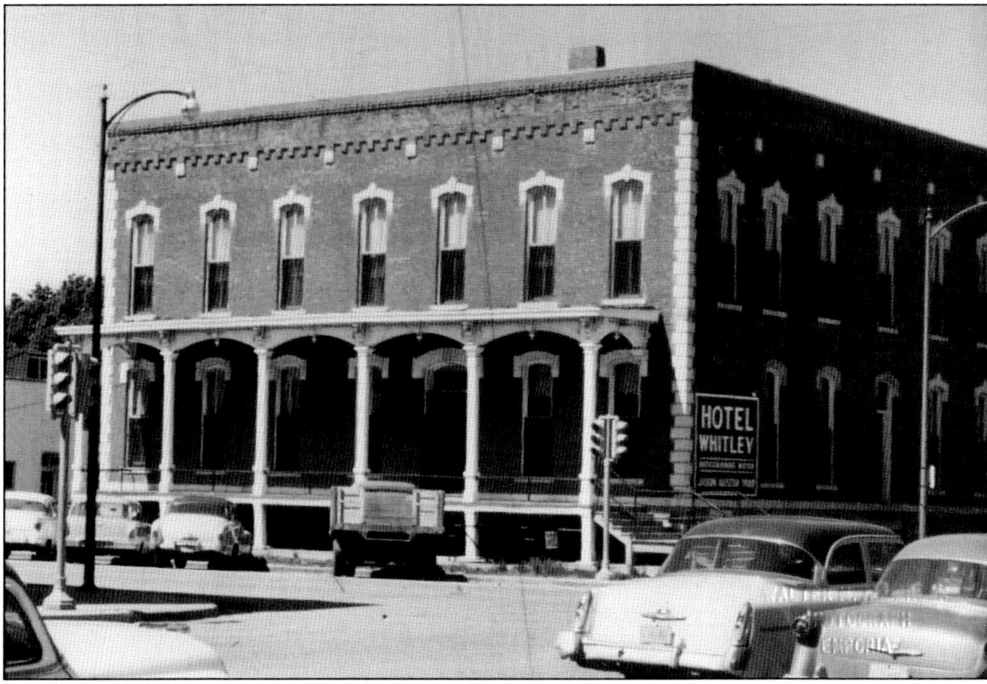

The Whitley Hotel, originally called the Fifth Avenue Hotel, was located at Fifth Avenue and Merchant Street. It was built around 1880 by a group of Emporians who wanted to develop Fifth Avenue as the key east-west commercial and business avenue. After a 1921 fire destroyed the Whitley Hotel at Sixth Avenue and Merchant Street, its owner, Col. H.C. Whitley, moved operations over to the Fifth Avenue hotel site, which took on the name Whitley Hotel. The hotel, pictured here around 1951, was sold to Fred G. Cline, owner of Cline Auto Supply, in 1959. (Courtesy of the Walter M. Andersen Collection, Emporia State University Special Collections Archives.)

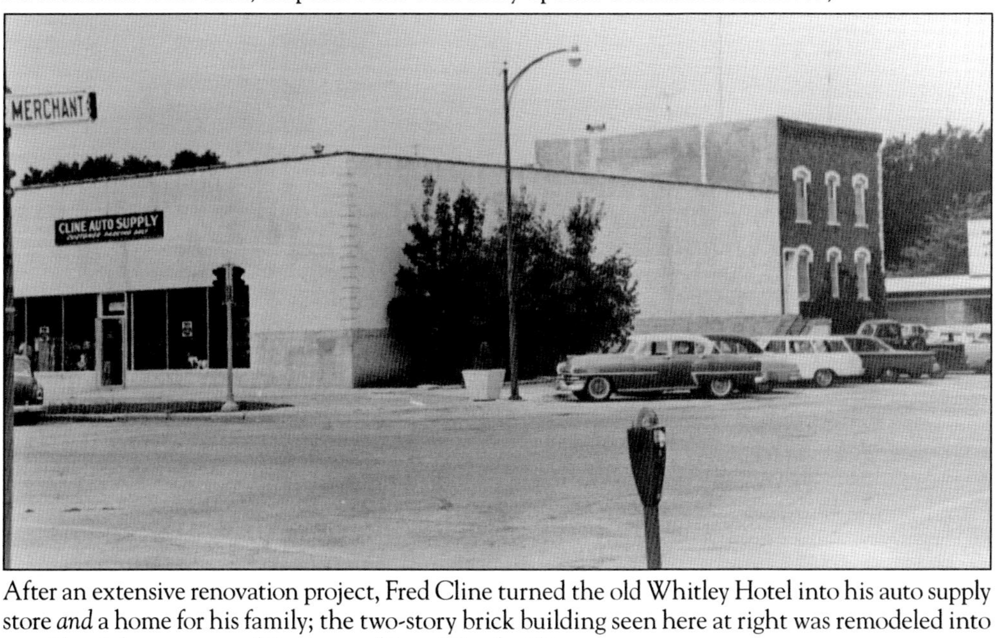

After an extensive renovation project, Fred Cline turned the old Whitley Hotel into his auto supply store *and* a home for his family; the two-story brick building seen here at right was remodeled into a residential apartment. (Courtesy of Ron Woodruff.)

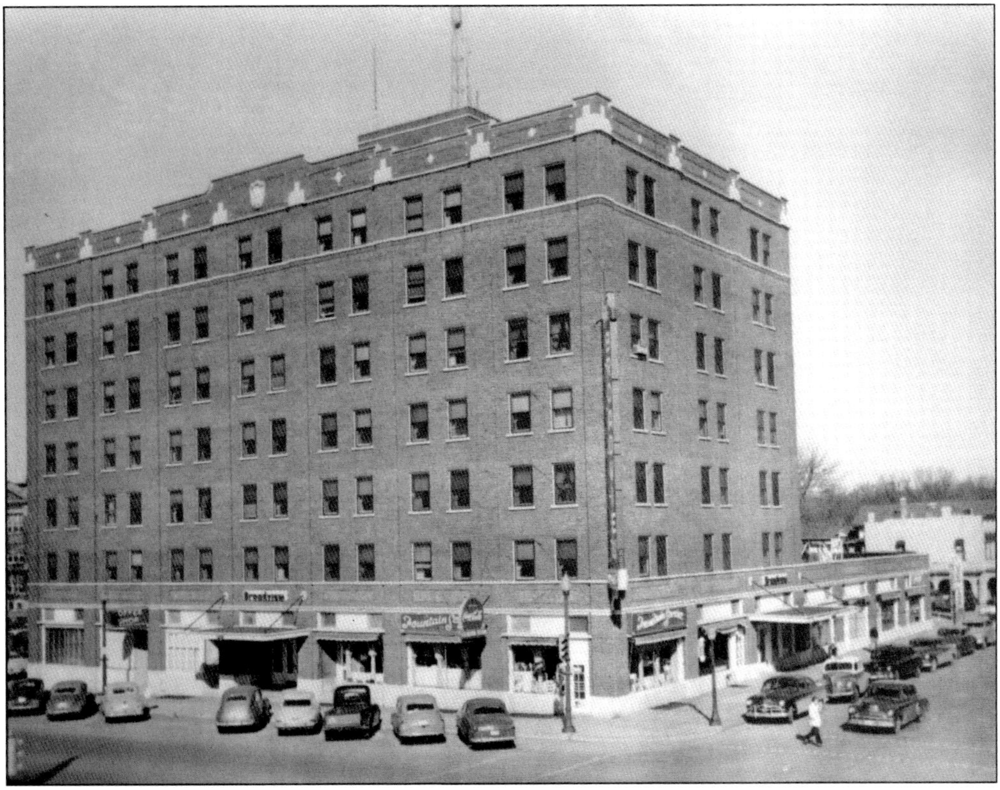

The Hotel Broadview located at 110 West Sixth Avenue opened to the public on September 21, 1923. The hotel was built to replace the Whitley Hotel, which burned on the same site in March 1921. The seven-story reinforced concrete structure is the tallest commercial building in Emporia. The Broadview had 150 guest rooms replete with all the modern conveniences of the Progressive Era. The hotel closed in 1964. In 1972, the building was sold to Broadview Towers Inc. for redevelopment to become one of the first Federal Housing Administration senior-housing projects. The building is in the Kansas State Register of Historic Places.

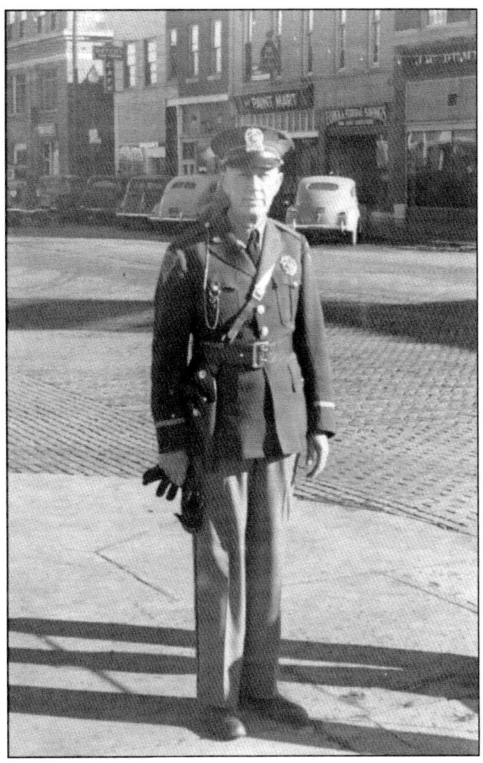

One of Emporia's most beloved policemen was Charlie O'Brien. For over 20 years, O'Brien was seen on the streets of Emporia providing protection and safety to the citizens as a traffic cop. His love and care for the children of Emporia earned him great respect. This image shows O'Brien on the corner of Sixth Avenue and Merchant Street in the 1930s.

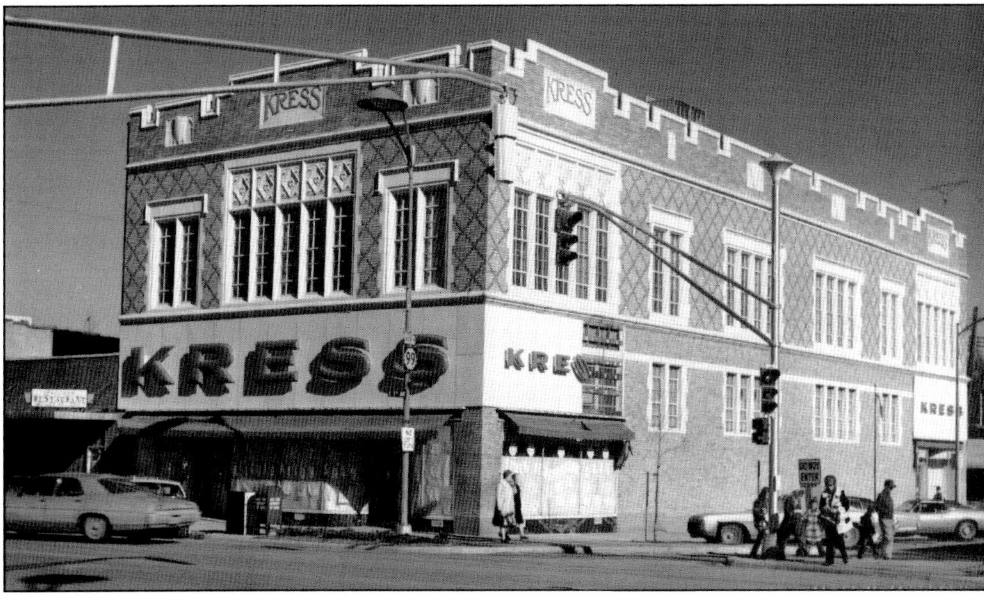

On November 16, 1929, Emporia's newest chain store opened at 702 Commercial Street. Originally located on the northeast corner of Sixth Avenue and Commercial Street and known as Kresge, the Kress Corporation had faith in the rising prosperity of Emporia in the 1920s. The brick facade had intricate designs representative of Elizabethan or Gothic styles. The interior featured coffered ceilings and Corinthian columns. This photograph was taken in 1973. Following the close of the Kress store, it was developed into offices and business suites that retained much of the original interior's integrity. (Courtesy of the Walter M. Andersen Collection, Emporia State University Special Collections Archives.)

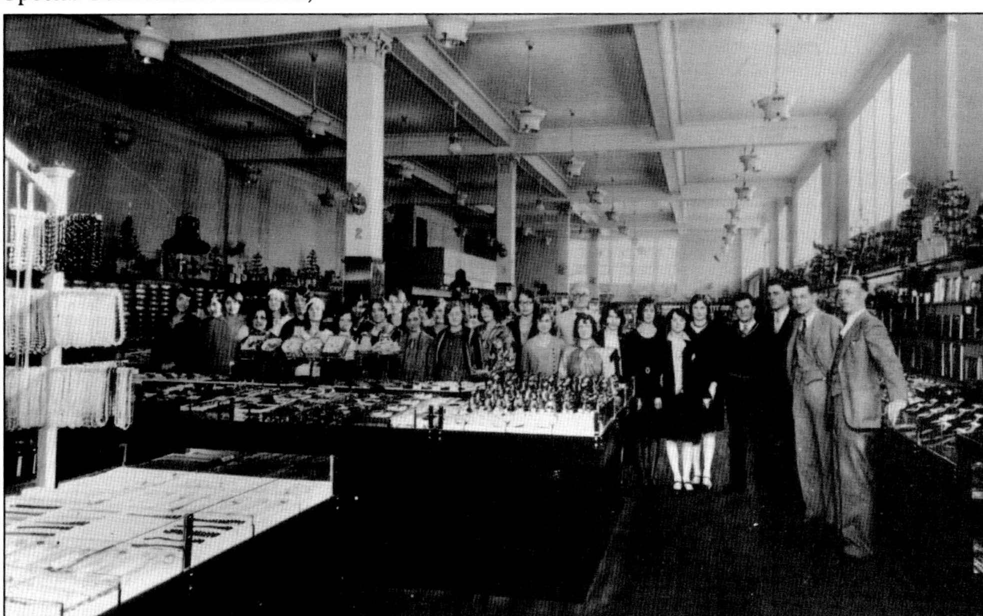

Pictured here are employees in the Kress store soon after its opening. The building is listed in the National Register of Historic Places. (Courtesy of the Walter M. Andersen Collection, Emporia State University Special Collections Archives.)

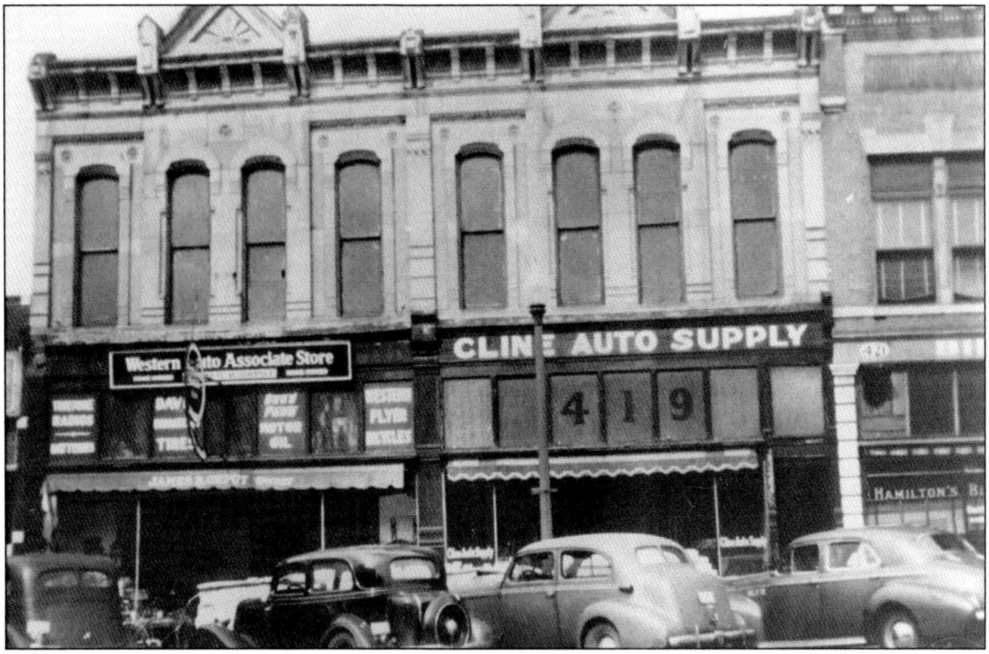

Many of the downtown buildings have seen a lot of businesses come and go under their roofs. For example, the building that housed the Cline Auto and Western Auto stores in this c. 1945 photograph was built in 1884 as a hardware store. Over the years, it also served as a stove shop, a carriage repository, a piano and printing shop, a grocery store and meat shop, and a restaurant. In 1950, the second floor of the building was remodeled to house Emporia Bowl, owned by Gaines Judsen. (Courtesy of Ron Woodruff.)

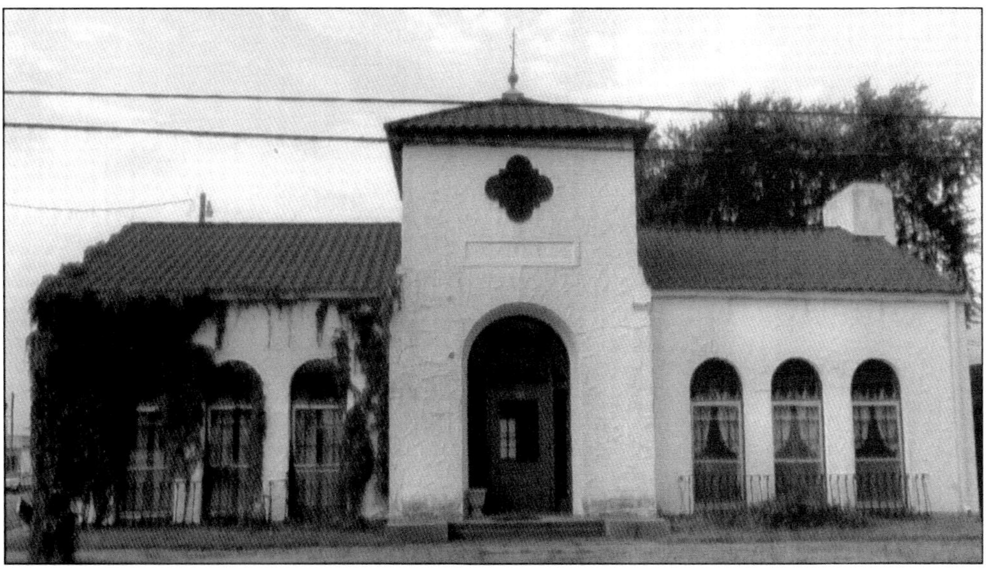

When the Social Service Club merged with the Emporia Welfare Society, it built the Welfare Building at 325 Merchant Street in 1927 to meet the needs of the community. Funds for the Spanish Mission–style building were provided by Margaret Warren, who was intensely interested in local welfare work. Original plans for the building included an entire development that would have featured 30 market stalls on the tract, macadam driveways, parking space, and a water garden.

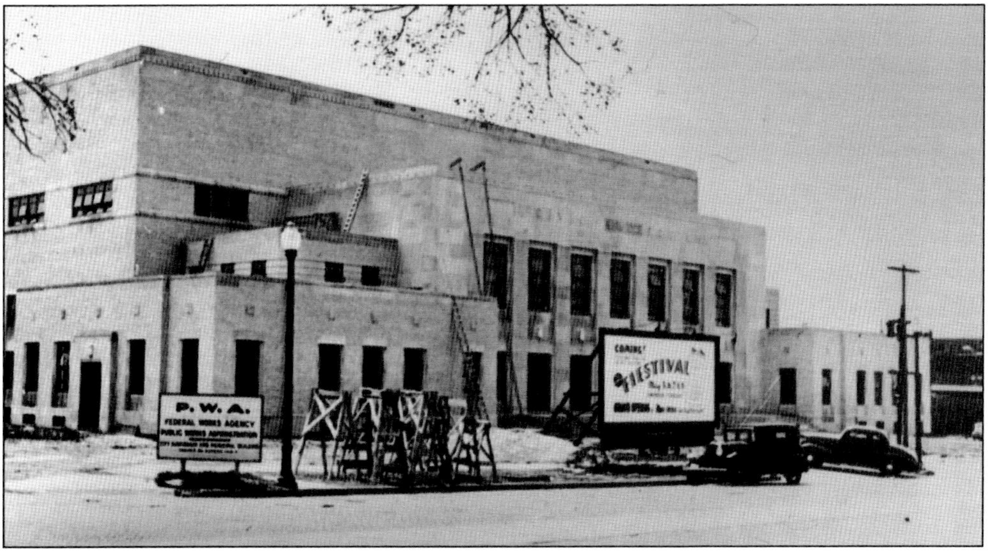

This image shows the civic auditorium nearing completion. Construction for the auditorium, which sits on an entire city block, began in 1938 following the Art Deco design of architects Henry Brinkman and Stan Hagan. The auditorium was completed in 1940 with the city hosting a grand five-day Fiestival to celebrate.

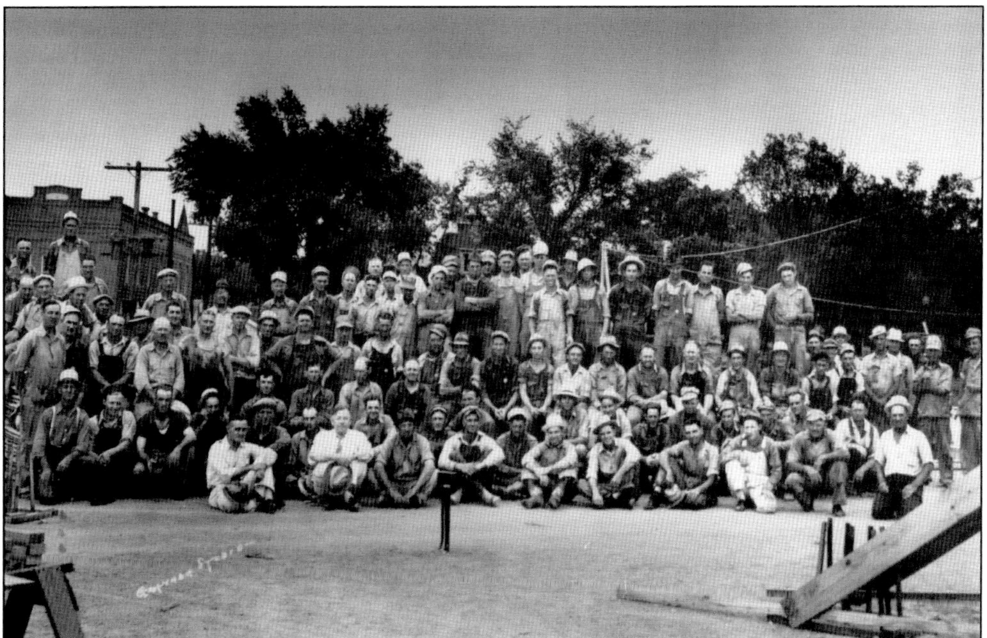

Thought by many Emporians to be an extravagant and oversized structure when first conceived, the civic auditorium has proven to be one of the city's best assets. In 1972, the auditorium was named the William Lindsay White Auditorium in honor of White's accomplishments and his support of the city. It has been home to Kansas state high school basketball tournaments for all but three years since 1955. Many celebrities have also performed on its stage. Besides the auditorium, the building houses the city municipal offices and the police and fire departments. Seen here is the construction crew that built the facility.

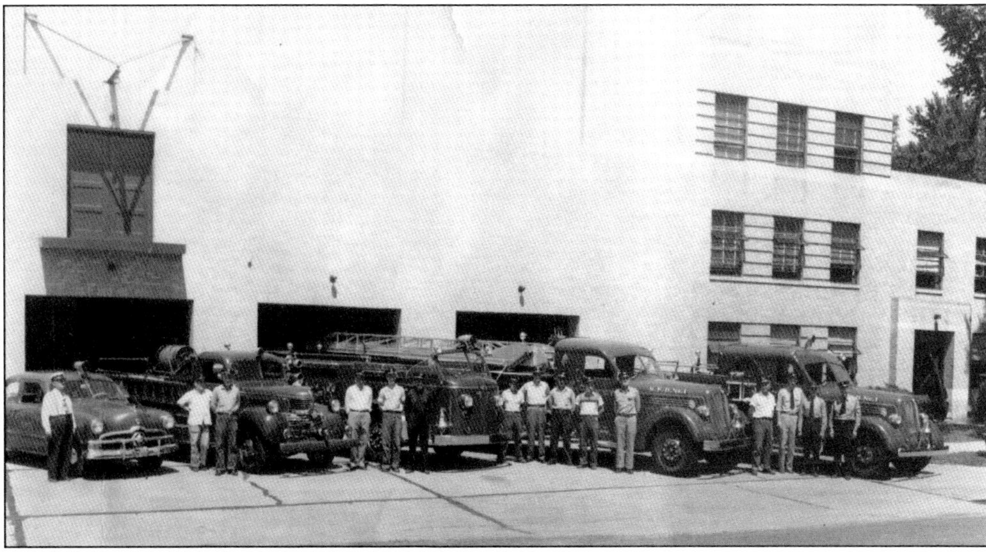

With the completion of the new civic auditorium in 1940, the Emporia Police and Fire Department moved to their quarters from the old city building at 20 East Fifth Avenue. The spacious new building provided both departments room for newer and more modern equipment. Today, both of these important city departments remain in the civic auditorium following renovations. These c. 1950 photographs capture the fire department crew and their equipment.

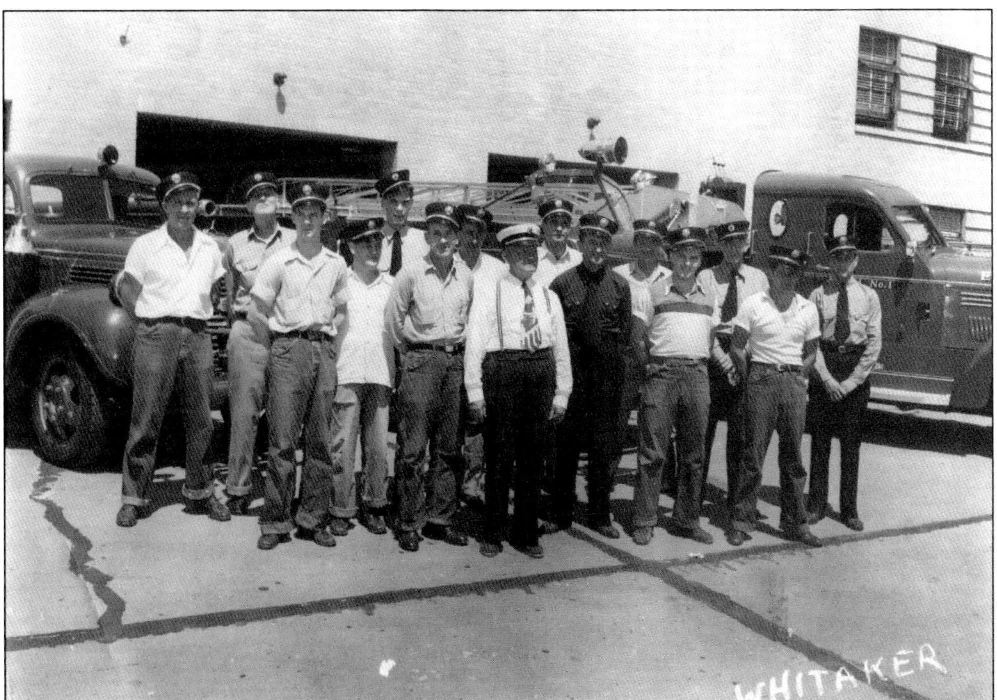

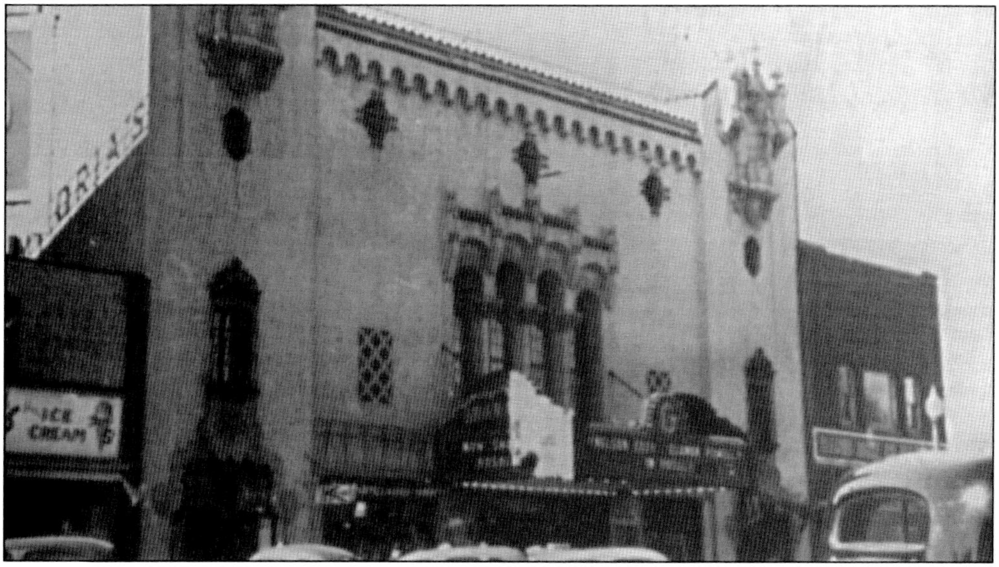

Thanks to a group of Emporia businessmen who rescued it from demolition in 1994, the Granada Theatre remains as Emporia's cinema treasure. The 1,400-seat theater was built in 1929 at a cost of $350,000. In addition to serving as a movie theatre, it was used for beauty contests and traveling vaudeville acts. Robert Boller, nationally known theater designer, designed the outside of the theater in the Spanish Colonial Revival style popular in the 1920s. The Spanish style was carried into the theater with alcoves surrounded by gilded plaster details and ornate plaster panels that lined the balcony rail and the proscenium arch.

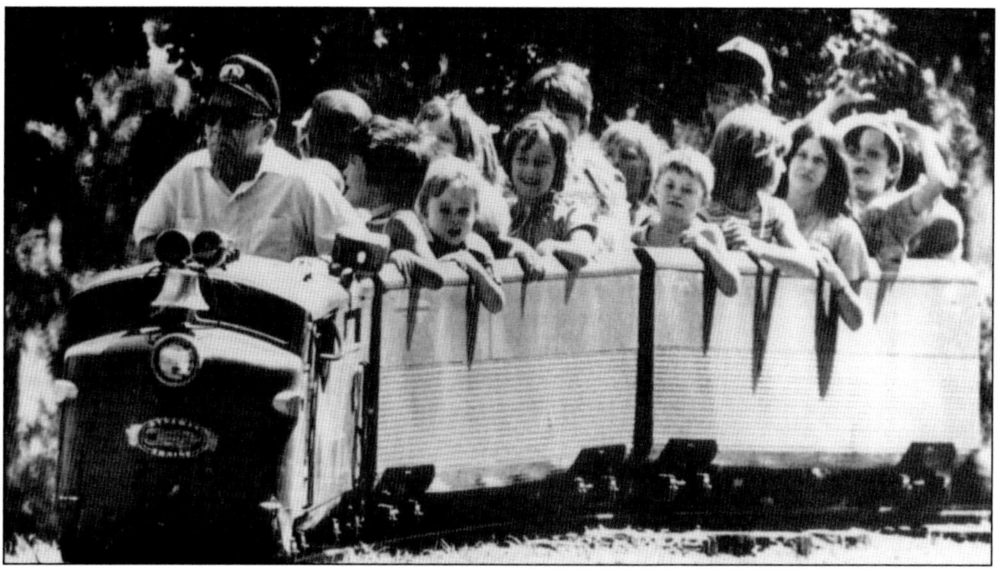

Ever since 1958, young and old alike have enjoyed the miniature train rides at Soden's Grove Park, and they have Dr. Fred McCabe to thank for the happy memories. When the Emporia Chamber of Commerce backed out of the plan to bring the miniature train to Soden's Grove, McCabe became trustee of the project and coordinated the fundraising and building projects. The train made its first run in August 1958, with P.E. "Hap" Reser as the driver. Train rides cost 10¢. In 2001, the Emporia Sertoma Club took over the operation of the train and made improvements to the track, storage buildings, depot, and boarding platform.

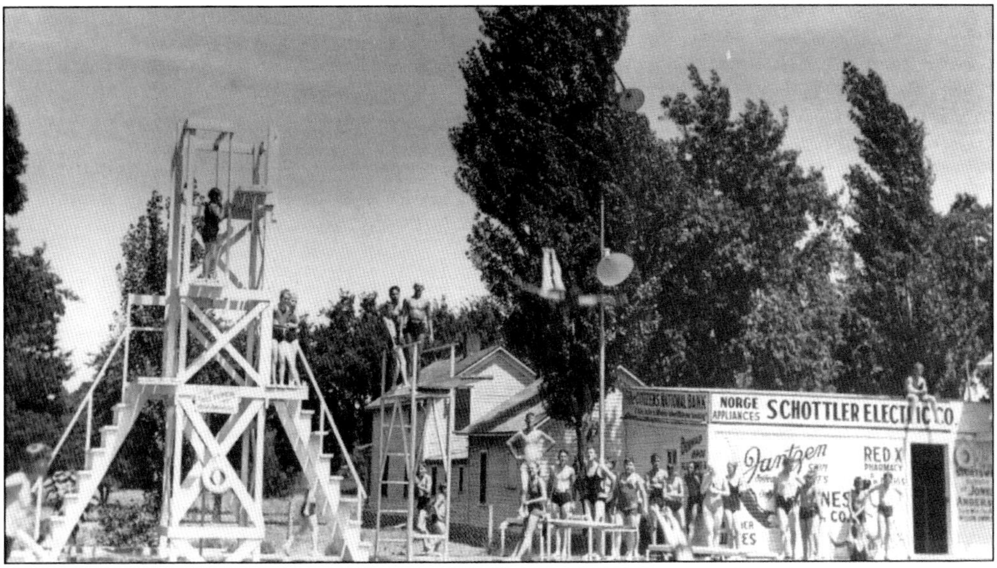

During the dog days of summer, Emporia's children could escape the heat by swimming at the Emporia Swimming Pool (pictured around 1937), owned and operated by John Lawrence. The pool, located across the street from Peter Pan Park at 302 South Congress Street, featured a 10-foot steel diving platform, a large water wheel, springboards, slides, and merry-go-rounds. Refreshments were available at a concession stand nearby. The cost in 1935 was 25¢ for adults and 15¢ for children 12 and under.

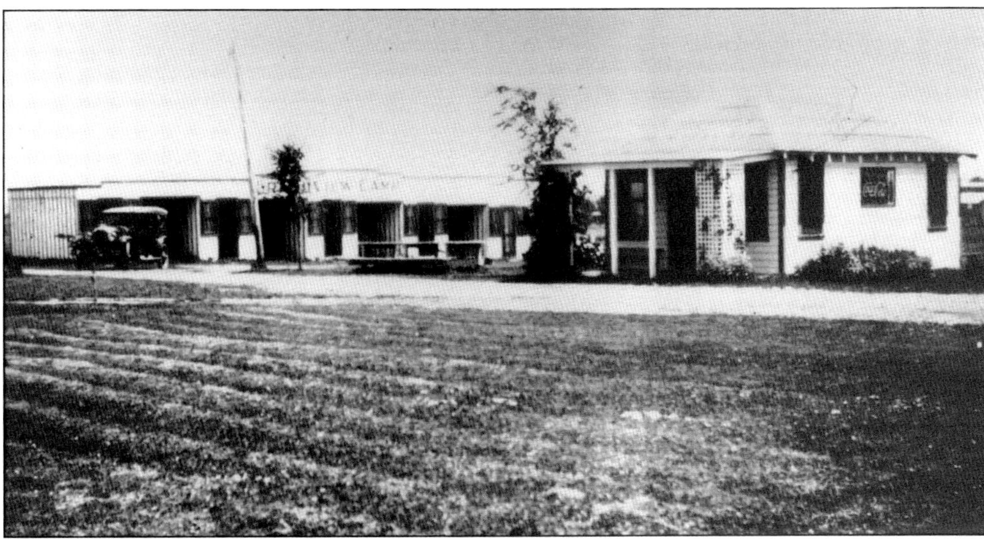

As Americans became more mobile and traveled across the country, auto camps like the Grandview Tourist Camp became popular places to stop and spend the night. The Grandview Tourist Camp was opened in July 1927 by William Collins and was located one and a half miles east of Emporia. The camp consisted of cabins with lights and running water, a gas station, and a lunch counter. (Courtesy of the Walter M. Andersen Collection, Emporia State University Special Collections Archives.)

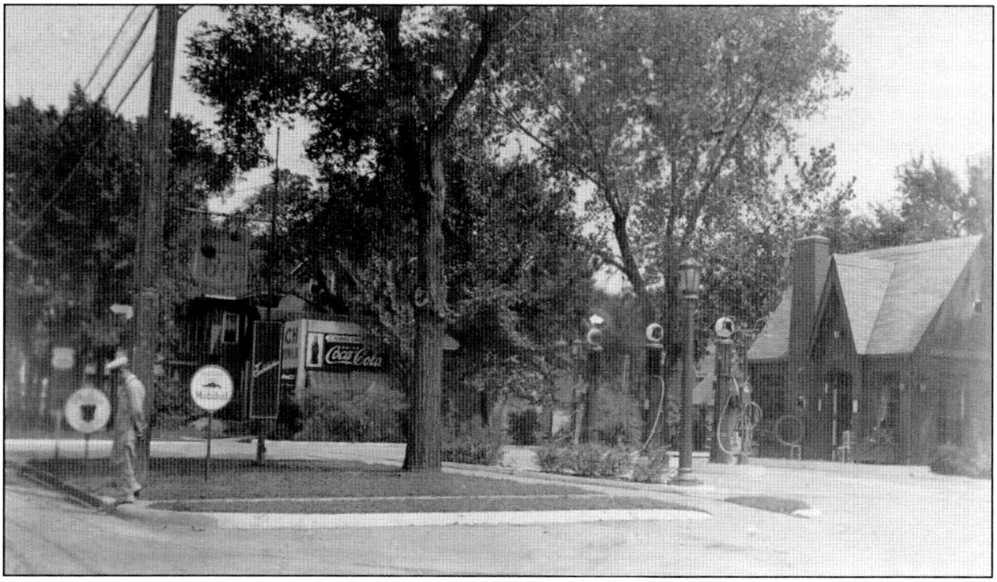

With the automobile becoming the most common mode of transportation in the first half of the 20th century, gas stations sprang up on intersections near highways and businesses. Emporia was no exception. Most of the stations were located on Sixth Avenue (US Highway 50), Commercial Street, and near the colleges. The architectural design for the stations was varied and often reflected the residential building styles. Emporia has several Spanish-, Tudor-, Cottage-, and Modern-style stations that remain from the 1920s–1940s. Today, many of these stations have been adapted for other uses, such as liquor stores, beauty salons, restaurants, and gift shops. The two stations shown here were within four blocks of each other. The image above shows a Tudor-style station that was located at Sixth Avenue and Rural Street. Below is a more modern station that was located at Sixth Avenue and Congress Street.

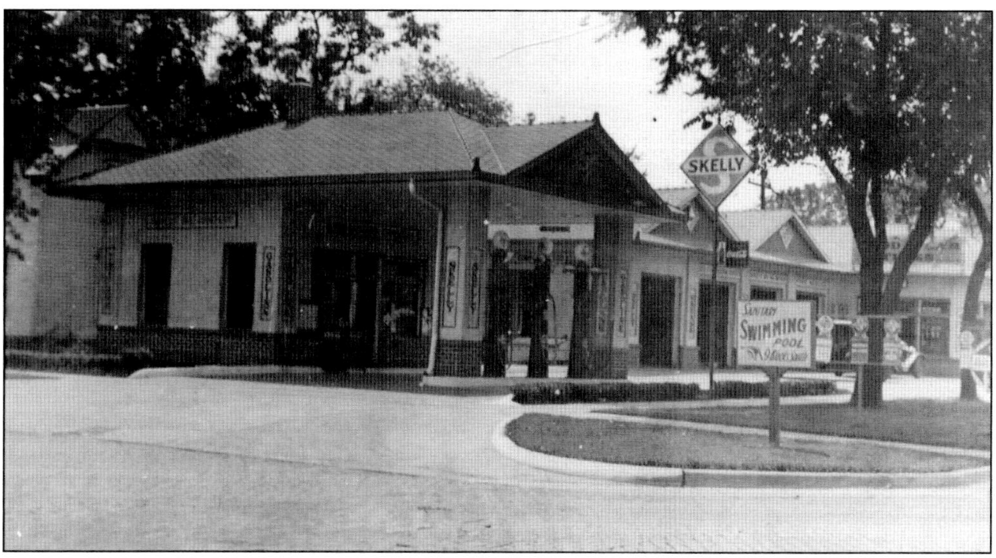

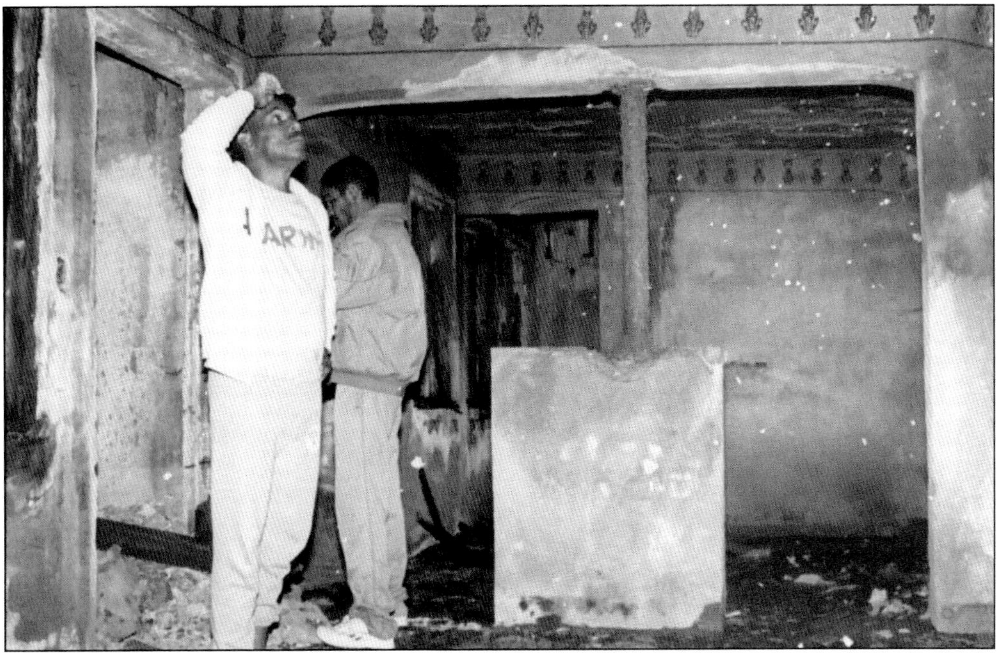

The Black Cat Café was hidden for years underneath the sidewalk between Commercial and Merchant Streets at Seventh Avenue. Exterior stairs led to the two-room café, which was originally public restrooms; it was converted into the café by George and Grace Wells in 1927. The Wellses offered lunches, pastries, and fountain services. The underground café was short lived and the Wellses opened another café above ground. Eventually the stairs, along with the history of the public restrooms and café, was sealed over with cement. (Courtesy of the Walter M. Andersen Collection, Emporia State University Special Collections Archives.)

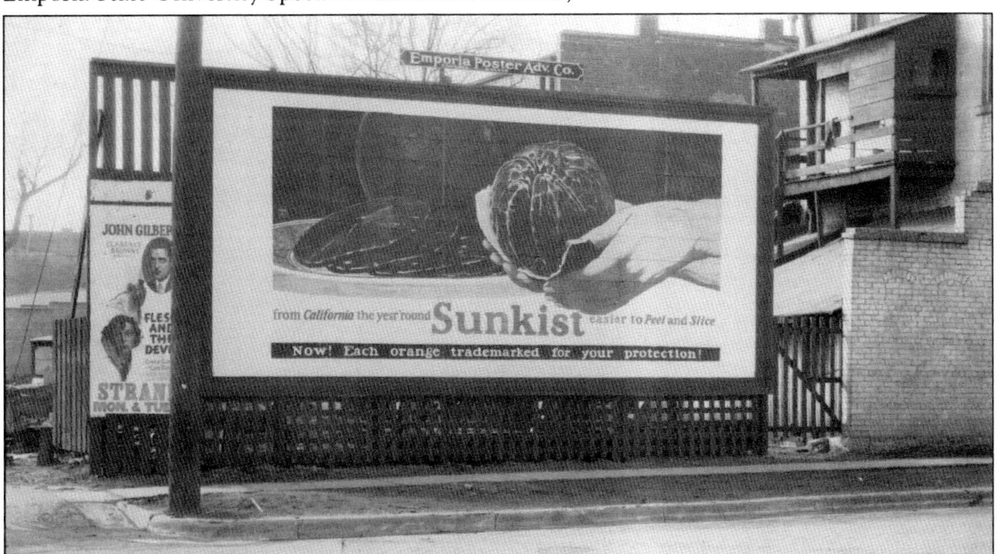

Billboard advertising became popular as more people traveled to work and on vacations in their automobiles. The Emporia Poster Advertising Company produced signs for billboards that were located throughout the city and countryside. This poster near a building downtown is advertising fruit at a local market.

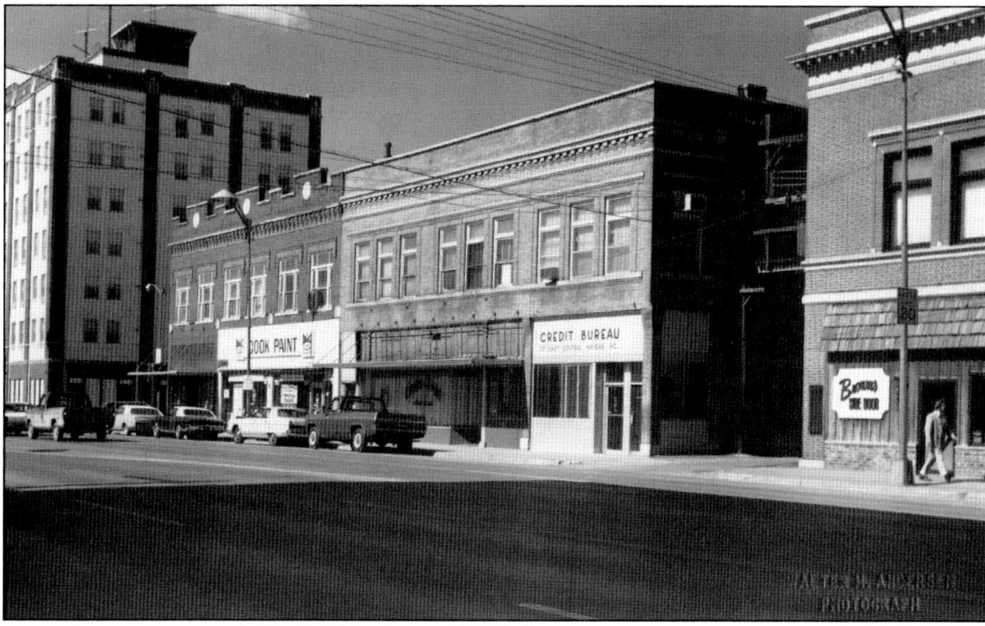

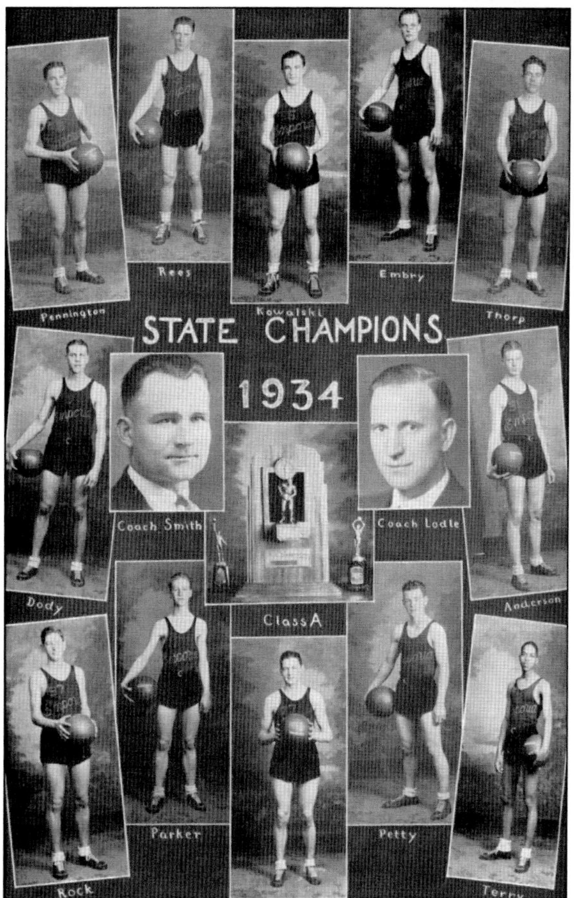

This 1975 photograph of the northeast corner of Sixth Avenue and Merchant Street reflects downtown changes over 100 years. Once the site of the Whitley Opera House from 1881 until it burned in 1913, it was replaced with more modern structures. As time passed and the need for parking increased, these buildings were demolished for a parking lot. (Courtesy of the Walter M. Andersen Collection, Emporia State University Special Collections Archives.)

In 1934, Emporia High School won its second state basketball championship. The team was coached by Alfred Smith, the father of legendary basketball coach Dean Smith (center left). Smith encouraged Paul Terry (bottom right), an African American, to join the varsity team. Terry was used as a valuable defensive player and sixth man, and was the first African American to play basketball in the Eastern Kansas Conference. Terry was inducted into the Emporia High School Hall of Fame.

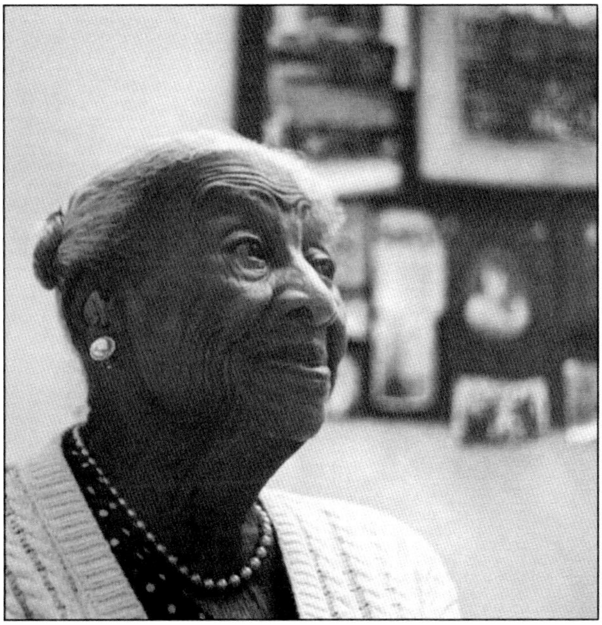

When she died at the age of 111 on December 18, 2010, Catherine Williams Carter had the distinction of being one of the oldest women in the United States, having lived a life that spanned three centuries. Catherine moved to Emporia from Burlingame, Kansas, in 1919 with her two brothers, Elijah and Clayton. She married Allen "Lee" Carter at the Mount Olive Church on October 12, 1926. Lee worked at the Santa Fe roundhouse for 45 years. One of the jobs Catherine worked during her 91 years in Emporia was as a dishwasher in Newman's Tea Room. She remained at her home on East Street until she reached the age of 100 and moved to the Emporia Presbyterian Manor.

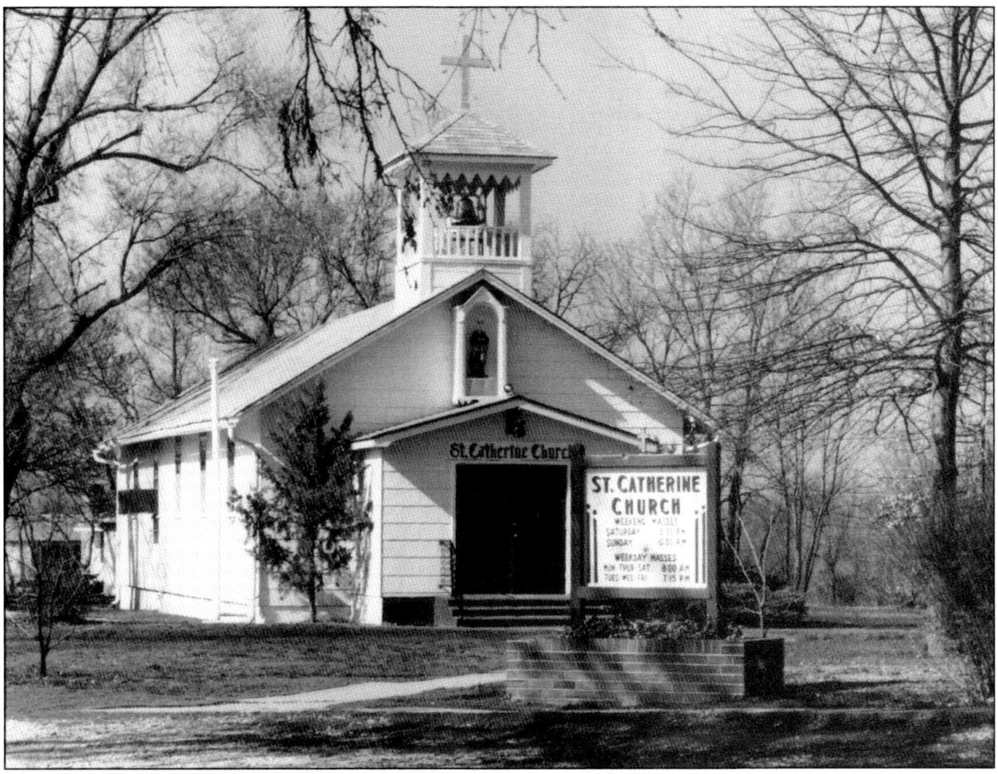

In 1923, the Emporia Catholics and the Catholic Church Extension Society of Chicago purchased lots at 130 South Pine Street to build a chapel for their Mexican American parishioners who missed their Spanish-language religious ceremonies. The new church was blessed as St. Catherine of Alexandria. In 1942, it was moved to South Lawrence Street on the grounds of the old Riverside School.

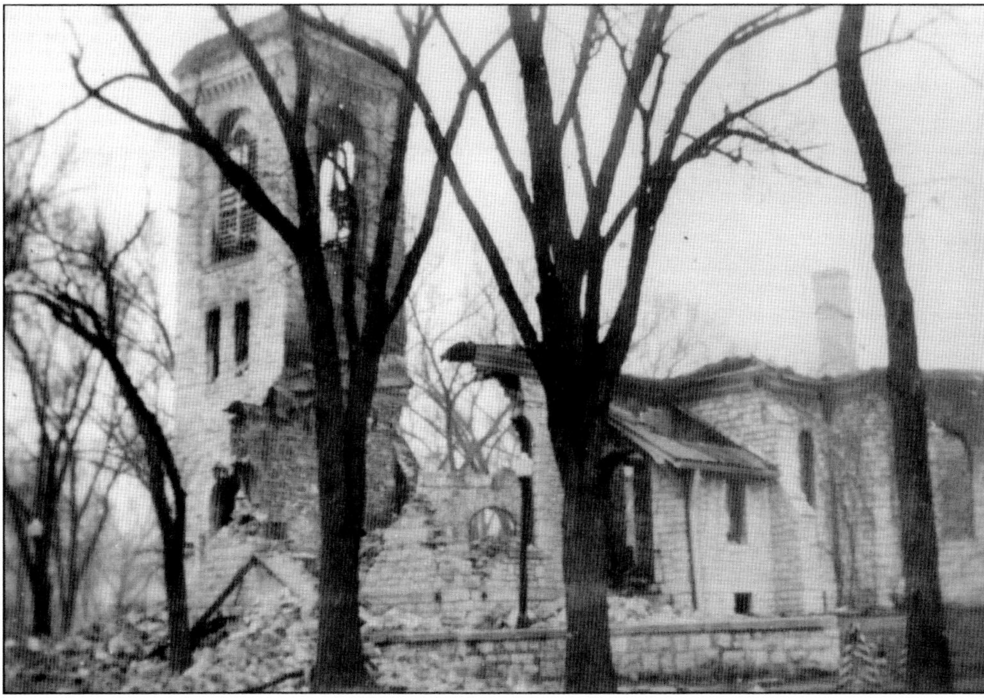

On the morning of December 20, 1942, a fire destroyed the First Congregational Church at Eighth Avenue and Mechanic Street. The loss was estimated at $95,000. Seven years later, the church was rebuilt at the site of G.W. and Nellie Newman's home at Twelfth Avenue and State Street, where it is still located today. Coincidentally, the Newmans were active members of the church when they were alive. (Courtesy of the Walter M. Andersen Collection, Emporia State University Special Collections Archives.)

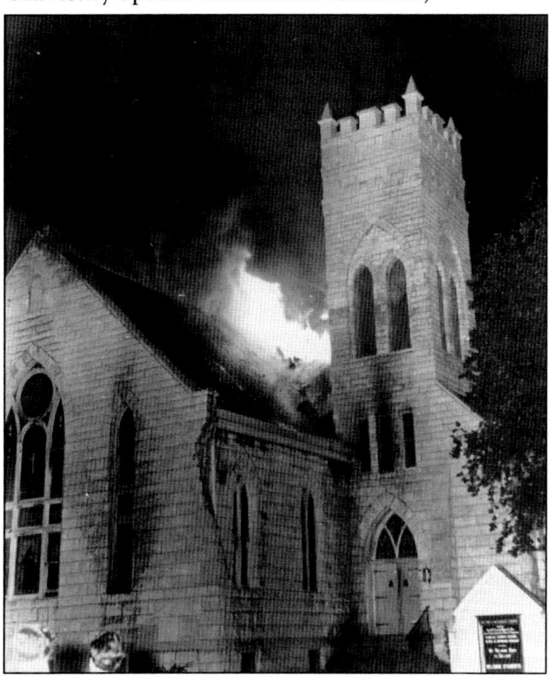

On September 14, 1957, the First United Methodist Church, located at 823 Merchant Street, was destroyed by fire. This was the second time the church had been destroyed by fire as the previous structure had burned in 1901 and was replaced by the building pictured here in 1903. After the 1957 fire, church services were held in Albert Taylor Hall on the ESU campus until the church was reopened in May 1961. (Courtesy of the Walter M. Andersen Collection, Emporia State University Special Collections Archives.)

Described in the *Emporia Gazette* as "a gem of Gothic architecture of well-balanced proportions and carefully wrought details" and "a monument to Emporia labor and Emporia perseverance," the Sacred Heart Church was dedicated on September 15, 1912. H.W. Brinkman designed the building, which, along with the furnishings, cost around $45,000 to build. The church, located at 101 Cottonwood Street, replaced a two-story church that was built in 1881.

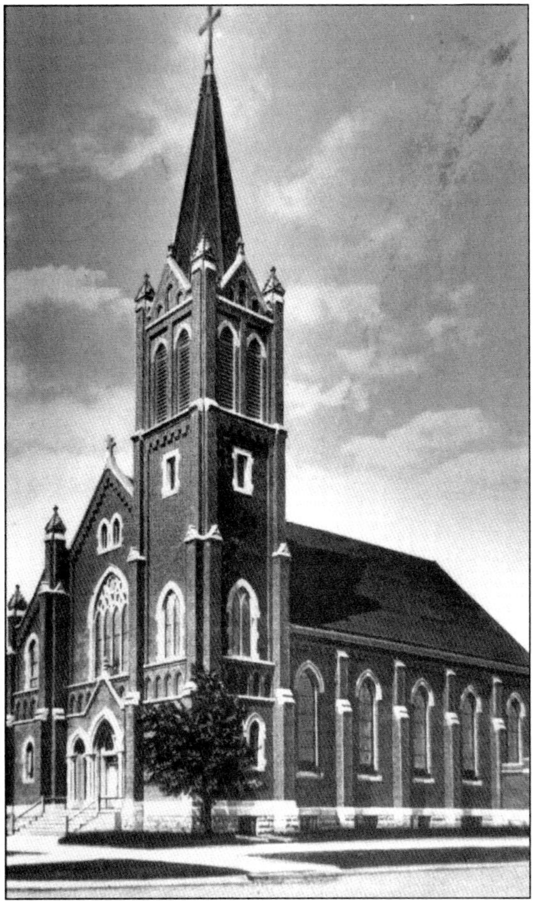

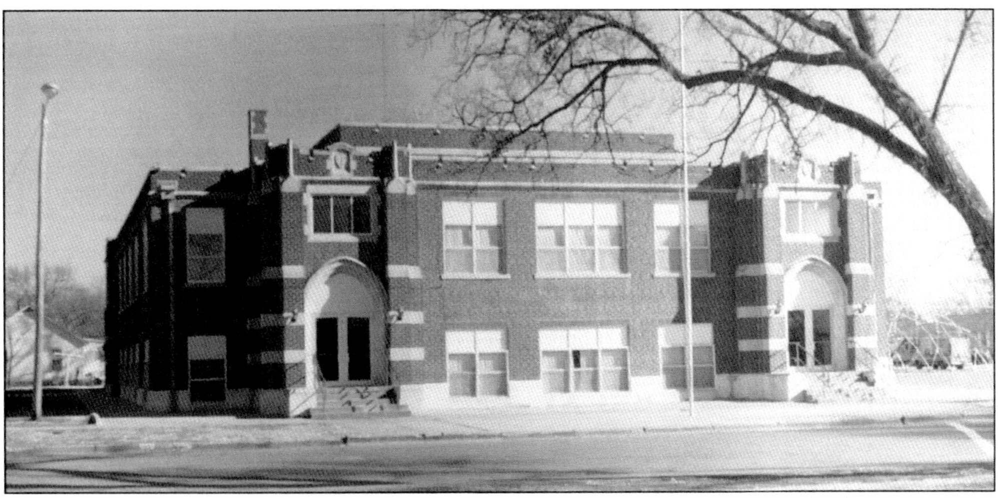

The current Sacred Heart School, located at 102 Cottonwood Street, was built in 1926 at a cost of $50,000. The architects, Brinkman & Hagan, were tasked with planning a two-story building that could be used for both educational and parish activities. The classrooms and a large auditorium were built on the second floor, while the first floor contained parish meeting rooms, a large dining hall, and a kitchen.

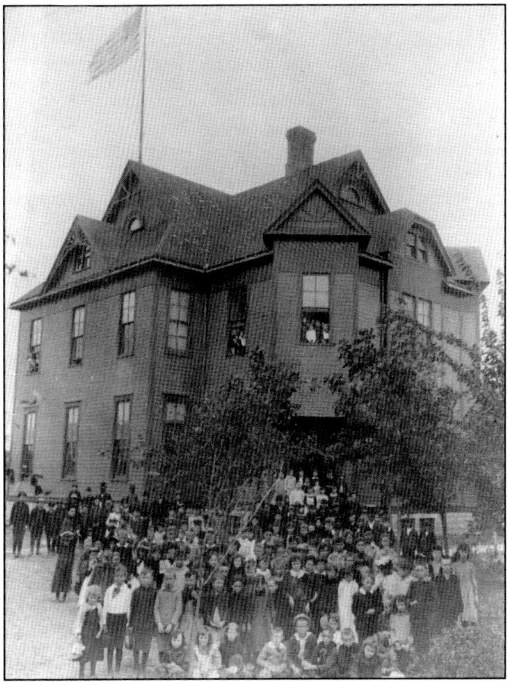

Students take time to pose for an all-school photograph at the first Walnut School. The school, built in 1885 on the southwest corner of Walnut Street and Eighth Avenue, represents the original four-room, two-story ward buildings that were built in the early days. (Courtesy of the Walter M. Andersen Collection, Emporia State University Special Collections Archives.)

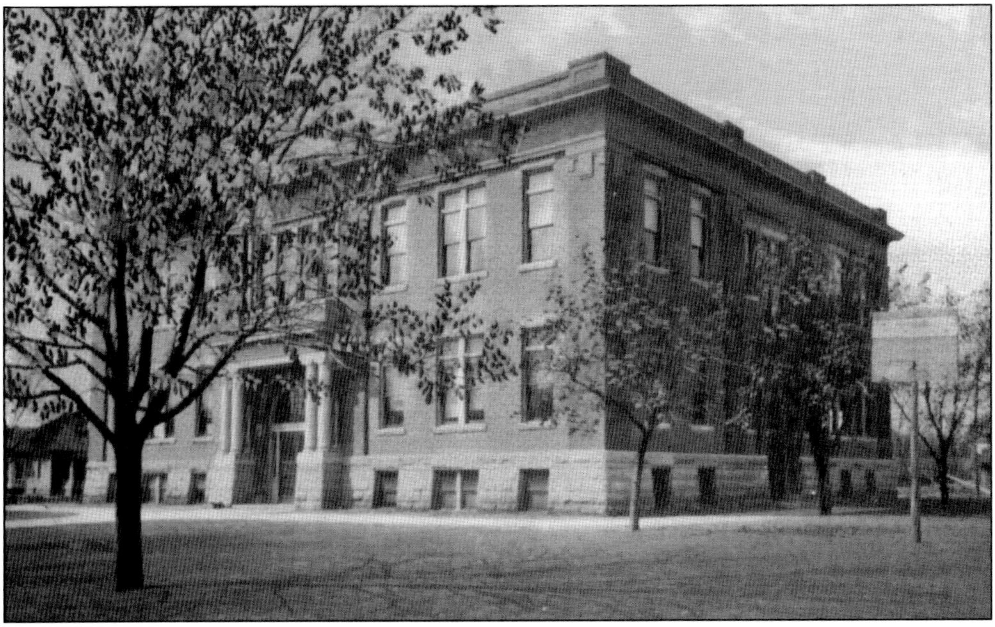

The second Walnut School was built in 1910 and located at 800 Walnut Street. Described as the handsomest school in town, it contained eight recitation rooms (four on each floor), spacious closets, roomy halls and stairways, and lots of windows. While the new school was being built, the students attended classes in the old frame building that had been moved to the back of the lot. Overcrowding led to the construction of the third Walnut School at 801 Grove Avenue, which opened in October 1950. Warren Brinkman was the architect for both the second and third buildings. (Courtesy of the Walter M. Andersen Collection, Emporia State University Special Collections Archives.)

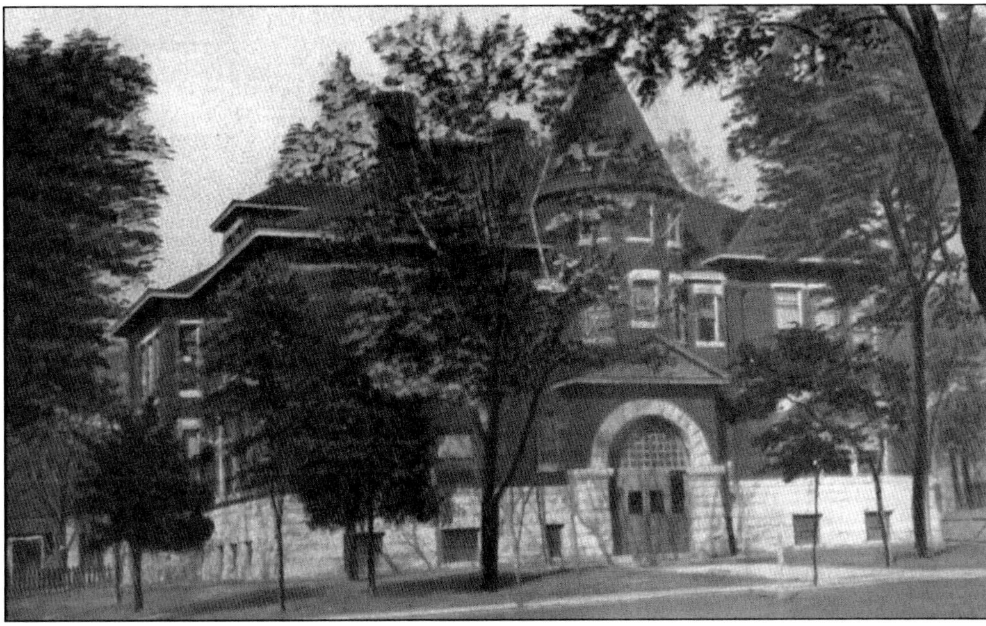

Union School was located at Fourth Avenue and Union Street. Originally built of wood in 1868, it was replaced by brick in the 1880s, then rebuilt as pictured here in 1901. It was closed in 1950 after William Allen White School was opened. (Courtesy of the Walter M. Andersen Collection, Emporia State University Special Collections Archives.)

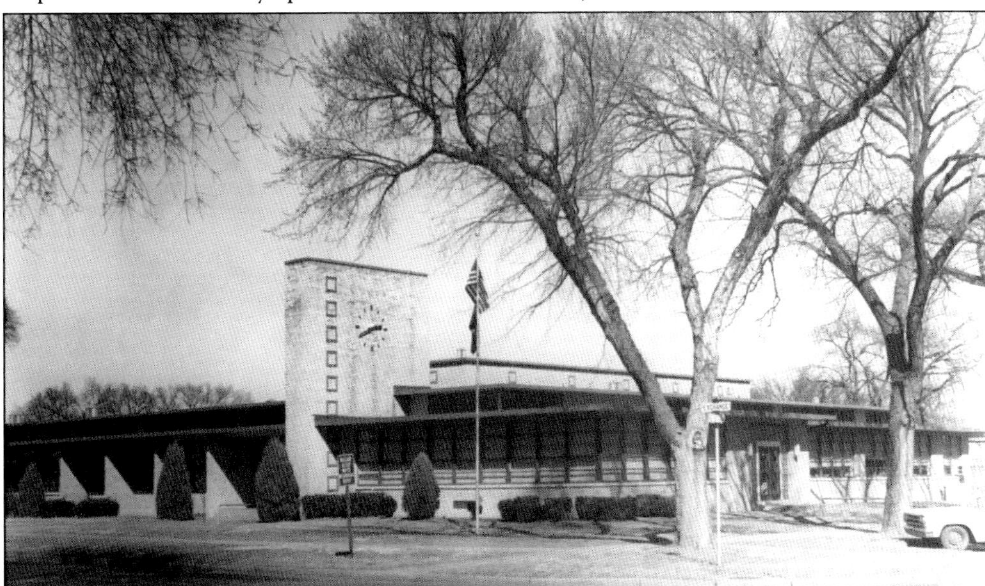

Named after *Emporia Gazette* editor William Allen White by the students of Union School, the William Allen White School opened in November 1950. Some of the features of the $337,000 building designed by architects Buck and Lewis included 10 classrooms, a principal's office, a nurse's clinic, a teacher's lounge, a kitchen, and a combination gymnasium and auditorium. The school is located at 902 Exchange Street, which is across the street from Red Rocks, the home of William Allen White. (Courtesy of the Walter M. Andersen Collection, Emporia State University Special Collections Archives.)

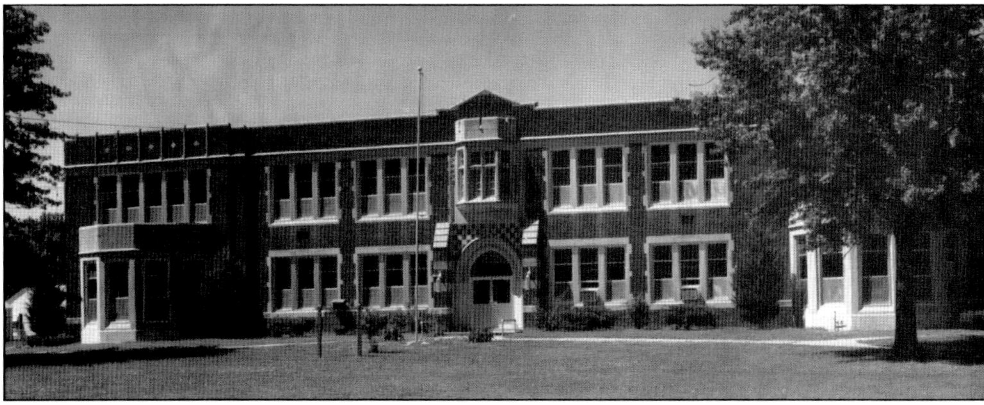

Opened in January 1930, Mary Herbert School was named after Mary Herbert, a teacher and principal who had worked in the Emporia School District for over 45 years. It was built to replace the Lincoln School, which was located on the southwest corner of Lincoln Street and Sixth Avenue. Designed by Brinkman and Hagan, it cost $100,000 to build. Today, it serves as the Unified School District No. 253 Board of Education office. (Courtesy of the Walter M. Andersen Collection, Emporia State University Special Collections Archives.)

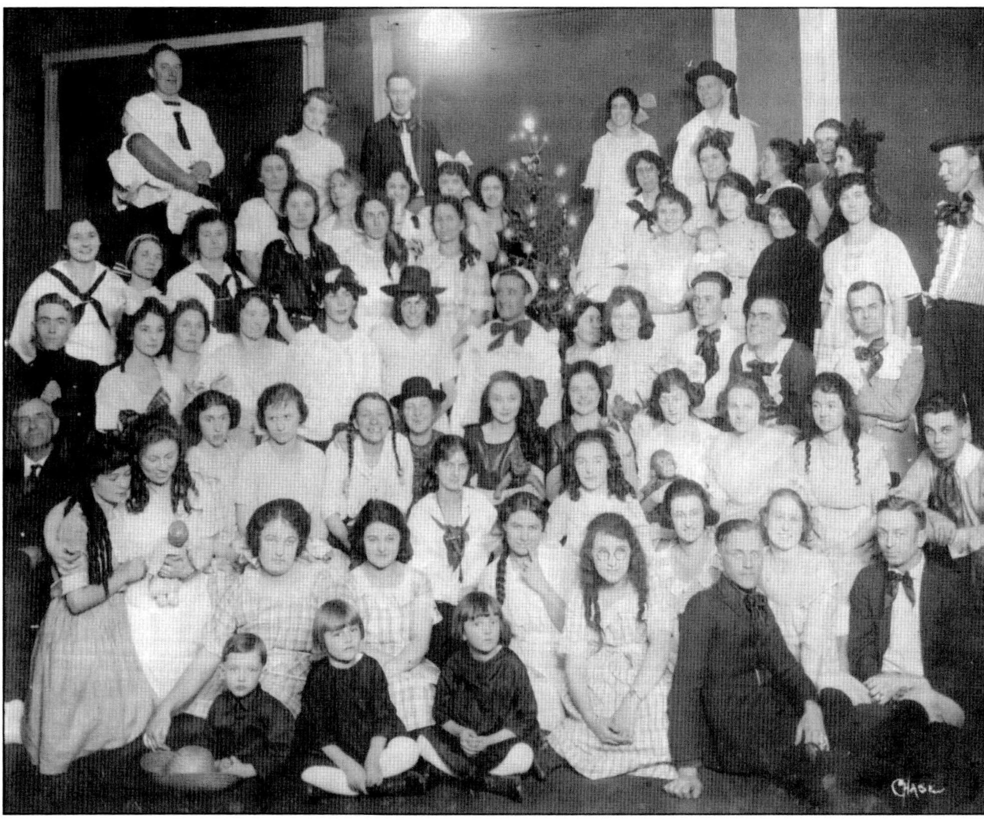

Celebrating the Christmas season has long been a tradition in the Emporia School District. The program was organized by the school music department and featured students from grades six through twelve. The seasonal celebration is now performed two nights before a capacity crowd in the civic auditorium. In this 1920s photograph, students are posing after a performance. (Courtesy of the Walter M. Andersen Collection, Emporia State University Special Collections Archives.)

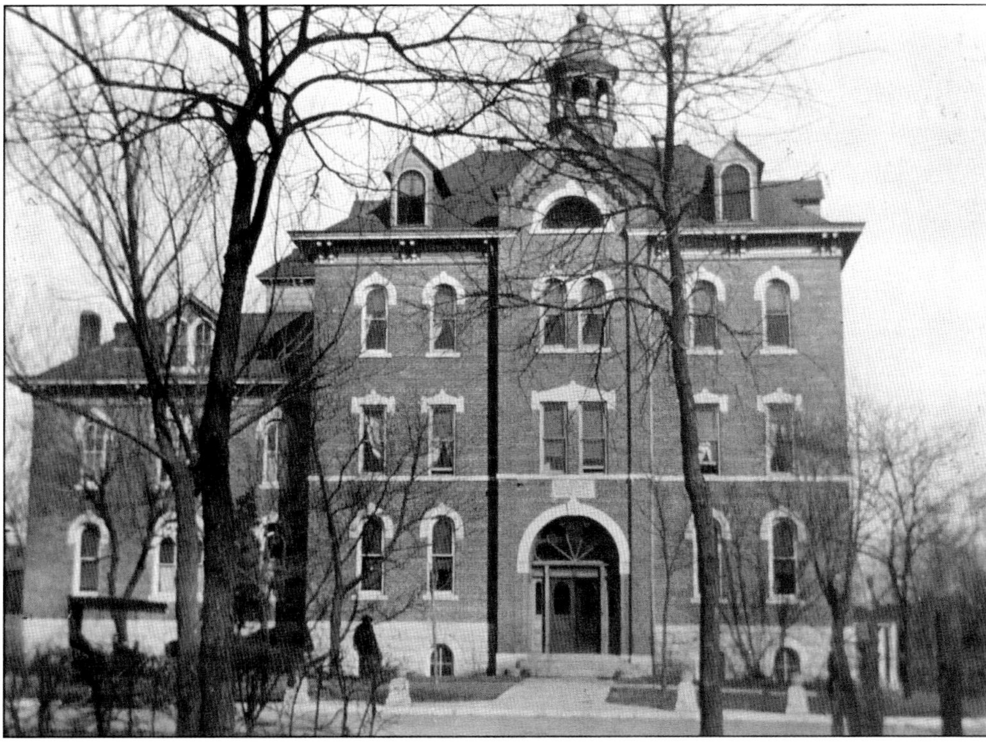

For 40 years, St. Mary's Hospital, founded by the Sisters of St. Francis, served as Emporia's only hospital. The 15-bed facility was opened in 1883 at 122 Exchange Street. In 1907, the hospital underwent a $25,000 expansion, but an excess of patients and a flooded basement in 1926 prompted the sisters to build a new hospital. This old building was razed in 1937.

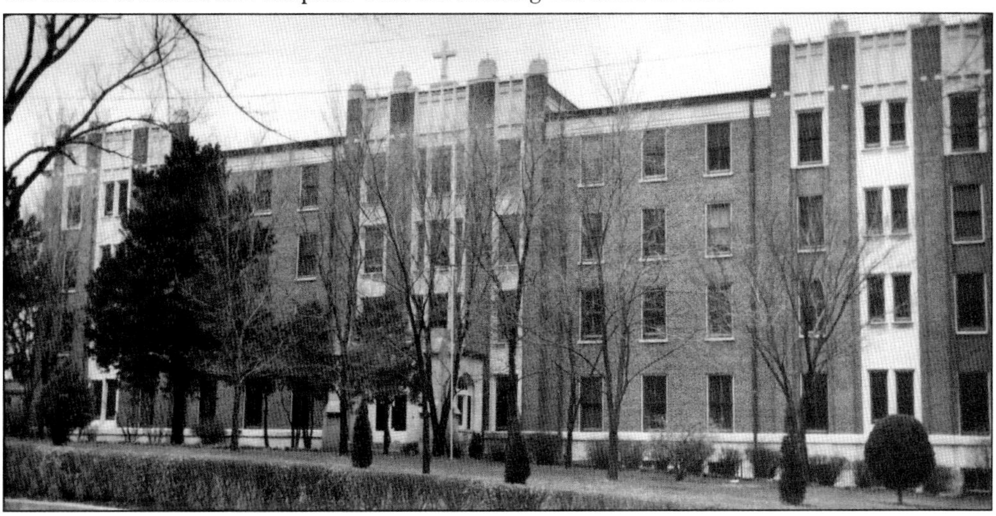

The Sisters of St. Francis opened the "new" St. Mary's Hospital at Fifteenth Avenue and State Street on November 21, 1928. The four-floor hospital cost approximately $250,000 to build. A newspaper account described "bright airy rooms for patients," operating rooms furnished with "some of the best equipment in the state," and an interesting baby department on the third floor that was adjoined by a sun porch. The hospital closed in 1991. Today, the Hillcrest Apartments and the Flint Hills Community Health Center occupy the site.

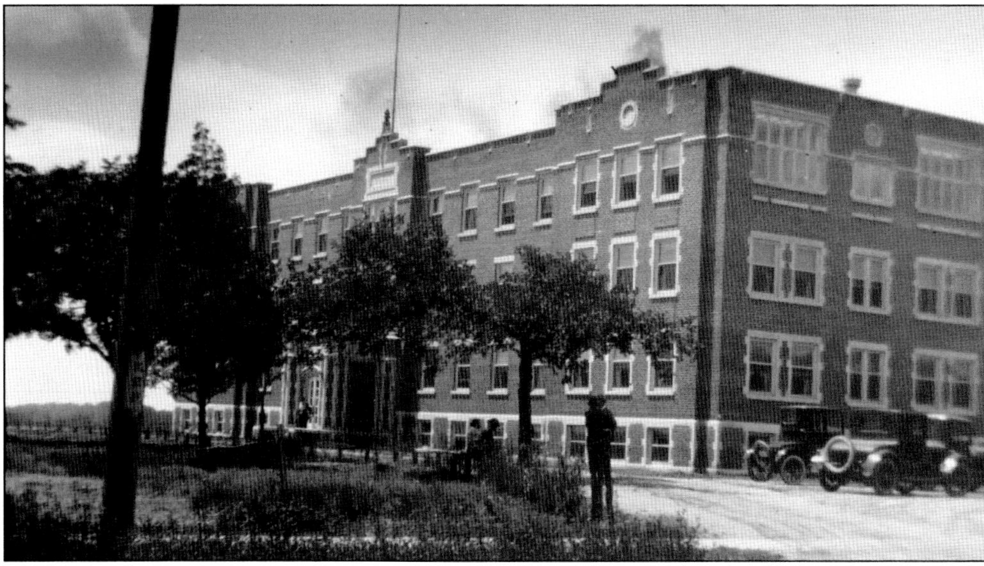

Thanks to a generous $50,000 bequest from the George W. Newman estate, the 81-bed Newman Memorial County Hospital, pictured here in approximately 1925, was built in 1922. The rest of the $300,000 cost was paid for with a two-mill tax levy and contributions from individual citizens and various clubs and organizations. In the first six months of the hospital's existence, 28 babies were born, and 106 major and 135 minor surgeries were performed.

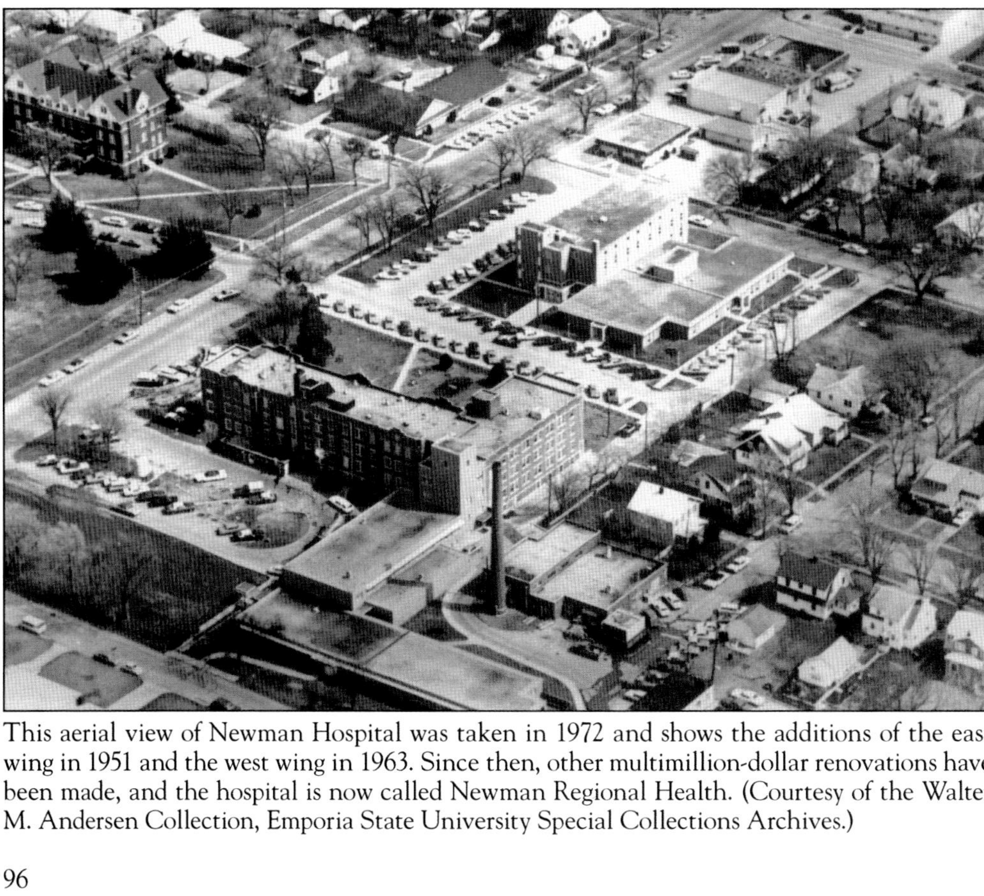

This aerial view of Newman Hospital was taken in 1972 and shows the additions of the east wing in 1951 and the west wing in 1963. Since then, other multimillion-dollar renovations have been made, and the hospital is now called Newman Regional Health. (Courtesy of the Walter M. Andersen Collection, Emporia State University Special Collections Archives.)

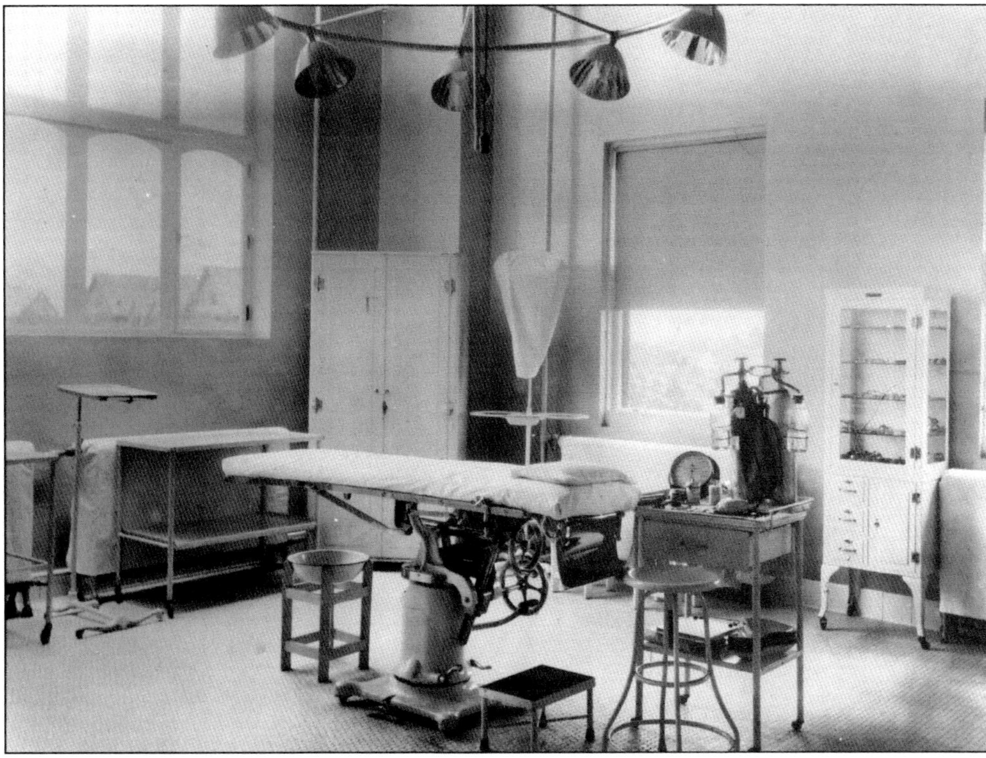

While George W. Newman's generous gift set in motion the creation of a county hospital, the project's completion relied on tax dollars and generous donations. One such generous donation came from S.H. Warren, who gave $5,250 to furnish the operating and sterilizing department, including all the equipment in the two operating rooms and the sterilizing room. This photograph shows one of the main operating rooms at the hospital in about 1924. (Courtesy of the Walter M. Andersen Collection, Emporia State University Special Collections Archives.)

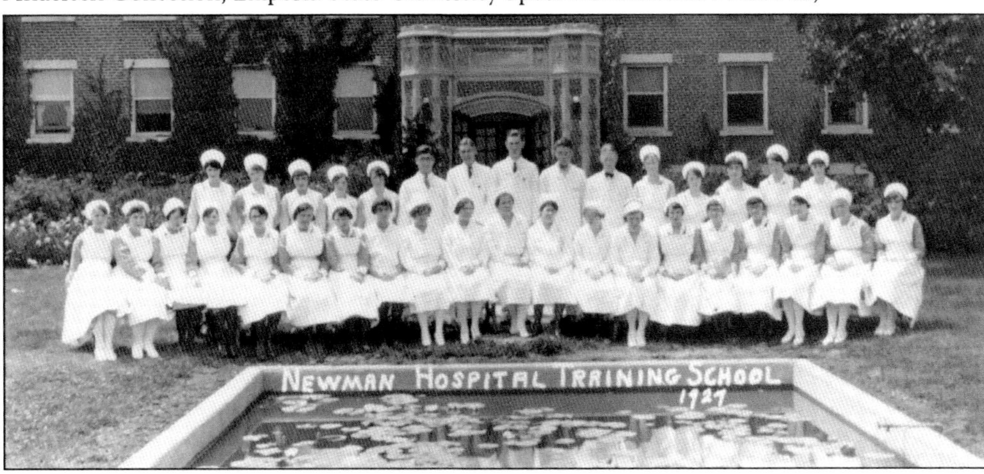

Pictured here is the 1927 class of the Newman Hospital Training School. These students learned the theory and practice of nursing under the direction of Cora Miller, superintendent of the hospital. Today, the Newman Division of Nursing is housed in the Cora Miller Hall located on the grounds of Newman Regional Health. (Courtesy of the Walter M. Andersen Collection, Emporia State University Special Collections Archives.)

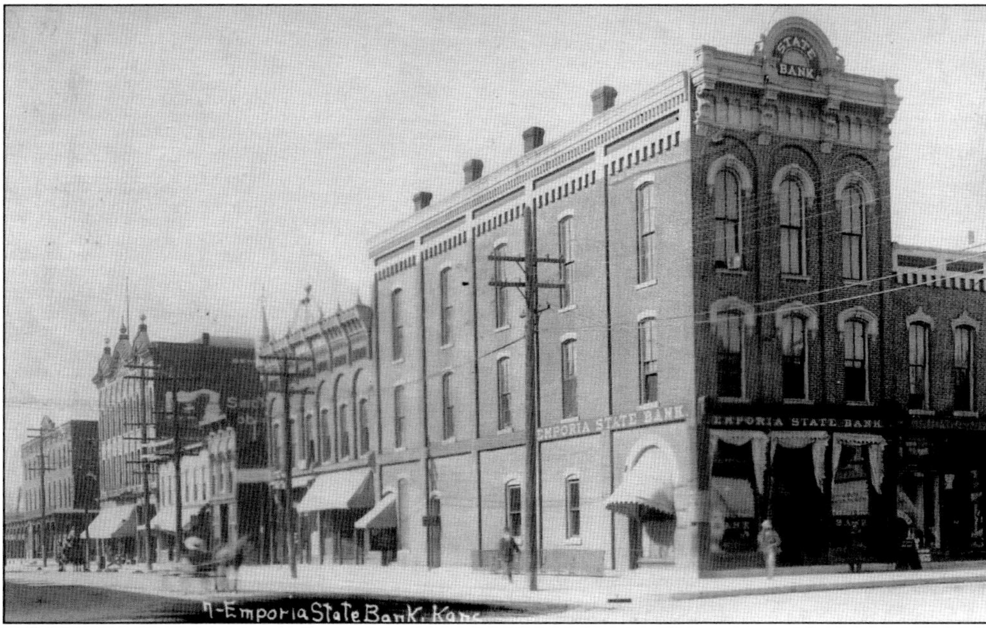

Emporia State Bank, the only family-owned bank still in existence in Emporia today, was founded in 1901 by William Wayman. It was located at the northwest corner of Sixth Avenue and Commercial Street in the Addis building. In 1914, the building underwent an extensive remodeling project. The third floor was removed, and the ceiling lowered. Marble imported from Italy, France, and Belgium was used in the redesign. In 1965, the bank was relocated to Eighth Avenue and Merchant Street.

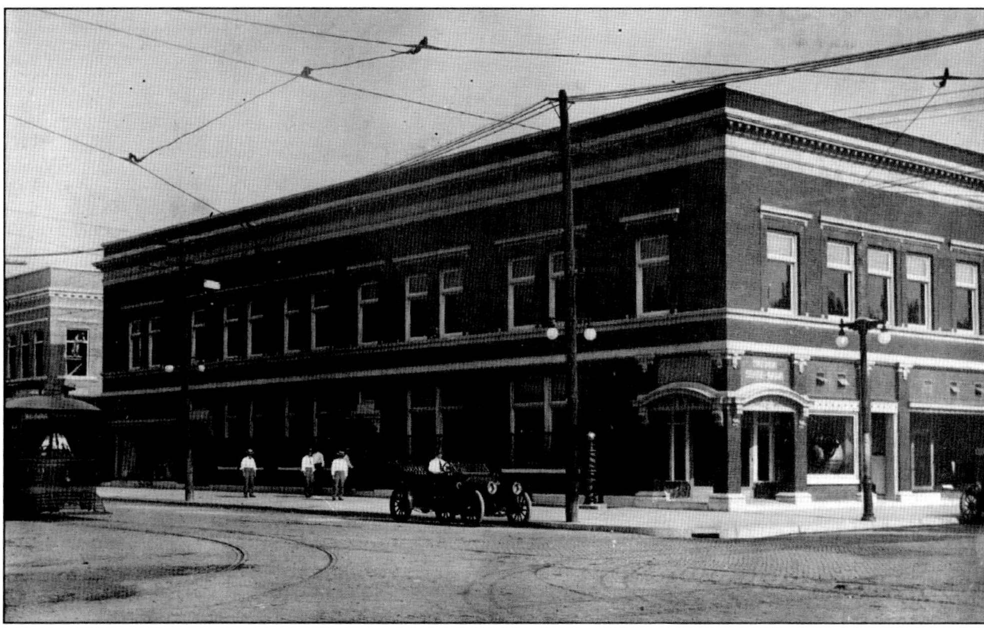
This photograph shows what Emporia State Bank looked like around 1920 after an extensive remodeling project in 1914 removed the third floor of the building. It also illustrates the change in mode of transportation from horse and buggy in 1901 to streetcars and automobiles in 1920. (Courtesy of the Walter M. Andersen Collection, Emporia State University Special Collections Archives.)

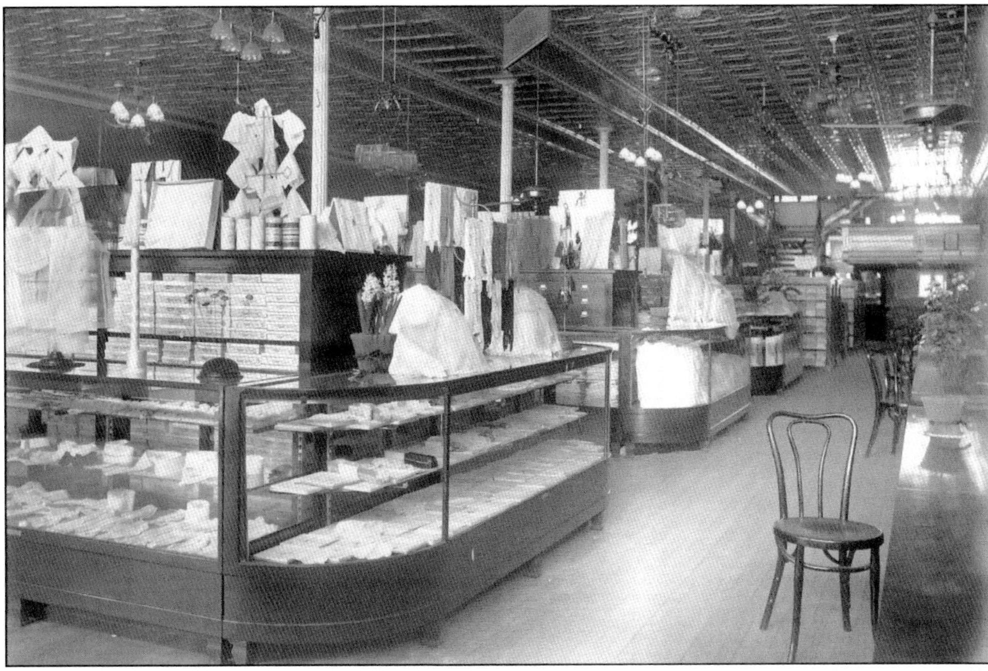

Part of G.W. Newman's formula for success with his department store was pleasing his customers by procuring the very latest and most-up-to-date products and knowing how to display those products in his store, as both of these photographs show. Visible above are ribbons, handkerchiefs, gloves, and collars. Note the pulley baskets that were used to transport merchandise throughout the store. The view below shows thread, pillows, lace runners, buttons, and beaded handbags.

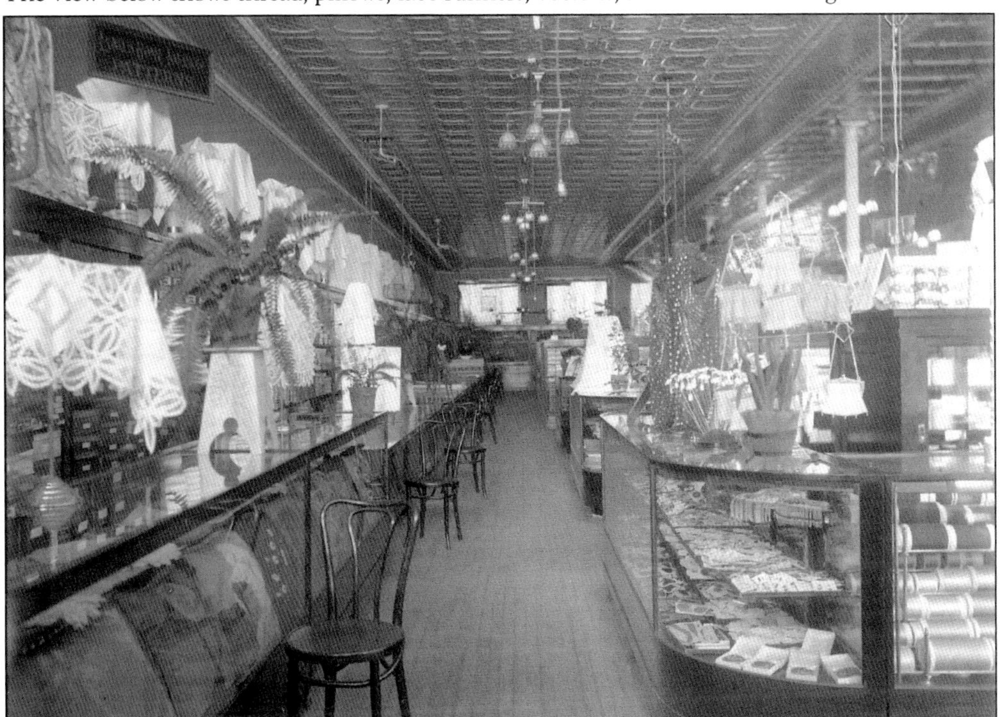

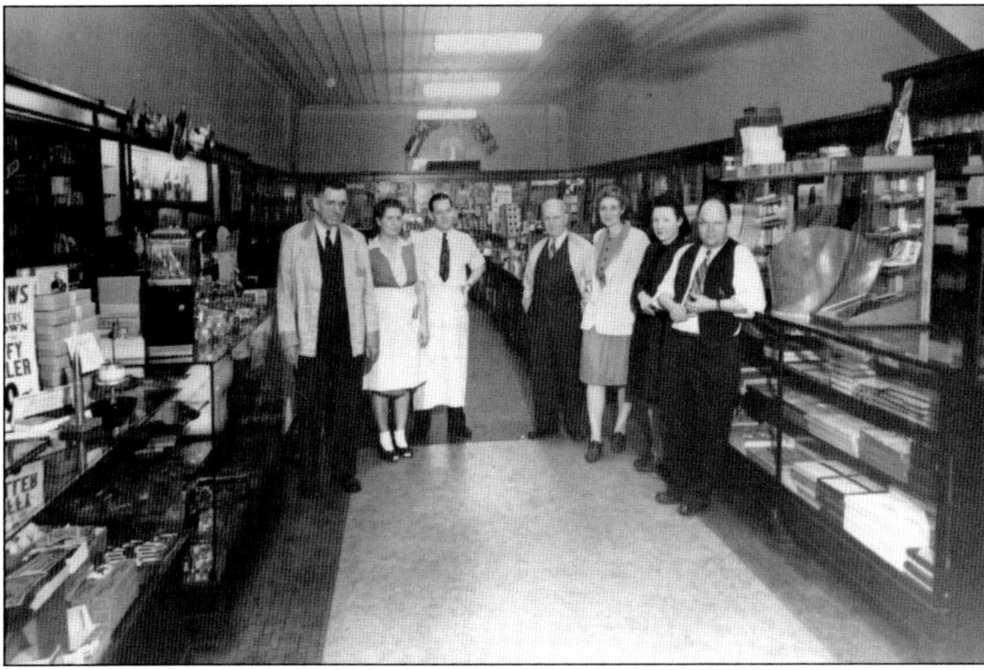

For many years, the Red X Pharmacy was not only a pharmacy but also a popular hangout for sodas and conversation. Located at 624 Commercial Street, it was owned by Joseph Kowalski. This 1945 photograph shows an interior view of the Red X Pharmacy with several of Kowalski's employees. Display cases and shelves filled with items are visible along both sides of the store. (Courtesy of the Walter M. Andersen Collection, Emporia State University Special Collections Archives.)

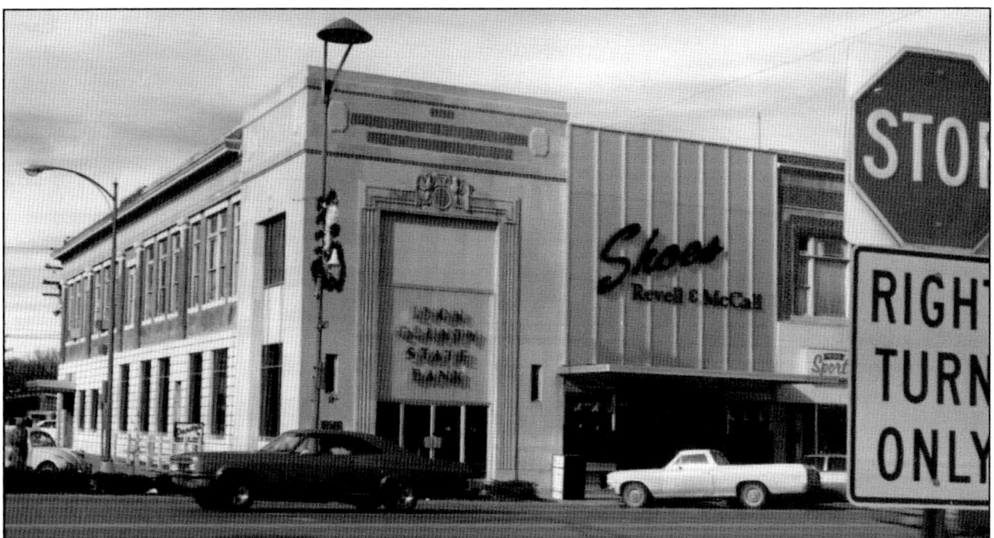

The Lyon County State Bank was chartered on June 27, 1913, with Sen. William Price as president. The bank was first located at 508 Commercial Street, but moved to the location shown here at 701 Commercial Street in 1956. The impressive structure reflects the strength and character of a banking institution. In 1975, the bank moved to a new building in the 900 block of Merchant Street. (Courtesy of the Walter M. Andersen Collection, Emporia State University Special Collections Archives.)

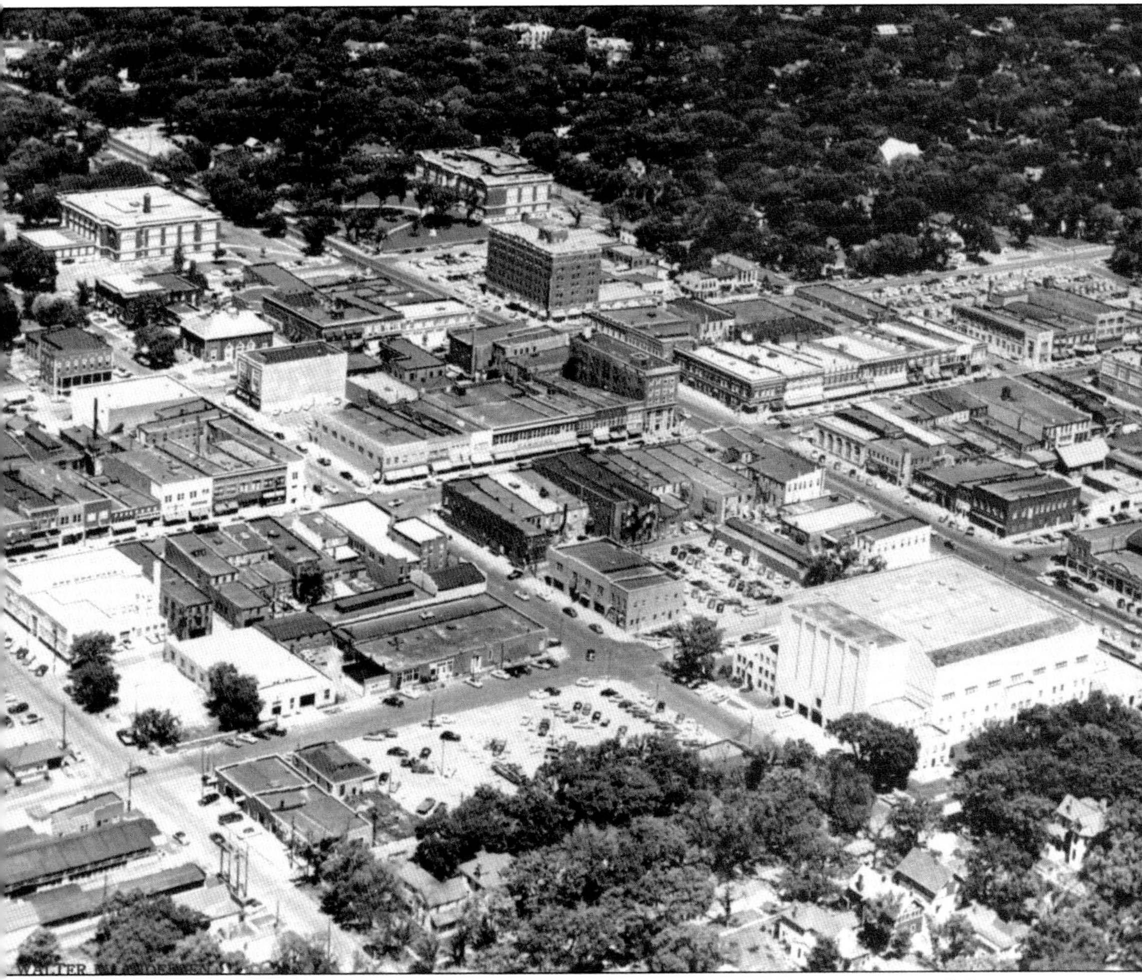

This 1950s aerial view of downtown Emporia shows the growth and progressiveness of the city following World War II. The large building on the right is the civic auditorium. The tall building in the upper center is the Broadview Hotel. The two buildings to the west of the hotel are the junior and senior high schools. The county courthouse is located at far left center.

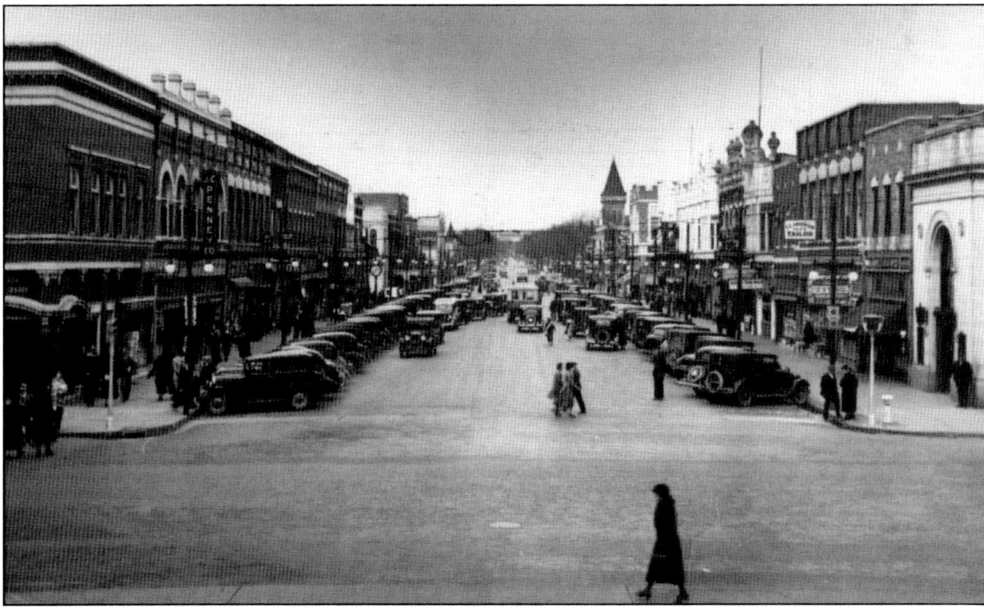

These two photographs show how the 600 block of Commercial Street changed during a 20-year span from 1932 to 1952. The view above shows a bustling city during the early years of the Great Depression. Although economic trouble was spreading across the country, this downtown view shows cars parked up and down the street. Architectural remnants of the 1880s–1890s building boom can be seen on the top stories. Below, the architectural battlements on top of the J.C. Penney's building have been removed. As the Victorian-era buildings and their elaborate facades aged, many of the architectural details were removed for fear they would fall on customers walking down the sidewalks.

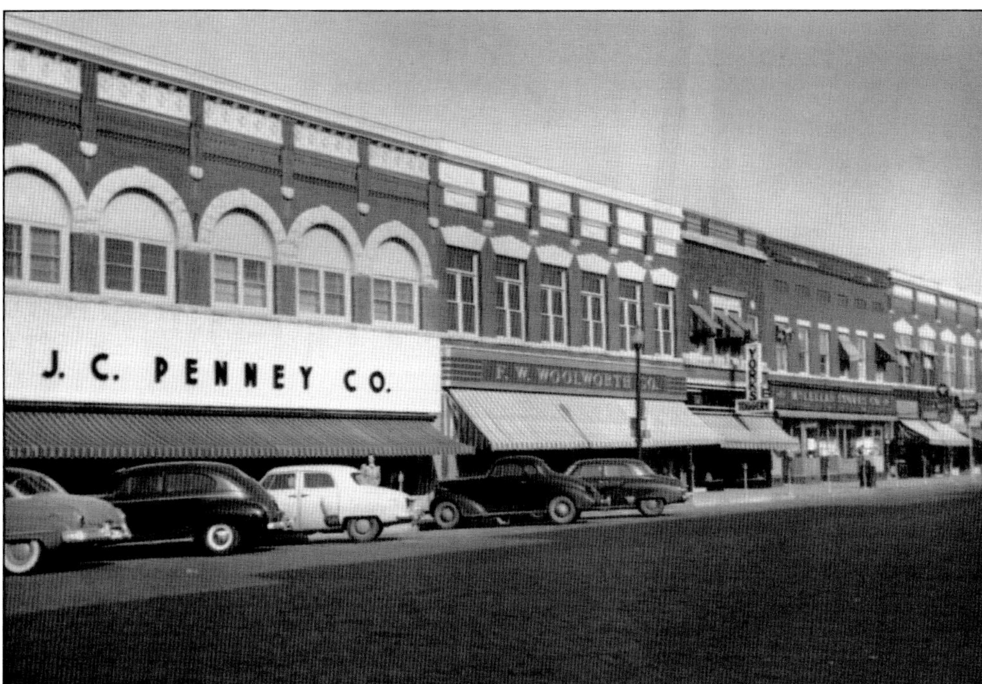

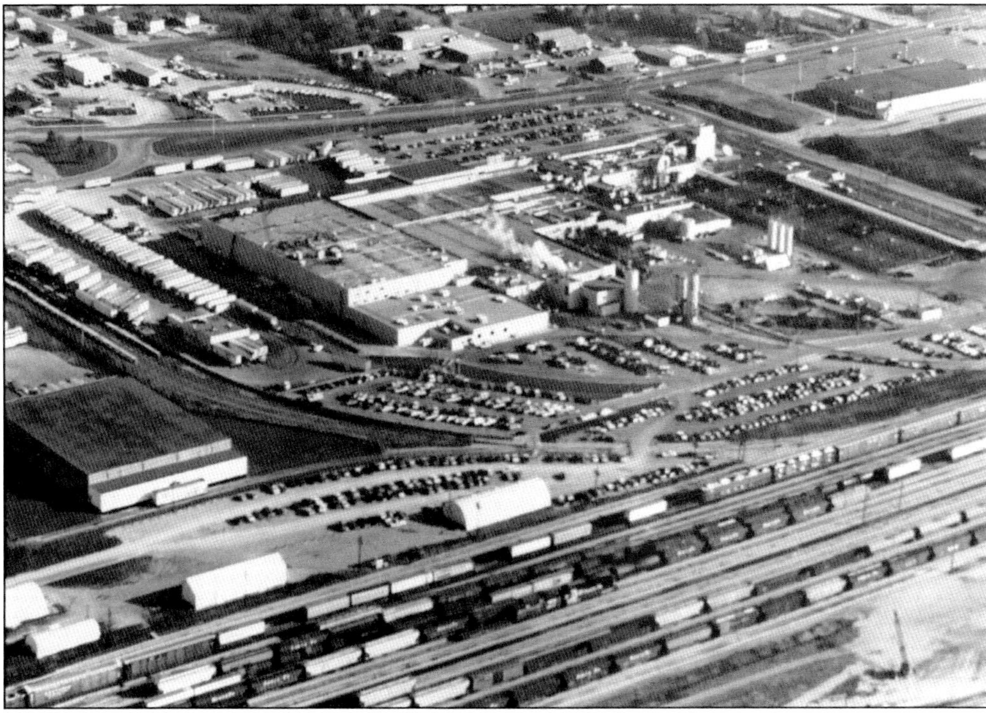

In 1969, the Iowa Beef Processors (IBP) plant was opened in Emporia at Sixth Avenue and Prairie Street. The slaughtering and packing plant soon became the largest employer in the city. The plant brought many Mexican and Asian workers who made Emporia their home. In 2001, IBP was purchased by Tyson Foods. This 1985 aerial view shows the plant in full production. (Courtesy of the Walter M. Andersen Collection, Emporia State University Special Collections Archives.)

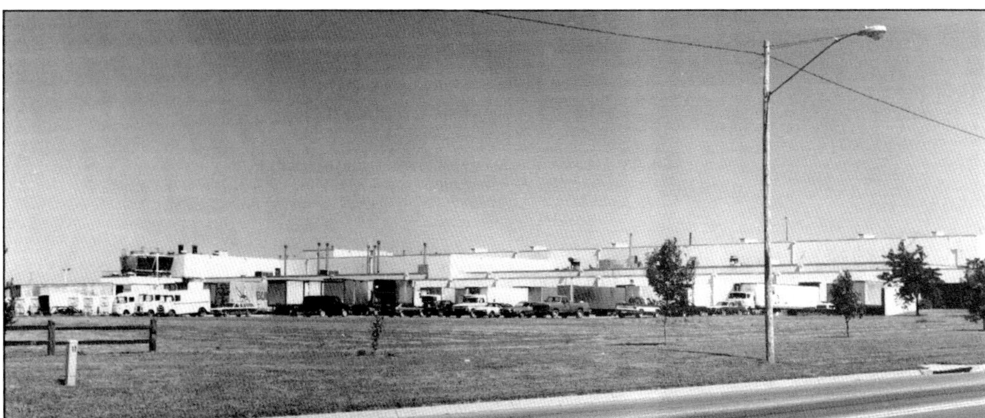

Interstate Bakeries, known to most people as "Dolly Madison," built a plant in Emporia about the same time as Iowa Beef Processors. These two major companies brought economic growth to Emporia, supplementing local companies such as Didde Web Press, Sauder Tanks, and Hopkins Manufacturing. Surviving financial struggles, the bakery now operates under Hostess Brands and is the leading plant for Twinkie production in the nation. The bakery is pictured here in 1976. (Courtesy of the Walter M. Andersen Collection, Emporia State University Special Collections Archives.)

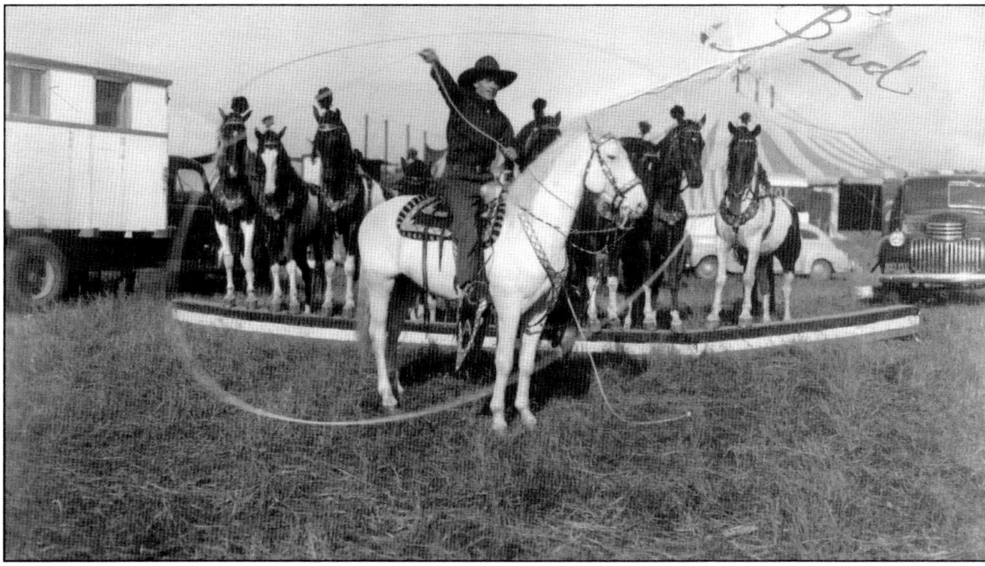

For 35 years, native Emporian Bud Anderson, pictured here with one of his show horses around 1936, entertained crowds all over the Midwest and West with his three-ring circus. Highlights of the program included three-member family acts of jugglers and aerialists, an elephant act, and Anderson's act with his well-trained ponies and horses. Anderson was killed in 1950 when the circus truck he was driving overturned near Miles City, Montana.

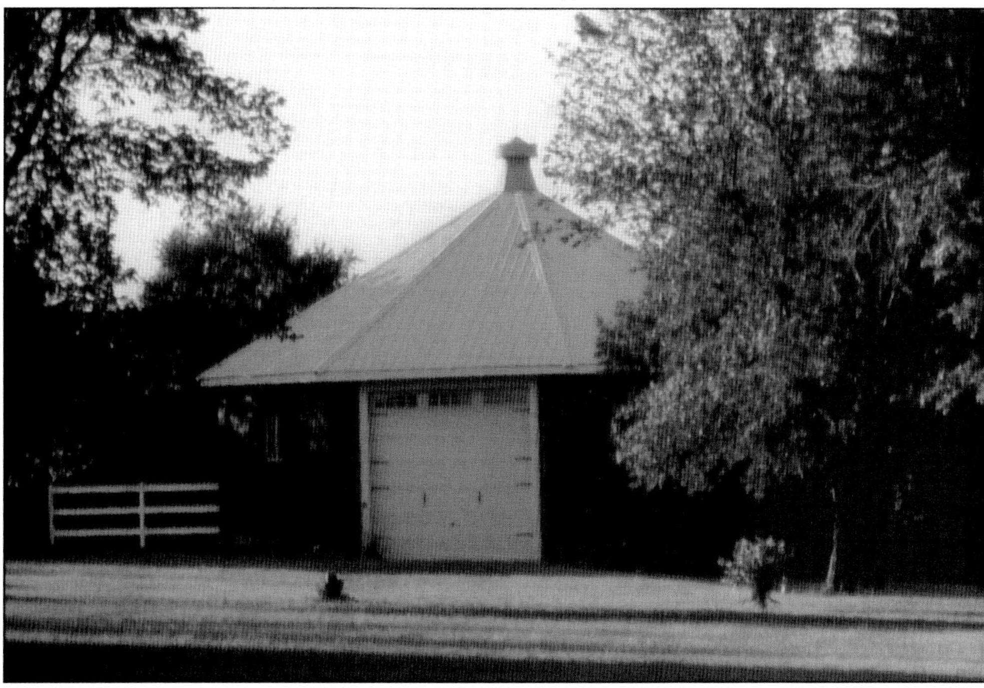

A part of Emporia's past can still be seen while driving east on the original Highway 50. Looking to the left, one can see several of the barns that were part of Bud Anderson's circus. The brick rectangular and round barns were used to house the circus animals and equipment during the winter months when the circus was not performing. Following Anderson's untimely death, the circus was bought by another company, and the barns are now used for storage.

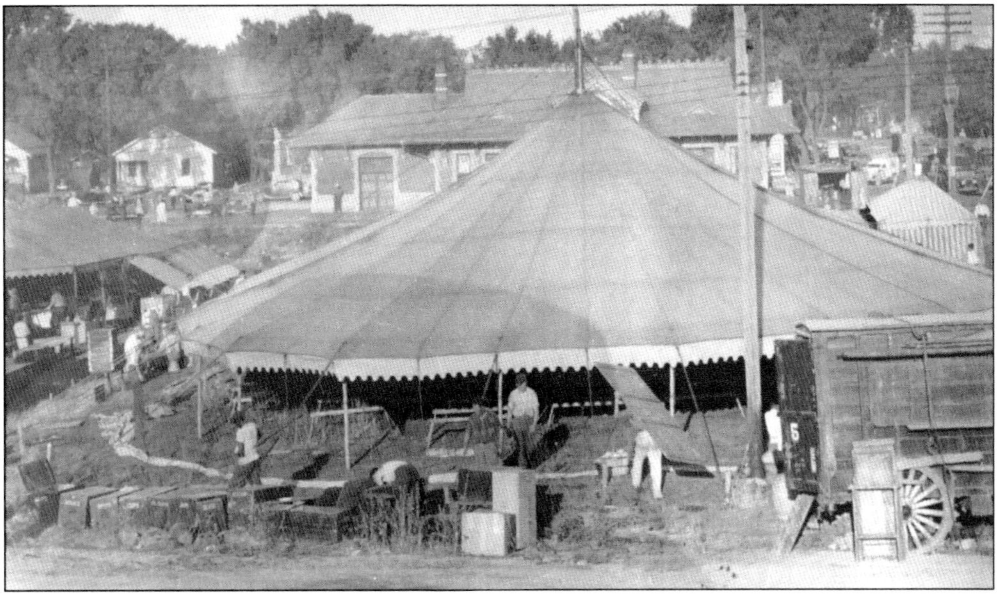

In the early 1900s, quite a few circuses set up their tents in the old circus lot east of the Katy depot. When the circus arrived early in the morning, large crowds of both young and old would gather to watch the fascinating work of unloading and setting up circus tents. (Courtesy of the Walter M. Andersen Collection, Emporia State University Special Collections Archives.)

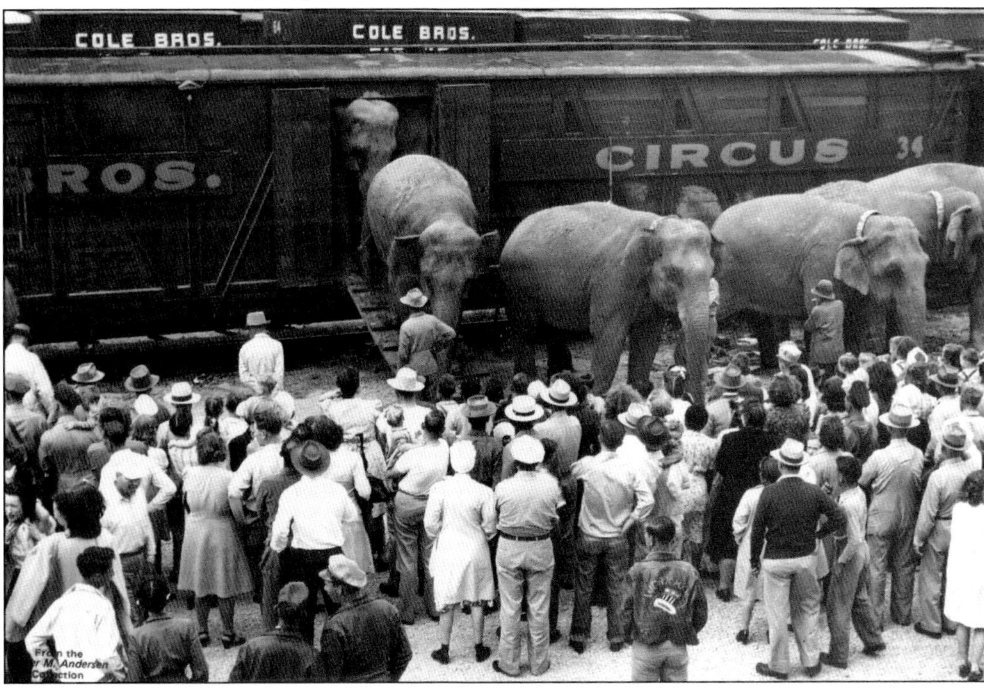

The unloading of circus elephants at Third Avenue and Commercial Street drew a large crowd on May 30, 1946. The Cole Brothers Circus, the largest circus to visit Emporia since before the beginning of World War II, was in town to give two Memorial Day performances. The circus was held on empty lots near the Katy depot on East Sixth Avenue. (Courtesy of the Walter M. Andersen Collection, Emporia State University Special Collections Archives.)

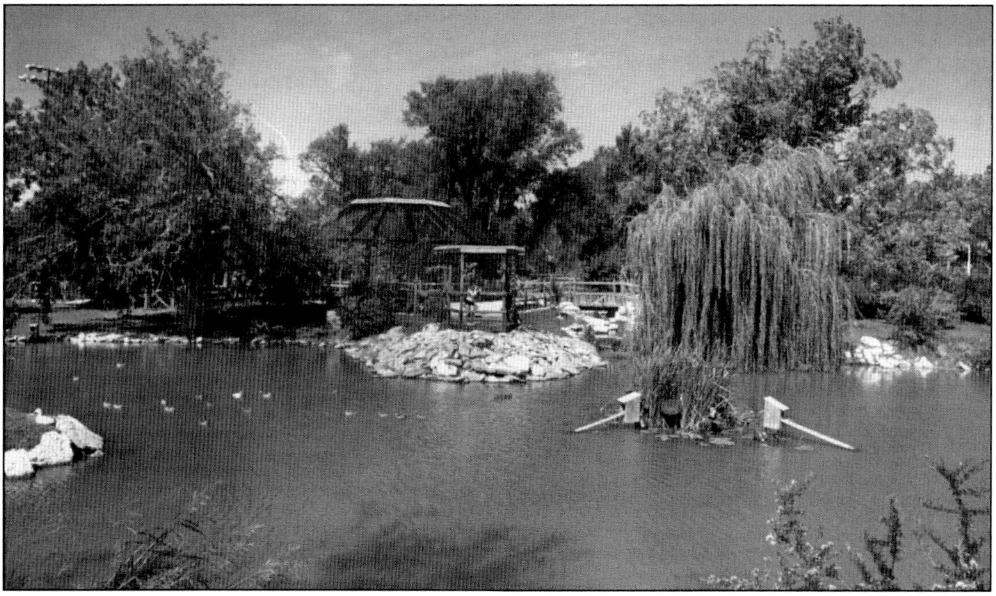

Emporia's David Traylor Zoo was founded around 1934 and has been accredited by the Association of Zoos and Aquariums since 1985. The 12-acre park, nestled in Soden's Grove, houses a variety of birds, mammals, and reptiles and features lush botanical displays and spectacular holiday lights. This photograph was taken during the summer of 1986, when the zoo was selected as Lawn of the Month by the Emporia Men's Garden Club. (Courtesy of the Walter M. Andersen Collection, Emporia State University Special Collections Archives.)

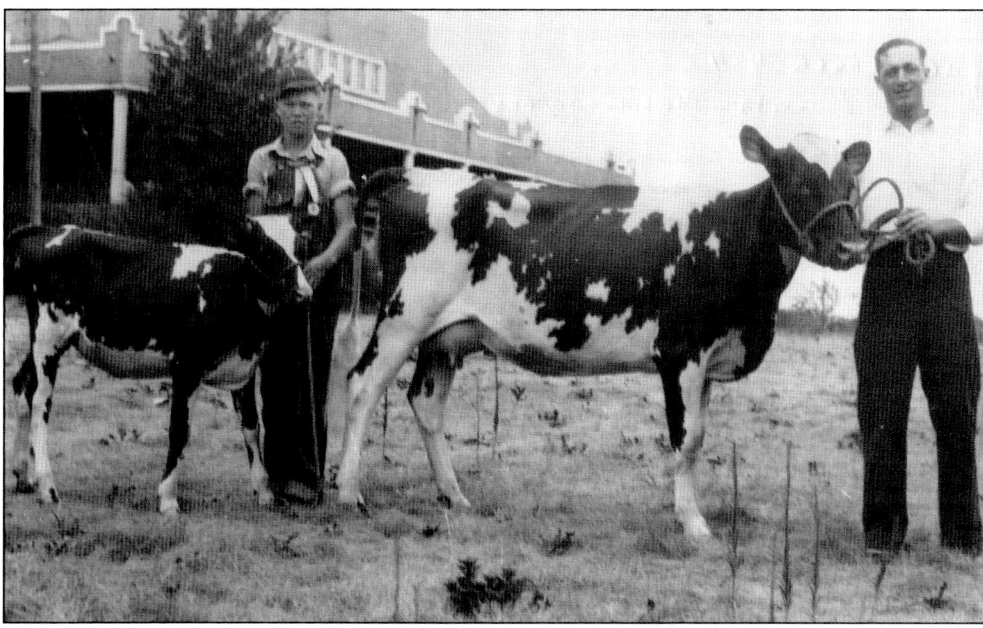

The Lyon County 4-H Fair is one of the most anticipated events of the summer. Today, the fair is held on land given by the E.T. Anderson family in the west-central part of Emporia. At one time, the event was held around the pavilion at Soden's Grove. The Hoch brothers are pictured here with their Ayrshire cow and calf in 1936. (Courtesy of the Walter M. Andersen Collection, Emporia State University Special Collections Archives.)

Five

A Great Place to Live

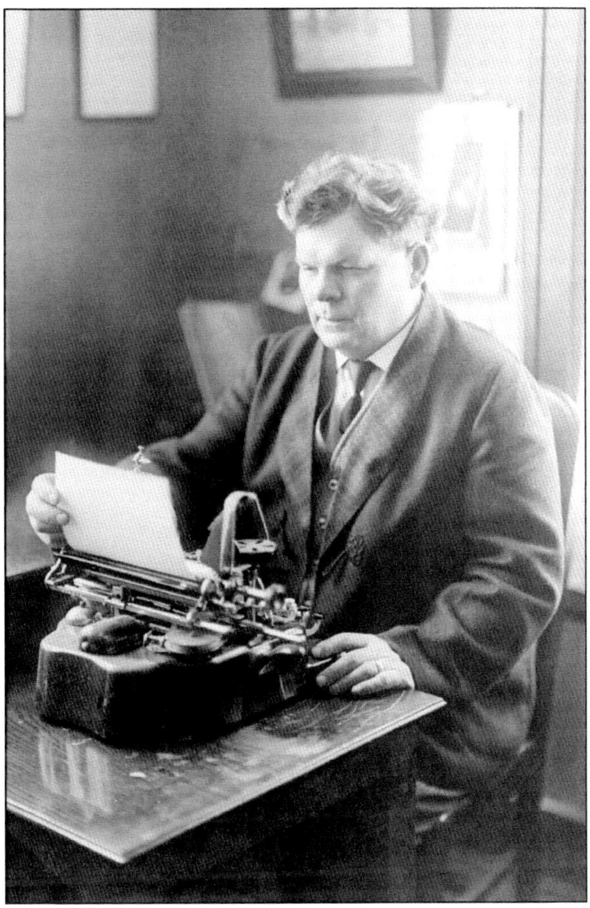

William Allen White once referred to "Uncle Walt" Mason, pictured here, as the poet laureate of American democracy. White brought Mason to the *Emporia Gazette* in 1907. Mason's poetry was used as filler for the section of the front page of the *Gazette* that contained local news. When Mason wrote a little poem advising people to go to church on Sunday, it was so popular that he kept writing poetry, which became a regular feature of the *Gazette*. One of his most famous poems is "The Little Green Tent," popular around Memorial Day. Emporia's spirit of education and democracy make it a great place to live.

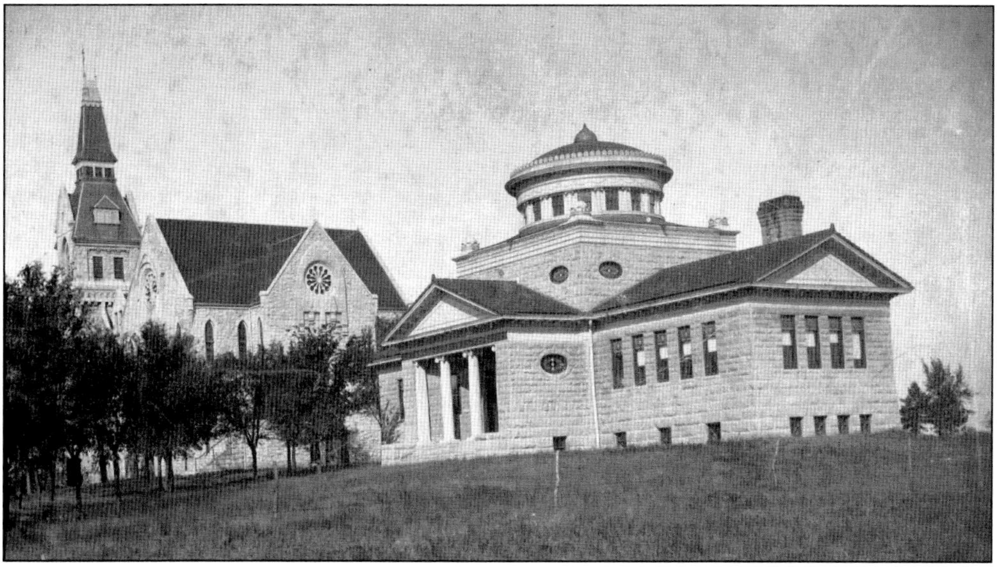

In 1882, the Presbyterian Synod of Kansas accepted Emporia's offer of $35,000 and 38 acres of land on the west edge of the city limits to establish a synodic college. On November 1, 1883, College of Emporia classes began in the upstairs room of the Addis building on the northwest corner of Sixth Avenue and Commercial Street. There were 15 students enrolled. This photograph shows the first two buildings on the new campus: Stuart Hall (left) and the Anderson Library.

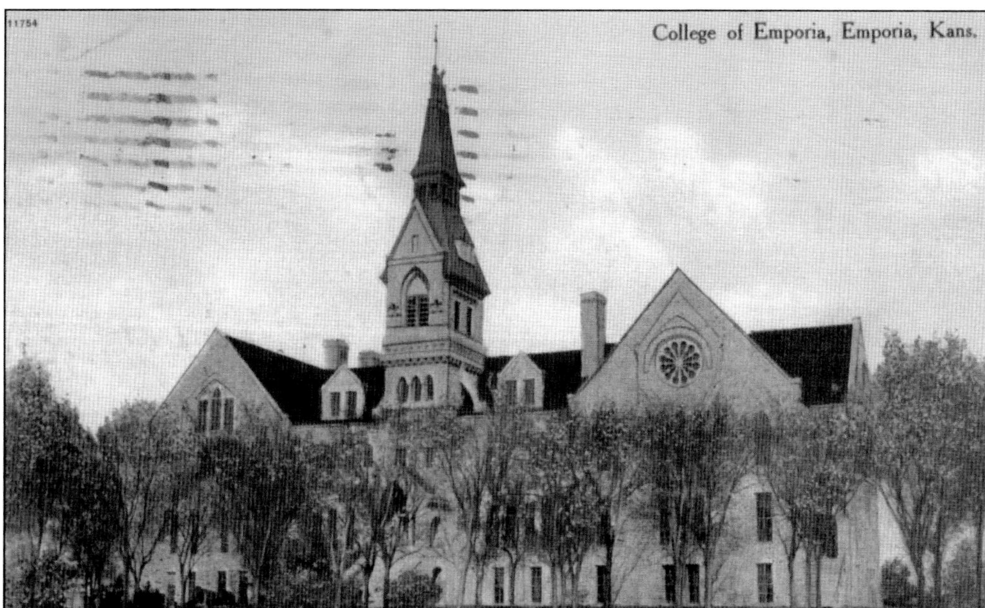

In 1886, the college moved to its permanent location at 1400 West Twelfth Avenue. Classes began in the nearly completed Stuart Hall, the first building on the campus, which is shown here. The building was named after Mary Stuart of New York, who gave $10,000 for its construction.

Disaster struck the College of Emporia on December 2, 1915, when Stuart Hall burned to the ground. President Culbertson, trying to save some records, was nearly killed when the bell crashed to the ground. The next day, a large sign appeared over the ruins with the words "C of E Fights!" This became the rallying cry of the college.

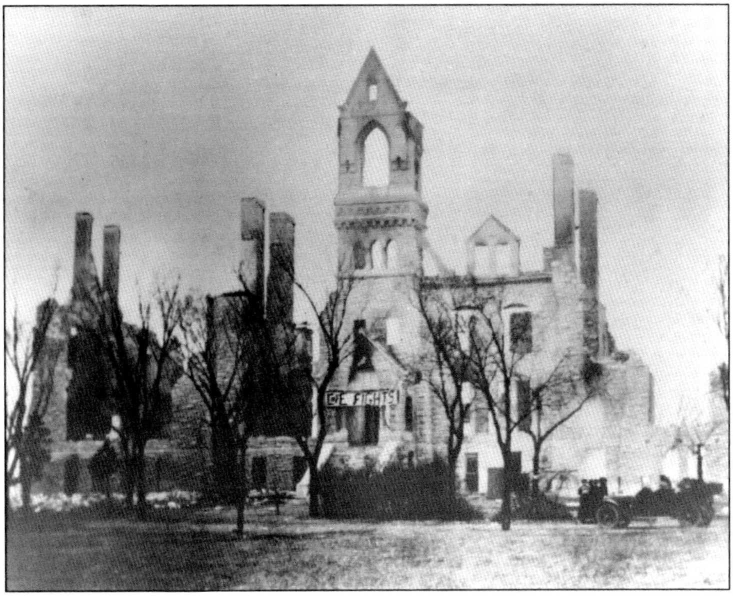

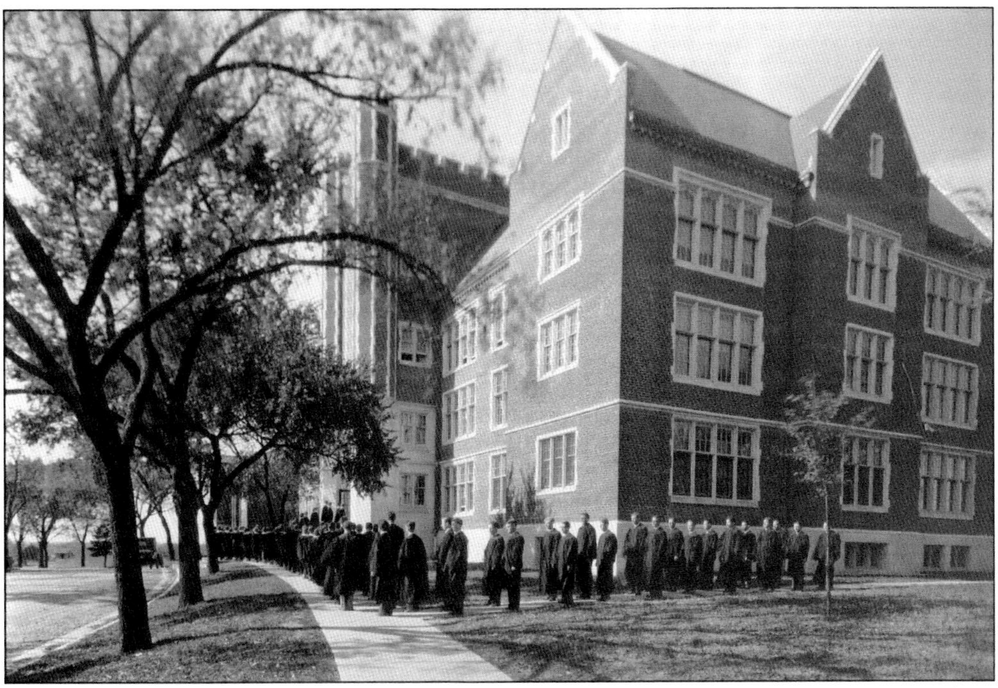

After the 1915 fire, plans were soon made to replace Stuart Hall. Because of a lack of immediate funds, it was not until 1919 that construction of the new administration building's basement and chapel was completed. By 1928, Kenyon Hall had been completed and named in honor of J.S. Kenyon, a wealthy Emporia benefactor who left $100,000 in his will to the college. This 1937 photograph shows graduates outside the building.

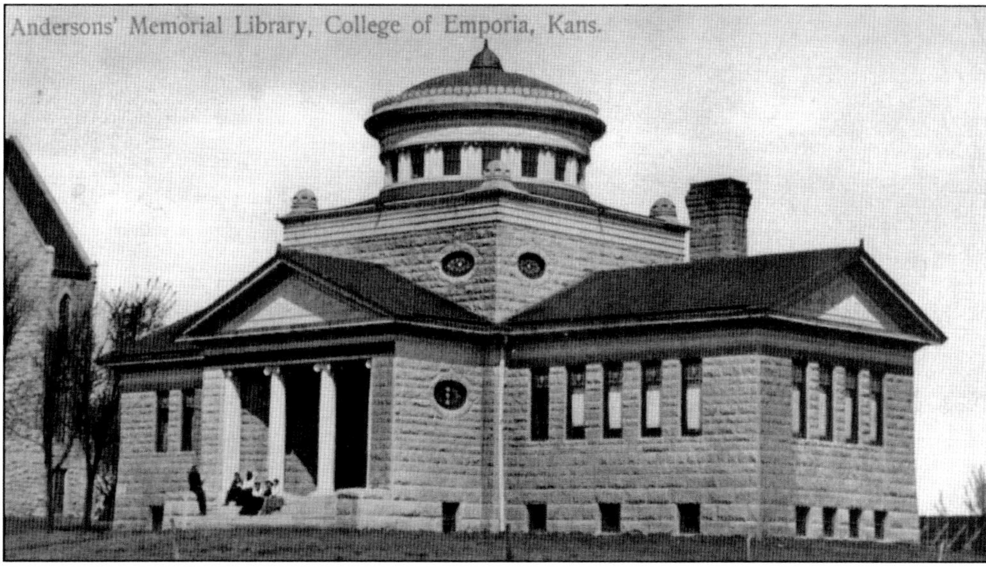

The Anderson Library on the College of Emporia campus is one of Emporia's most historic buildings. The library was completed in 1902 and is the first Carnegie library on a college campus west of the Mississippi River. It is named after John B. Anderson, who, at an early age, introduced Andrew Carnegie to books and the knowledge learned from reading. The dome of the limestone building designed by Charles Squires became a popular place for graduates to sign their names. The building is listed in the National Register of Historic Places.

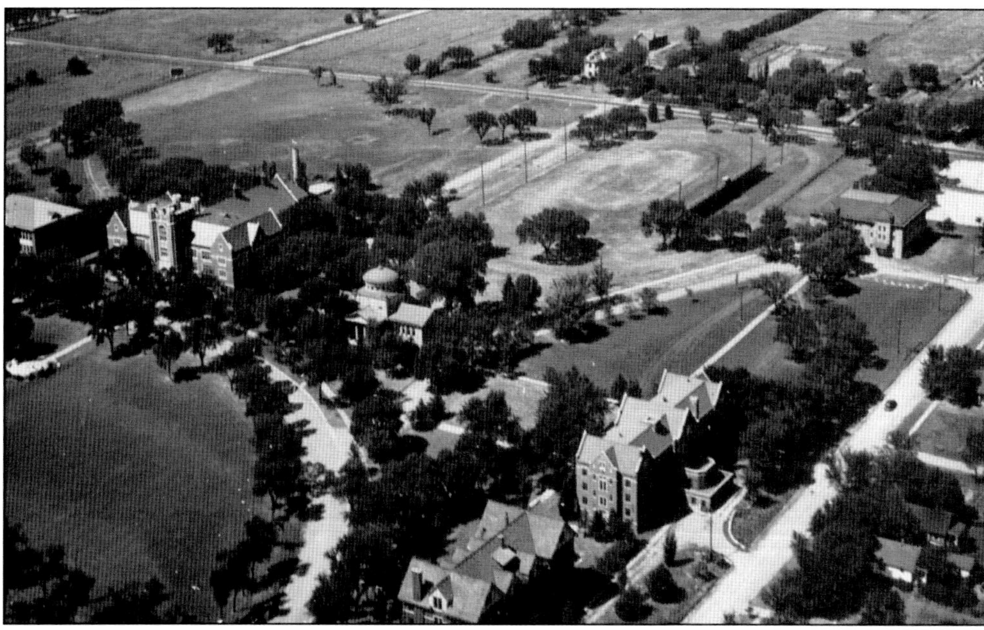

This aerial view of the College of Emporia campus was taken around the 1940s. At that time, there were several classroom buildings, the administration building, the library, Mason Gymnasium, and two residence halls. In the fall of 1974, the college closed its doors because of financial problems. The campus was purchased by The Way International, a nondenominational fellowship that retained ownership from 1975 until 1989. The property was then purchased by the College of Emporia Development Company for redevelopment.

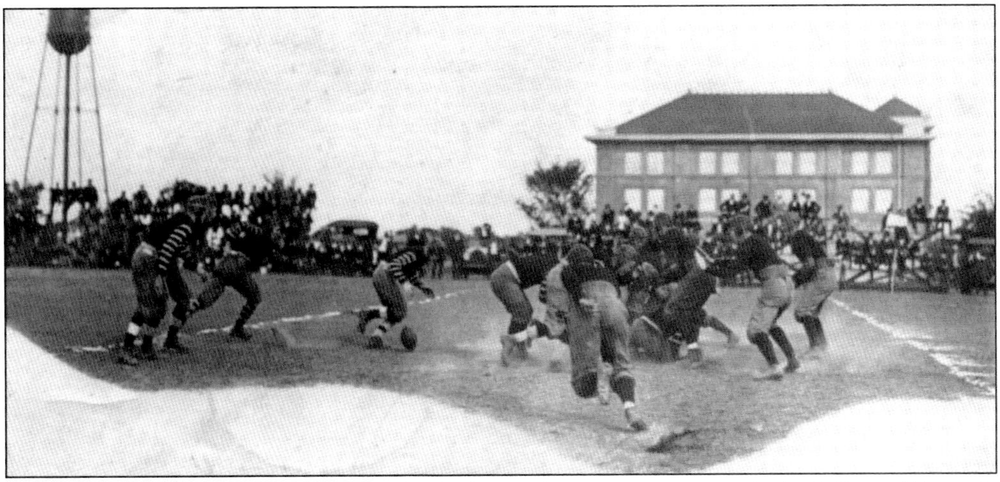

For several decades, the Thanksgiving football game between crosstown rivals College of Emporia and Kansas State Normal School was the most important game of the year. Perhaps the most anticipated game was in 1926, when both teams were undefeated. College of Emporia had won a record 19 straight games leading up to the dramatic day. The game ended in a scoreless tie.

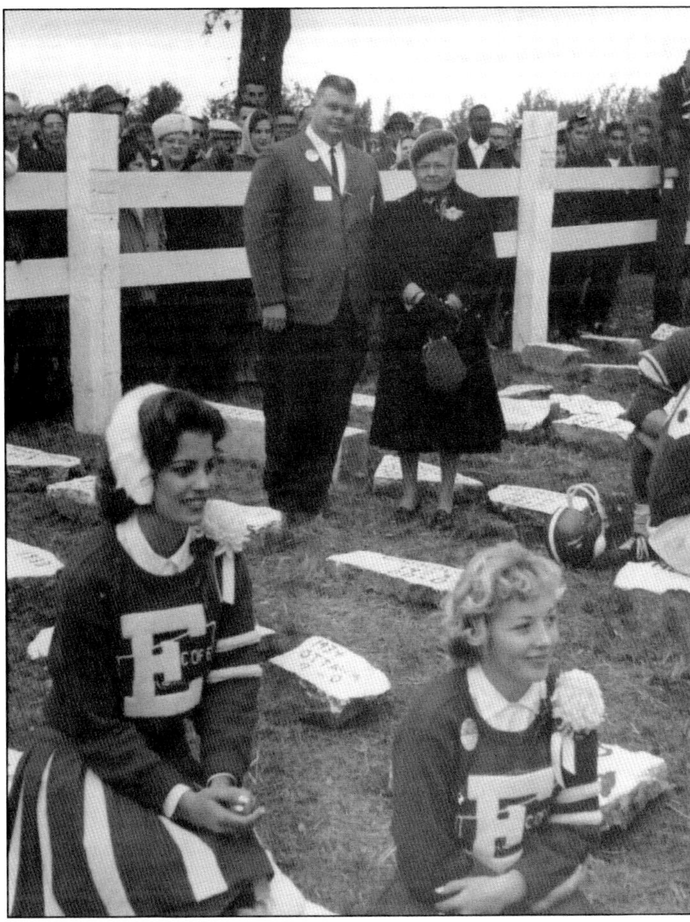

After a victorious football game, it was the tradition of College of Emporia students to conduct a funeral and mark the foe's burial with a tombstone that bore the name of the school, the year, and the score of the game. This tradition was started in 1918 in honor of football coach Gwinn Henry, whose school record was 34 wins, 4 losses, and 4 ties during his tenure. Seated in the cemetery are cheerleaders Patricia Kervick (left) and Jerilynn Jones Henrikson; standing are coach Raymond "Corky" Elbert and Amy Henry, wife of the former coach for whom the cemetery was named.

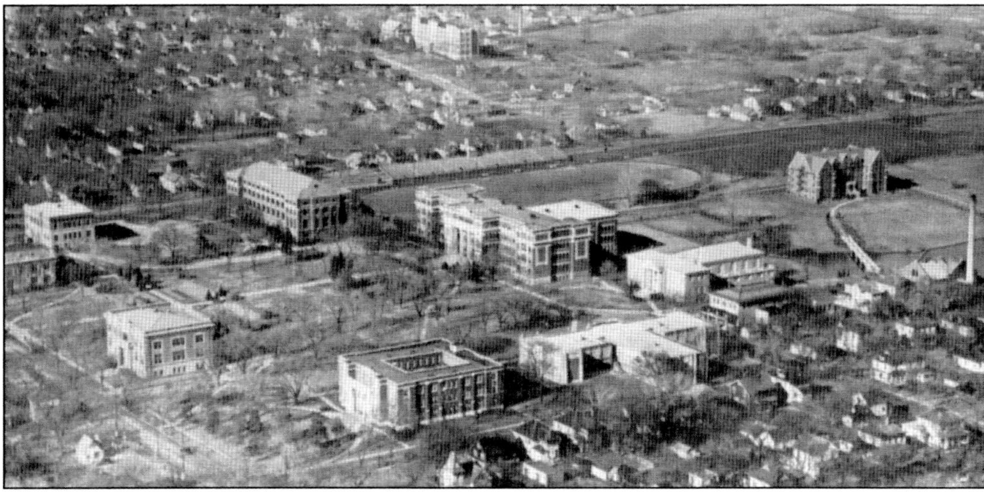

This aerial view of the Emporia State University campus, then Kansas State Teachers College, was taken in the early 1930s before the new stadium was built north of Wooster Lake. At that time, many of the older buildings were still on campus, including the Kellogg Library, Norton Science Hall, and the training school.

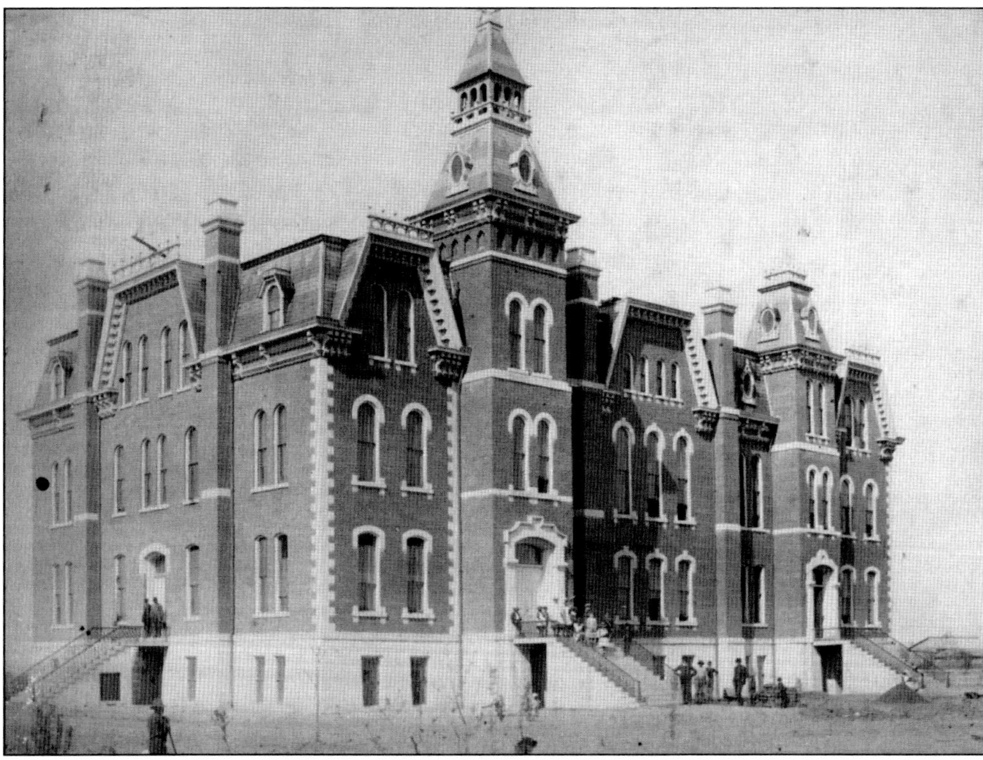

The Kansas State Normal School was established in 1863 by the Kansas legislature. It was not until February 1865 that the first classes were held in the public school building downtown. The first building on the campus located at Twelfth Avenue and Commercial Street was a two-story stone structure completed in 1867. The school soon outgrew the facility, and a new building, shown here, was erected in 1873. The structure burned in 1878, but was rebuilt in 1880 along the same lines as the 1873 building.

This c. 1868 photograph collage shows the first normal school building and those who administered and taught classes. Clockwise from the top are Lyman B. Kellogg, principal; Abbie Homer and M.J. Stimpson, instructors; Jenette Gorham, preceptress; Mary Jane Watson, one of the first graduates and education instructors; and H.B. Norton, science instructor.

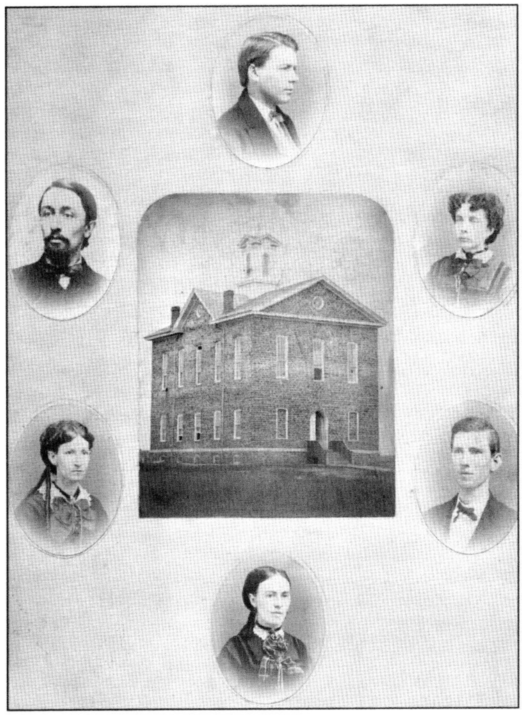

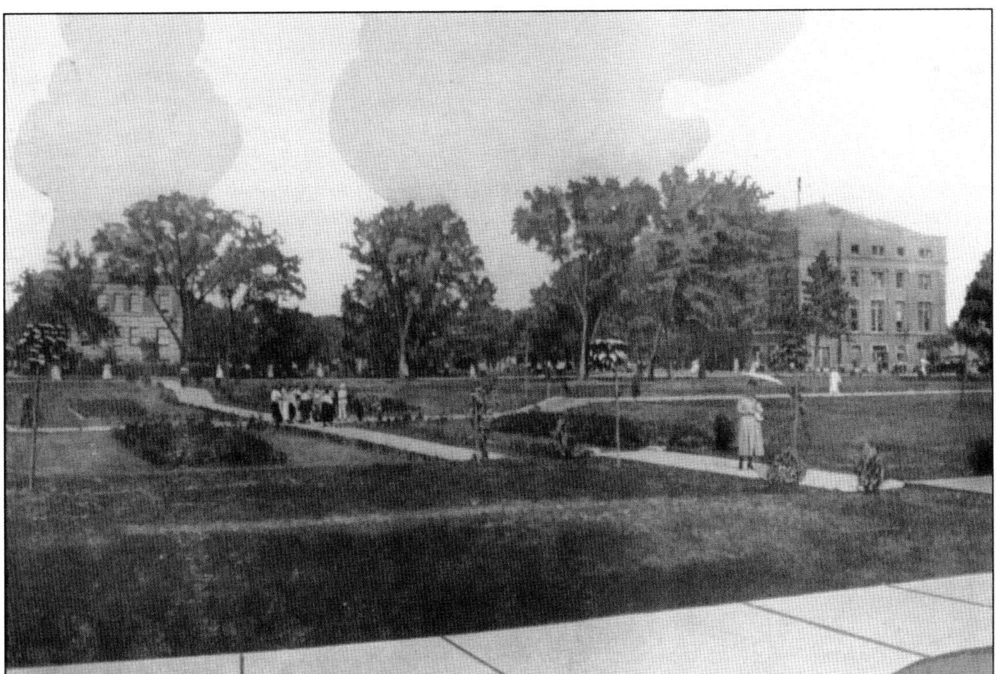

In 1917, a new administration building named Plumb Hall was built to replace the old 1880s main building, which had deteriorated beyond repair. The old structure was demolished, leaving a large hole in the ground. A decision was made to landscape this area, turning it into a sunken garden. The hole was filled to within three feet of ground level, and trees, shrubs, and flowers were planted in the area. Later, a water fountain was added to the park-like garden.

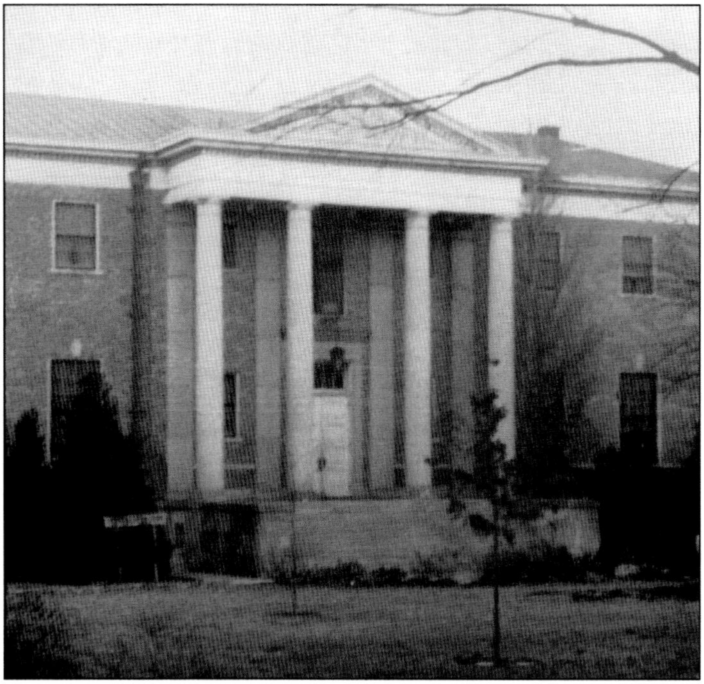

Like the city of Emporia, the university was cognizant of the sacrifices made by the country's men and women during World War I. To honor veterans and those who sacrificed their lives, the students and alumni decided to construct a building in their memory. In August 1922, the state of Kansas issued a charter—the first west of the Mississippi River—to the Memorial Union Corporation. Through student, alumni, and community donations, the Memorial Union building was open for use by the end of 1924.

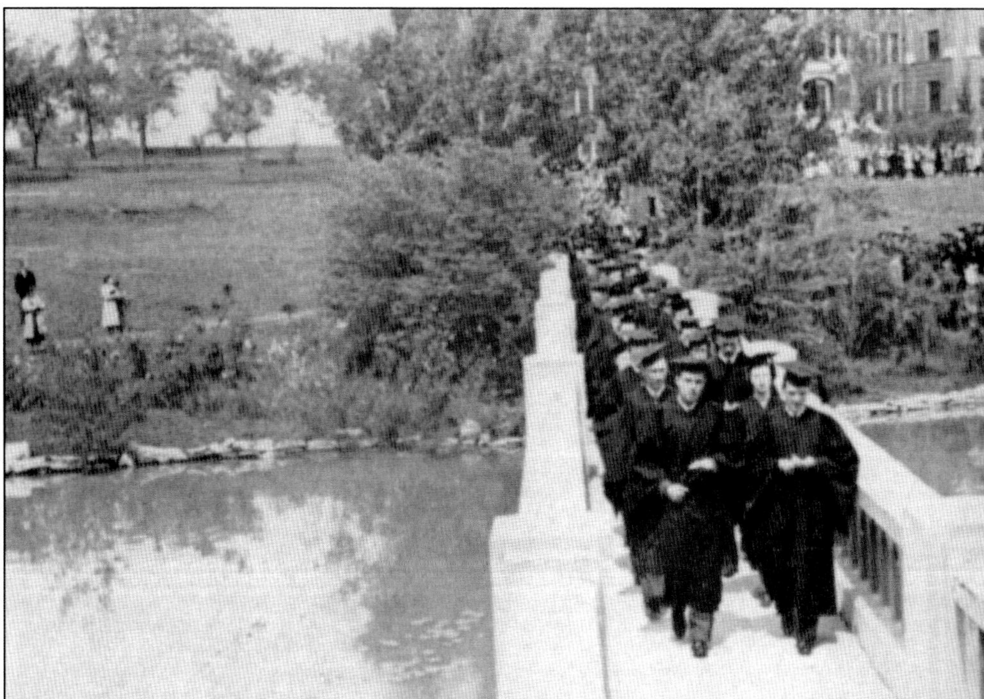

Wooster Lake and Wooster Bridge on the ESU campus hold many traditions. The lake was enlarged from a smaller pond after the completion of Plumb Hall in 1917. In 1928, the bridge was constructed to carry steam pipes from Morse Hall to the cafeteria. During Senior Walk, the graduating class would walk around campus and stop at buildings where they were greeted by the faculty. This image shows the Senior Walk across Wooster Bridge around 1938.

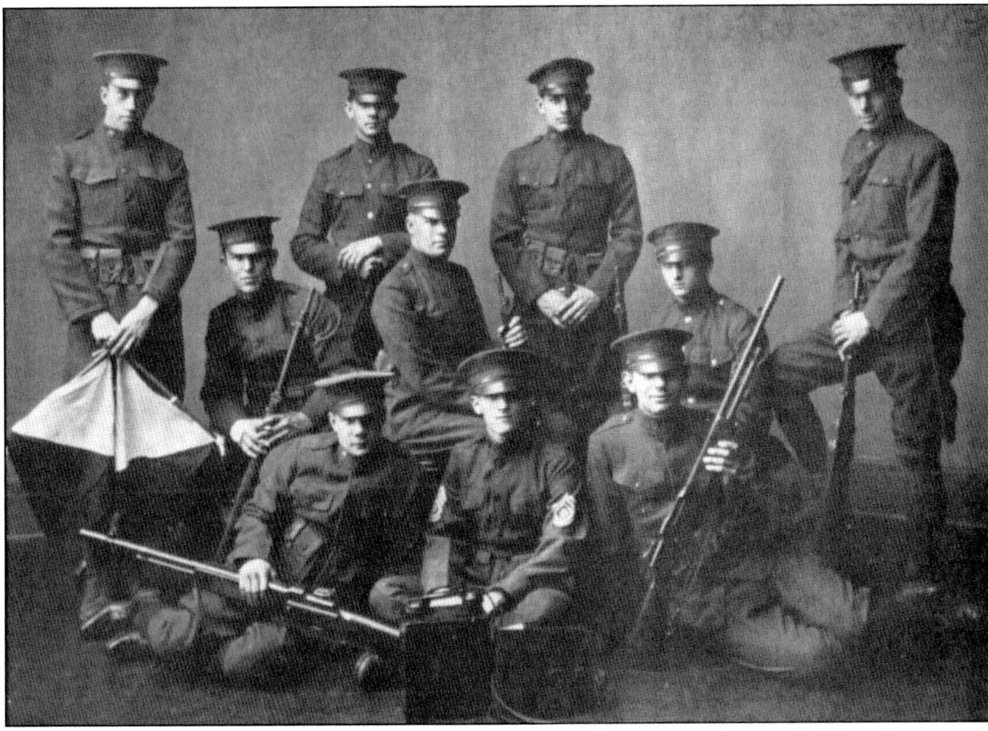

Following World War I, many college students joined the National Guard. This photograph from 1924 shows Company B of the 137th Infantry Division of the Kansas National Guard. The company was composed almost entirely of college students from the Kansas State Teachers College and the College of Emporia, as well as local high school students. The athletic grounds provided an ideal training location for the company.

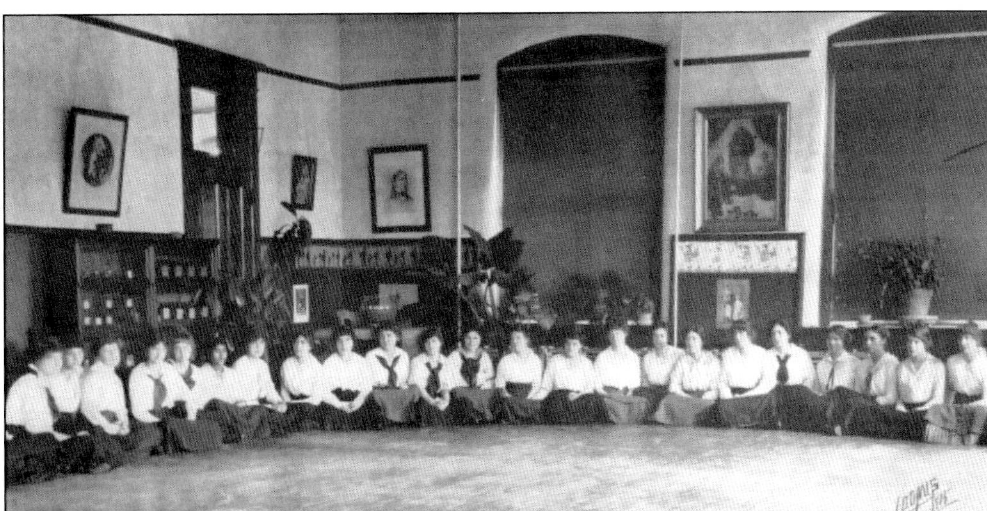

The normal schools were established to train teachers who were so desperately needed to teach in new settlements across the country. To meet this need, men and women could obtain a good education and teaching certificate at the Kansas State Normal School. This 1915 photograph shows a group of young women in a normal school classroom who would soon be kindergarten teachers.

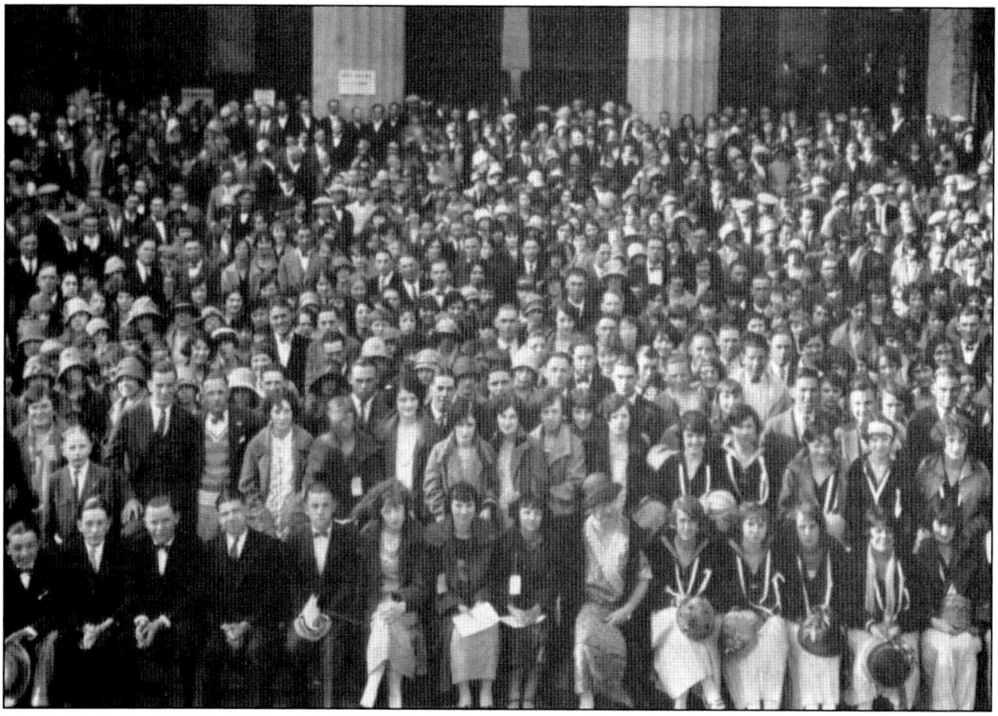

In 1912, music professor Frank Beach invited music teachers and students from around the state to the Kansas State Normal School for a recital to showcase the music department. From this gathering, the All-Kansas Music Festival evolved into one of the state's finest competitions for high school music departments. This 1925 photograph shows the 3,000 contestants gathered on the campus for the festival.

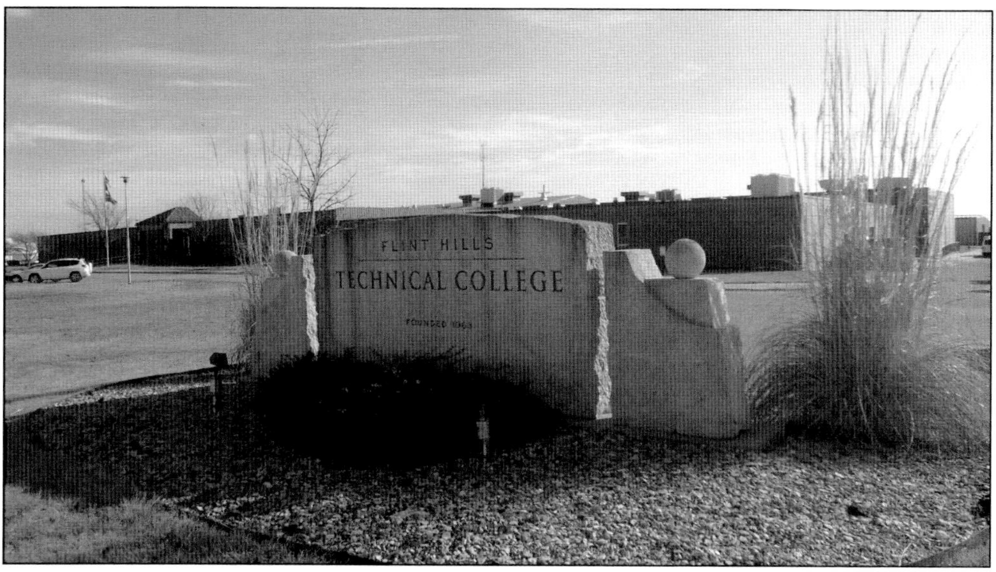

In 1963, the Kansas State Board of Education approved the application of the Emporia Board of Education to establish a two year technical college. The college was constructed on the western edge of Emporia. In 2007, the Higher Learning Commission accredited the college. Today, the college offers a variety of associate degrees, certificates, and licenses for real world skills.

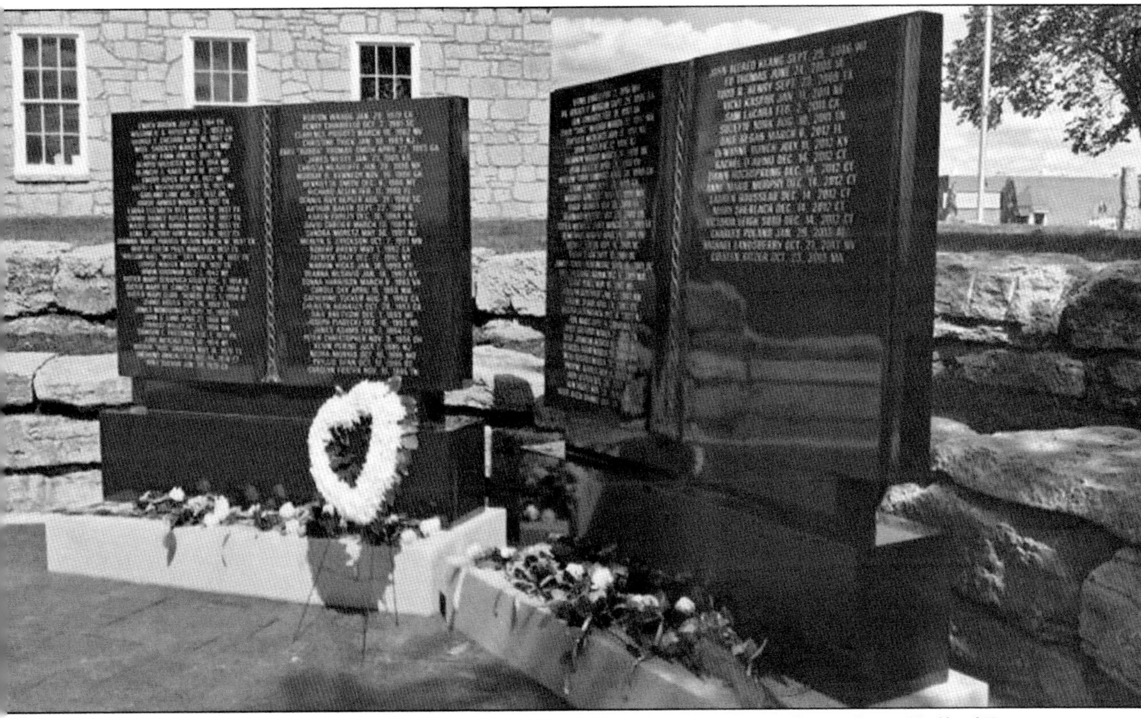

In keeping with Emporia's tradition of honoring the fallen, the National Teachers Hall of Fame conceived the idea of a tribute for teachers who have lost their lives teaching and working in America's schools after the horrific shootings at Newtown, Connecticut, in 2012. Located on Emporia State University's campus, the Memorial to Fallen Educators consists of two large black granite monuments shaped like open books with the names of the fallen educators inscribed in gold letters. The memorial was dedicated on June 12, 2014. (Courtesy of Emporia State University.)

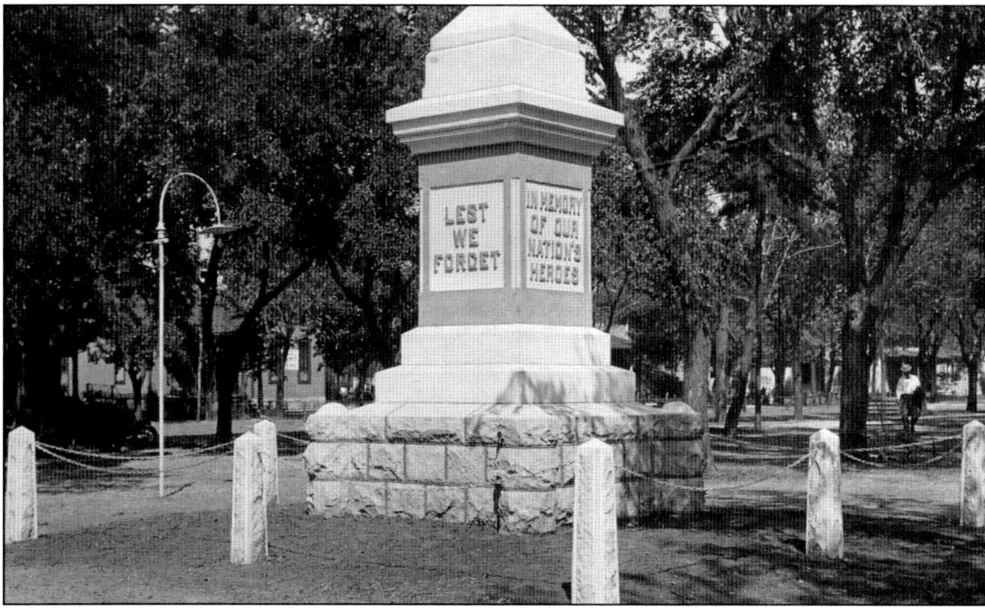

Emporians began honoring war veterans over 100 years ago by placing monuments in city parks. This square granite spire monument was erected in 1913 by the Women's Relief Corps and the citizens of Emporia. The inscriptions on this monument read: "To Our Silent Victors," "In Memory of our Nation's Heroes," and "Lest We Forget." It is located in Fremont Park at Fourth Avenue and Union Street.

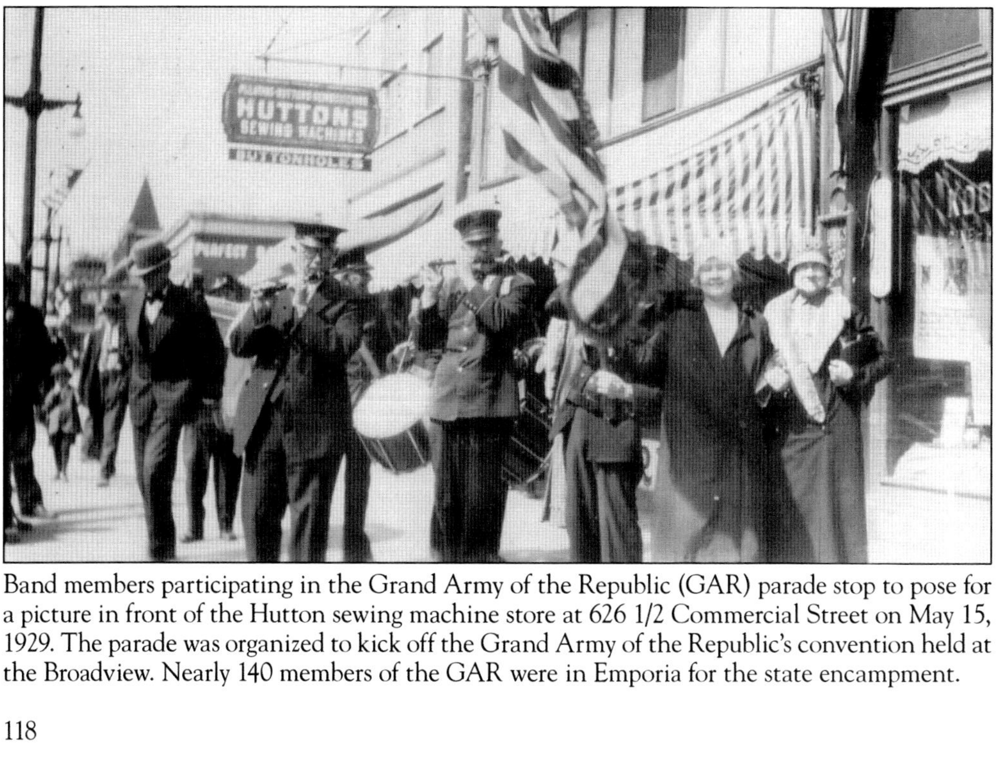

Band members participating in the Grand Army of the Republic (GAR) parade stop to pose for a picture in front of the Hutton sewing machine store at 626 1/2 Commercial Street on May 15, 1929. The parade was organized to kick off the Grand Army of the Republic's convention held at the Broadview. Nearly 140 members of the GAR were in Emporia for the state encampment.

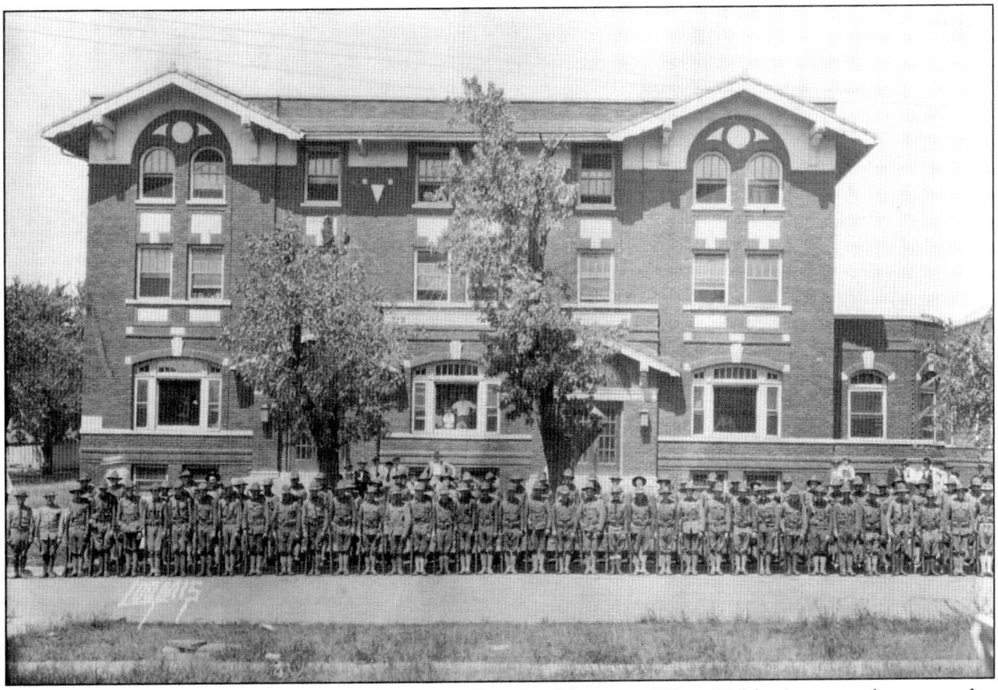

The YMCA, located behind the old post office building on West Fifth Avenue, became the headquarters of Company D, 4th Kansas Infantry, Kansas National Guard, in September 1918. In preparation for the possibility of their unit being called into action during World War I, regular drills were held every Monday night in the gymnasium during cold weather, and equipment was stored in the handball room.

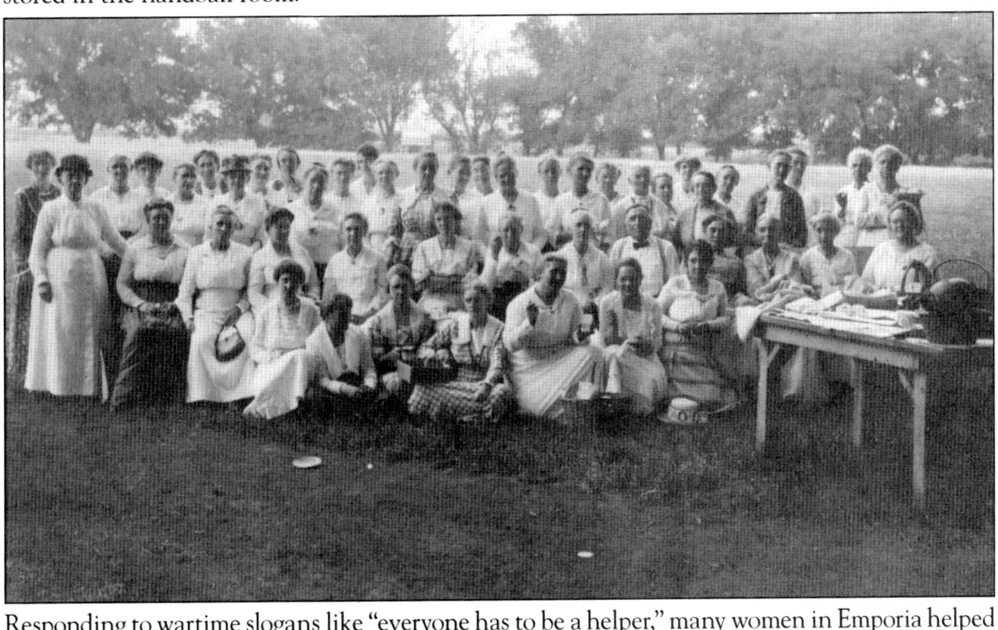

Responding to wartime slogans like "everyone has to be a helper," many women in Emporia helped with the war cause by participating in sewing groups, like the one pictured here, either through the Red Cross or through other civic organizations. Some of the items sewn included bed shirts, pajamas, handkerchiefs, napkins, washcloths, and bandages for amputated limbs.

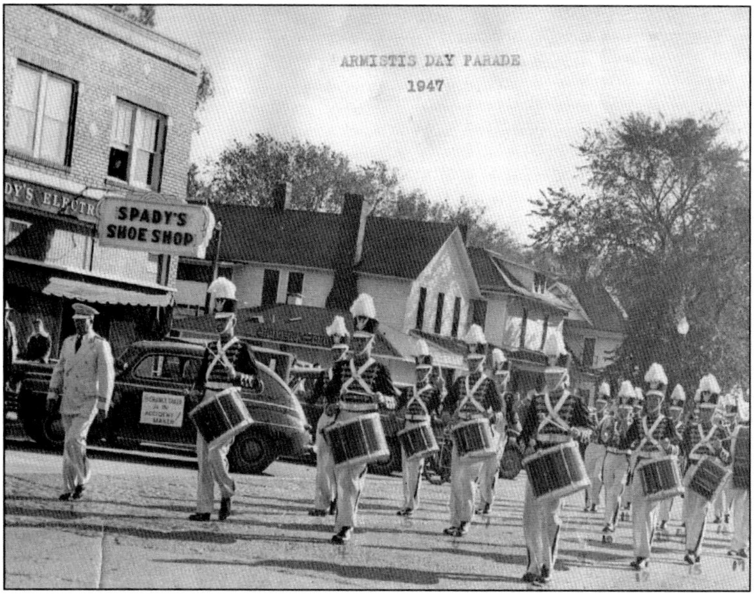

The Drum Corps marches in the 1100 block of Commercial Street as part of the Armistice Day parade in 1947. Emporians have taken great pride in honoring veterans since the Civil War. As the founding city of Veteran's Day, the community continues to honor the nation's veterans with an annual parade on November 11.

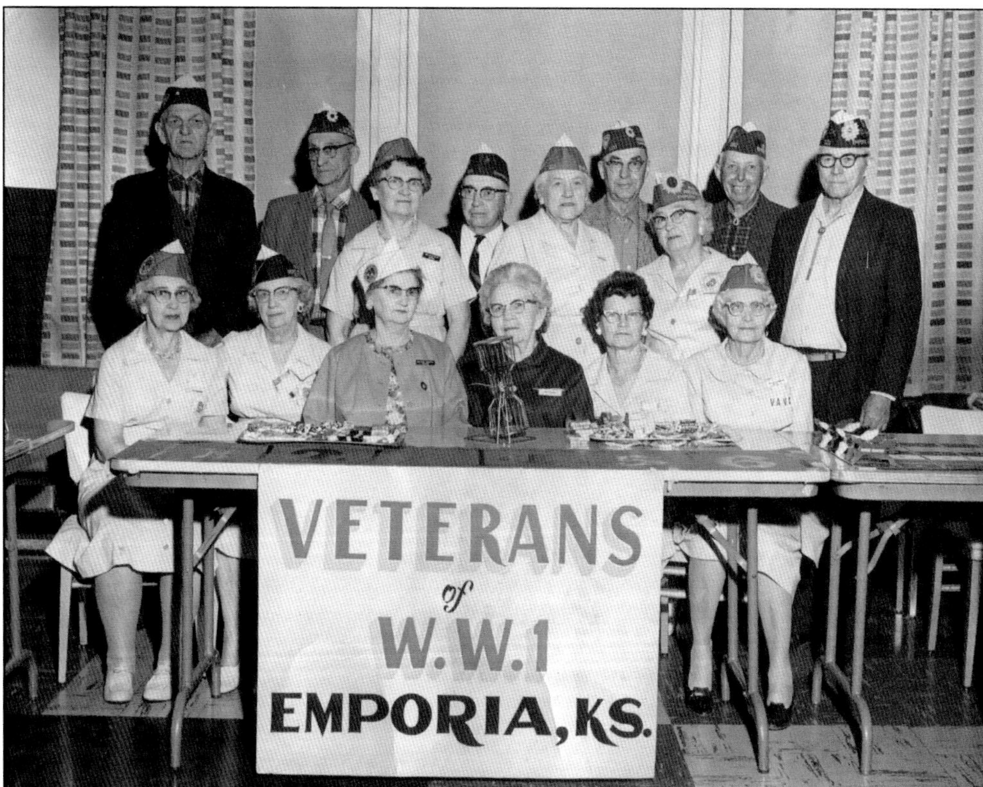

Veterans of World War I gathered for reunions annually to reminisce. Pictured in this 1966 photograph are, from left to right, (first row) Faye Barnow, Ella May Suddock, Hazel Knoeppel, Maud Hughes, Edith Humphreys, and Martha Jennings; (second row) Hallie Beath, Esther Schallehn, and Myrtle Rowland; (third row) William Barnow, Lloyd Milner, Fred Knoeppel, Harry Rowland, Seth Humphrey, and Dana Jennings.

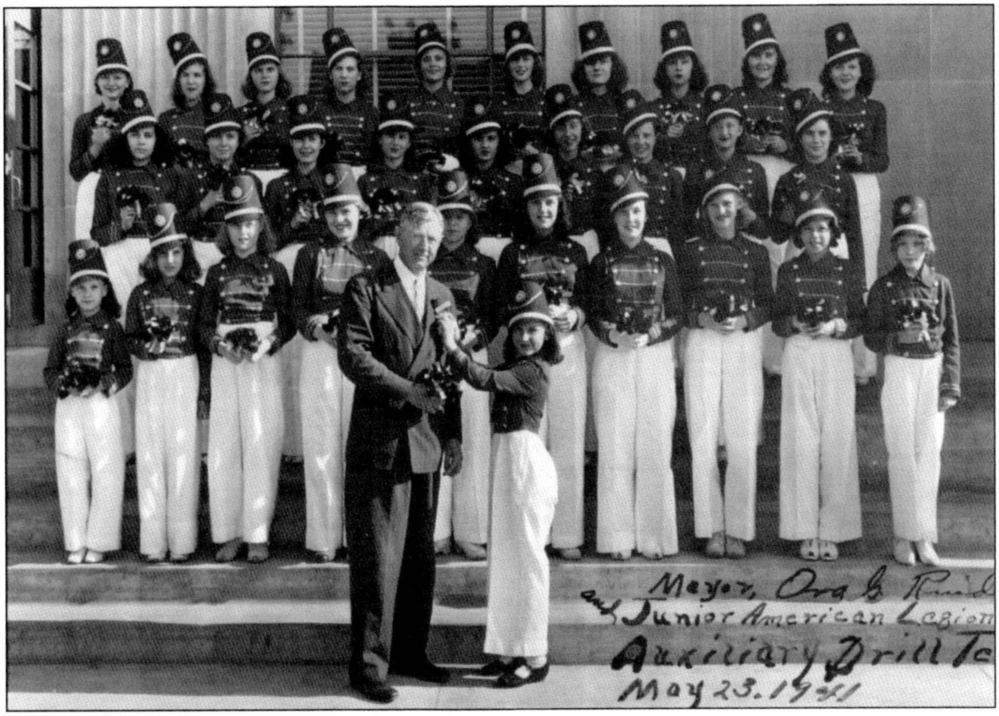

In 1919, Congress chartered the American Legion as a patriotic mutual support and community service organization. American Legion posts were established across the country. Many communities had Junior American Legion drill teams. Pictured here is Mayor Ora Rindom on the front steps of the civic auditorium holding the trophy won by the team in 1941. (Courtesy of the Walter M. Andersen Collection, Emporia State University Special Collections Archives.)

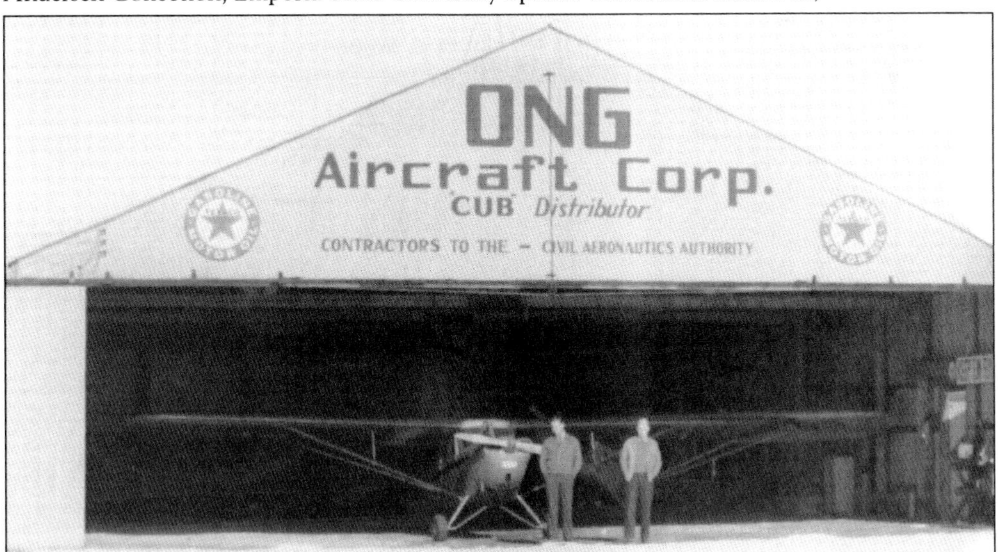

Aviation became increasingly popular in the 1920s and 1930s. In 1939, Emporia's first airport was located nine miles north of the city. It was used for flight training programs offered through Emporia State University and the Civil Aeronautics Authority. Although it was not a War Department program, many of the students would later become pilots in World War II.

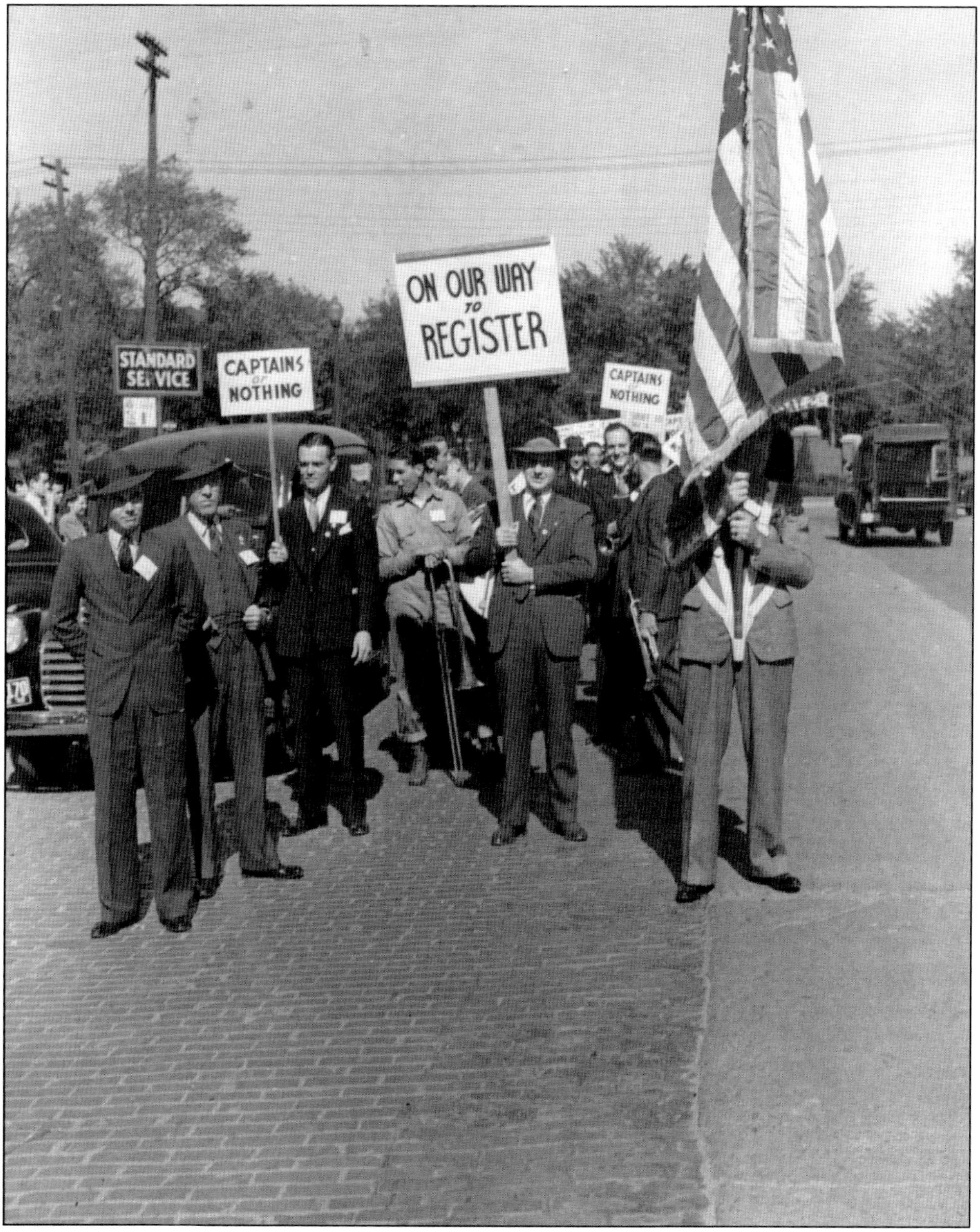

"I want to be a Captain" was the theme of this parade on October 16, 1940, with men carrying signs on their way to register for the first peacetime draft in the history of the United States. The parade was led by an American flag carried by Warren Jones, a five-piece band, and an "On Our Way to Register" sign carried by Sam Mellinger. Approximately 4,000 Lyon County men between the ages of 21 and 35 registered that day.

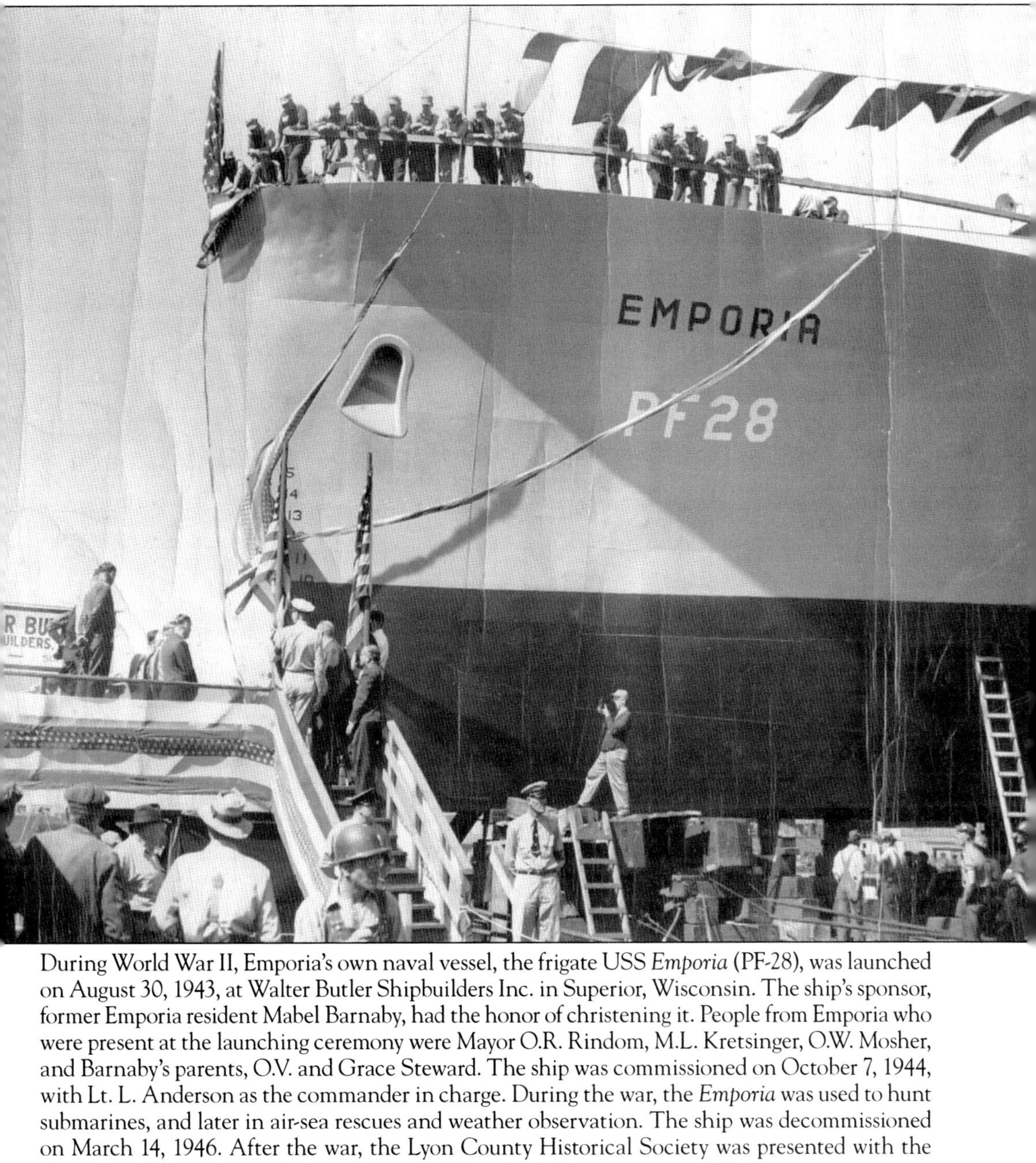

During World War II, Emporia's own naval vessel, the frigate USS *Emporia* (PF-28), was launched on August 30, 1943, at Walter Butler Shipbuilders Inc. in Superior, Wisconsin. The ship's sponsor, former Emporia resident Mabel Barnaby, had the honor of christening it. People from Emporia who were present at the launching ceremony were Mayor O.R. Rindom, M.L. Kretsinger, O.W. Mosher, and Barnaby's parents, O.V. and Grace Steward. The ship was commissioned on October 7, 1944, with Lt. L. Anderson as the commander in charge. During the war, the *Emporia* was used to hunt submarines, and later in air-sea rescues and weather observation. The ship was decommissioned on March 14, 1946. After the war, the Lyon County Historical Society was presented with the ship's flag, bell, and records during a special Fourth of July ceremony in 1950.

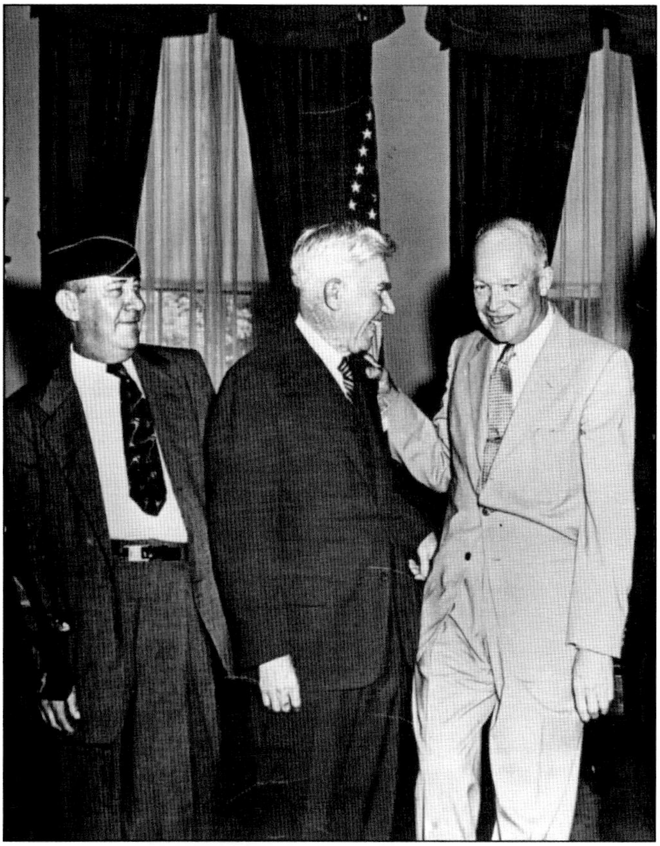

In 1953, Emporian Alvin J. King proposed that Armistice Day be changed to Veterans Day to recognize and honor all veterans from all wars and conflicts. Veterans Day was first organized and celebrated in Emporia in 1953. Kansas congressman Ed Rees, also an Emporian, then took King's proposal to Congress, and Pres. Dwight D. Eisenhower signed the bill proclaiming November 11 as Veterans Day. The first nationwide observance of Veterans Day was in 1954. Pictured here from left to right are King, Rees, and Eisenhower after the signing ceremony in Washington, DC. Below is President Eisenhower signing the bill into law.

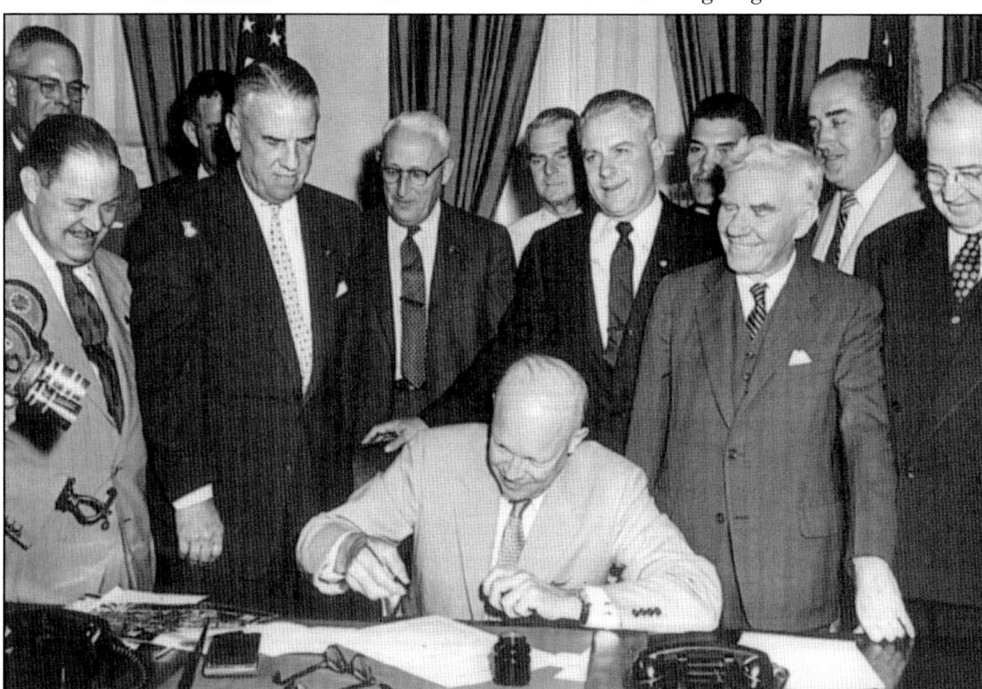

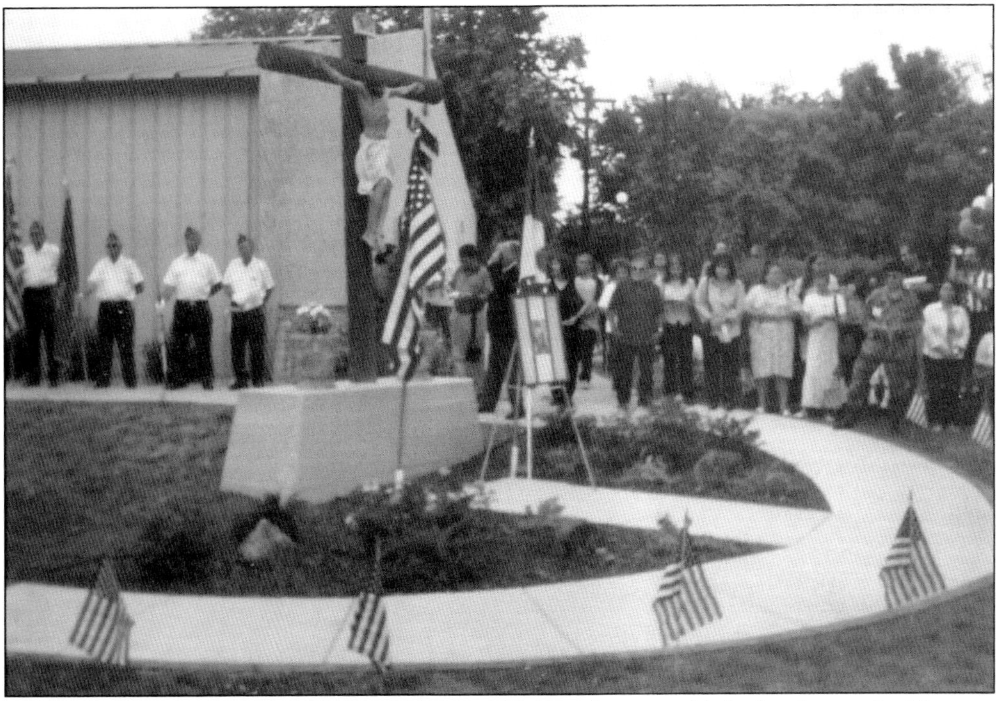

The Mexican-American World War II Veterans Memorial was established to honor the Mexican American men and women of Emporia who proudly served their country. The memorial also honors Jesse Garcia and Robert Ramirez, who were killed in action in World War II. In 2005, a rededication ceremony was held at St. Catherine's Church, 205 South Lawrence Street, where the memorial is located.

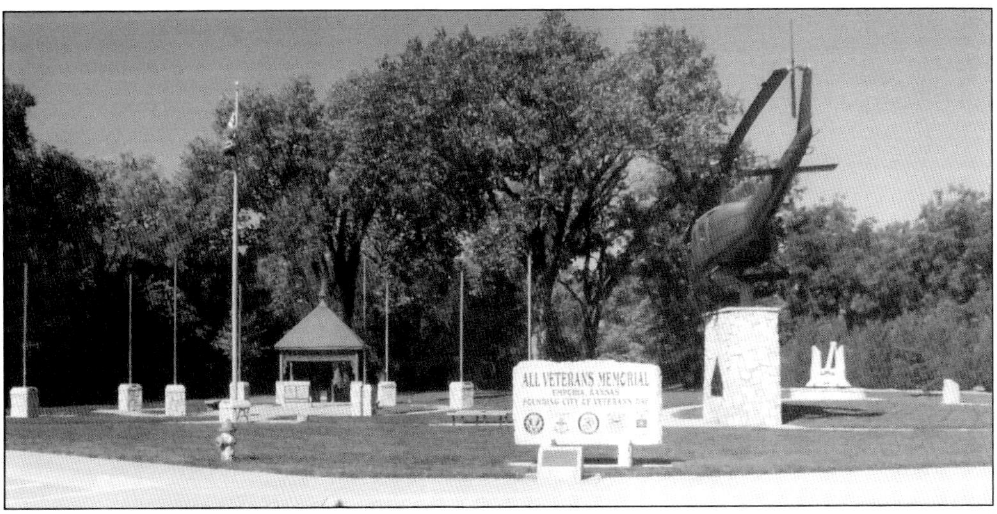

In 1991, Emporia became the first city in the United States to establish an All Veterans Memorial Park dedicated to veterans of all wars, conflicts, and peacetime service. The park is located at 933 South Commercial Street and contains a circular walkway with individual memorials that represent each of the major conflicts that the Unites States has fought in since Emporia was established in 1857.

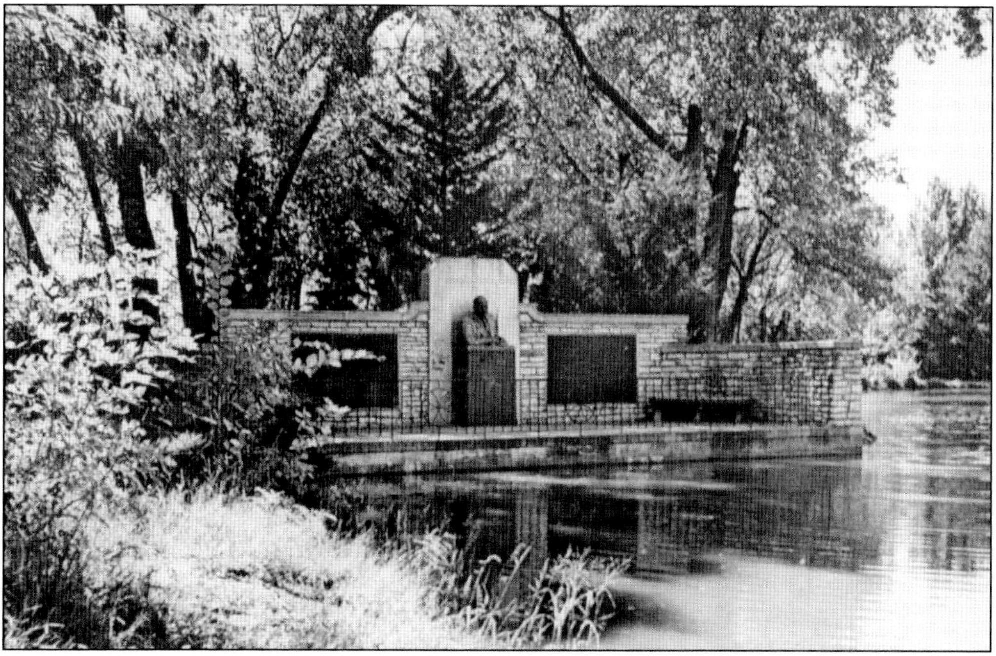

A memorial to William Allen White, famous Kansas newspaper editor, can be found on the southeast edge of Peter Pan Lake. The memorial features a bronze bust of White by sculptor Jo Davidson surrounded by two large bronze plaques on which the eulogy White wrote for his daughter Mary is carved. In July 1950, Pres. Herbert Hoover dedicated the park memorial.

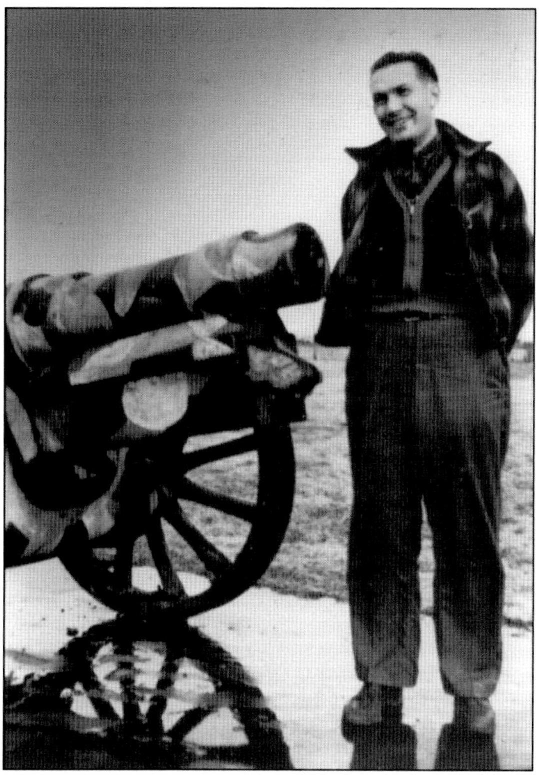

Much of the preservation of Emporia's visual history can be credited to Emporian Walter Andersen. As a young man, Andersen worked at a local theater and developed an interest in photography. Following service in World War II, he worked for the Santa Fe Railroad until his retirement in 1972. Creating a darkroom in his basement, he began photographing, collecting, and reproducing many photographs brought to him by local residents. He loved to share his collection with the community and produced calendars with Emporia scenes as holiday gifts. Following his death, the more than 12,000 prints and 20,000 negatives were given to the Emporia State University Libraries and Archives, where they can be researched and enjoyed for years to come. (Courtesy of the Walter M. Andersen Collection, Emporia State University Special Collections Archives.)

Bibliography

A Memorial to Pioneers of Lyon County: 1855–1875. Emporia Gazette, 1922.

Centennial, 1857–1957, Emporia, Kansas: 100 Years of Progress: Centennial Celebration, June 30–July 6, 1957. Emporia, KS: Emporia Centennial Inc., 1957.

Cutler, William G. *History of the state of Kansas*. Chicago: A.T. Andreas, 1883.

French, Laura M. *History of Emporia and Lyon County*. Emporia, KS: *Emporia Gazette*, 1929.

Gilson Scrapbooks. Emporia, KS: Lyon County Historical Society.

Stotler, Jacob. *Annals of Emporia and Lyon County: Historical Incidents of the First Quarter of a Century, 1857 to 1882*. Emporia, KS.

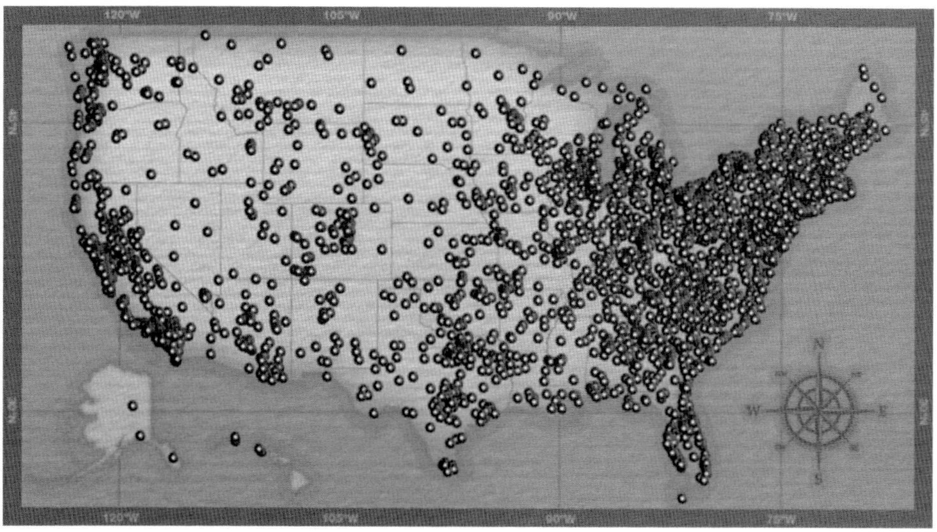

Consistent with our mission to preserve history on a local level, this book was printed in South Carolina on American-made paper and manufactured entirely in the United States. Products carrying the accredited Forest Stewardship Council (FSC) label are printed on 100 percent FSC-certified paper.

MADE IN THE USA